A Life of
PRAYER

SWINDOLL
LEADERSHIP
LIBRARY

A LIFE OF
PRAYER

CULTIVATING THE INNER LIFE
OF THE CHRISTIAN LEADER

PAUL CEDAR

CHARLES R. SWINDOLL, GENERAL EDITOR

WORD PUBLISHING
Nashville•London•Vancouver•Melbourne

A LIFE OF PRAYER
Swindoll Leadership Library

Unless otherwise indicated, Scripture quotations used in this book are from
the Holy Bible, New International Version (NIV).
Copyright © 1973, 1978, 1984 International Bible Society.
Used by permission of Zondervan Bible Publishers.

Published in association with Dallas Theological Seminary (DTS):
General Editor: Charles Swindoll
Managing Editor: Roy B. Zuck
The theological opinions expressed by the author are not necessarily the
official position of Dallas Theological Seminary.

ISBN 0-8499-1355-1

Printed in the United States of America
98 99 00 01 02 03 04 05 06 BVG 9 8 7 6 5 4 3 2 1

Dedication

With deep love and great admiration I dedicate
this book to my beloved wife
and prayer partner,

Jean Helen Cedar,

who has taught me more about prayer than any other person.
It has been a joyous adventure to share with her
over the years in our Lord's
"school of prayer."

Contents

FOREWORD

∘━✦━∘

İMAGINE WHAT it would have been like to hear Jesus pray, to eavesdrop on an intimate conversation between the Son of God and His heavenly Father. The Gospel of Luke records one disciple's response after watching Jesus pray. "One day Jesus was praying in a certain place. When he finished, one of his disciples said to him, 'Lord, teach us to pray'" (Luke 11:1).

What a fascinating request! The disciples lived in a religious culture that promoted prayer. They had heard people pray at the temple in Jerusalem . . . and in countless synagogue services. Before spending time with Jesus, I suspect each disciple would have thought he knew how to pray. But when they watched Jesus pray, they saw an intimacy, a fervency, a level of effectiveness that made their prayers seem feeble in comparison. With such a model before them, they wanted to learn how to pray like He did!

"Lord, teach us to pray." Those words have been repeated down through the centuries by Christians desiring a deeper intimacy with God. We all understand the power available to us through prayer, but how seldom we tap that power. Jesus challenged His disciples to persist in prayer, to "ask . . . seek . . . knock" (Luke 11:9). All of us long to accept our Lord's challenge, but where can we go to learn how to cultivate such disciplines and commitment to a life of prayer?

Thankfully, Paul Cedar provides us with some clear answers in this practical volume. While the disciples had the privilege of turning to the incarnate Word for direction, Dr. Cedar takes his readers today to the written Word. Combining the clear teaching of the Bible with illustrations from his own life, he gently guides his audience through the process of developing a life of prayer.

Want to know the purpose for prayer? Paul Cedar gives it. Confused about the proper posture for prayer? He shares some practical tips from the Bible. Discouraged by your struggle to maintain a consistent prayer life? He presents sensible, scriptural suggestions to get you back on track. Looking for ways to help your church become more focused on prayer? He offers some very specific, workable activities that can increase your church's emphasis on prayer. Every pastor ought to read this.

But be careful! This book will make a profound impact on your prayer life if you put these principles into practice. Have a pen and notebook ready beside you as you read . . . and jot down notes, specific suggestions, Scripture passages, and requests. Then find a quiet spot, free from all other distractions, and pray. As you do, remember the words penned by Joseph M. Scriven a century ago. They may seem simple and dated, but they remain ever relevant.

What a Friend we have in Jesus,
All our sins and griefs to bear!
What a privilege to carry
Everything to God in prayer!
O what peace we often forfeit,
O what needless pain we bear,
All because we do not carry
Everything to God in prayer!

Lord, teach us to pray!

—CHARLES R. SWINDOLL

General Editor

Acknowledgments

⊙━✦━⊙

WRITING A BOOK is both a privilege and a challenge. One of the greatest joys of my ministry over the years has been that of teaming with many brothers and sisters in serving our Lord Jesus Christ. Partnering with others in ministry has brought special joy to me.

This book has been that kind of joyous venture. I am deeply grateful for all who have been an encouragement and help to me as I have sought to be guided by the Holy Spirit in prayerfully preparing this manuscript.

My special thanks to Dean Merrill, who has served as preparation editor of my manuscript. Dean is a gifted writer who has served with distinction with David C. Cook, *Leadership Journal,* and Focus on the Family. He is now vice president and publisher of the International Bible Society and has been an invaluable source of counsel and editing.

I am deeply grateful, also, to my dear wife, Jeannie, and to our two sons, Daniel and Mark, for their significant help in reviewing the manuscript drafts, proofreading, and making suggestions that have been so helpful.

In addition, I am thankful for my sister, Ellen Ann Jones, other family members, the Mission America National Facilitation Team, and many others who serve on our personal prayer team. Each of these individuals has prayed faithfully for me during my preparation of this manuscript.

It has been a special honor for me to work with Dr. Charles R. Swindoll, general editor of the Swindoll Leadership Library, and Dr. Roy B. Zuck, managing editor, along with David Moberg and his staff at Word Publishing.

PAUL A. CEDAR

Introduction

My ADVENTURE in learning to pray began when, as a boy, I trusted Jesus Christ as my Savior and Lord. After my conversion at an early age, I became serious about my Christian life. I was blessed with wonderful parents, who were my first teachers in the "school of prayer."

My father was a committed evangelical who pastored rural Presbyterian churches for some forty years. He was a busy pastor who practiced prayer in his personal life and gave a high priority to prayer in his ministry.

Some of the finest training I received in prayer during my teenage years took place on Thursday evenings at church prayer meetings. In those meetings my father taught about prayer and then gave ample opportunity for us to put that teaching into practice. Large numbers of young people participated in those prayer meetings over the years. In fact, by far the majority of attendees were teenagers. It was, in a real sense, a school of prayer.

My mother was my more personal teacher and a quiet model of a praying Christian. Although she was a busy high school teacher during most of my formative years, she spent significant time in fasting and prayer. As a young man, my mother introduced me to some of the great pray-ers of all history, including "Praying Hyde," David Brainerd, and Andrew Murray. I still have biographies of such saints that she gave me as a teenager.

I do not remember having many discussions with my parents about praying. They simply did it and modeled it in their busy lives. Without fully realizing it at the time, prayer became deeply integrated into my life during my formative years.

By the time I left home for college, I was a young man who gave prayer a significant priority in my life. I did not do it out of a sense of religious duty. I prayed because it helped me stay close to God—and because I experienced answers to prayer over and over again.

I had planned to attend a Christian college, but God had other plans for me. He led me to a state college. Soon I was involved in the campus InterVarsity chapter. Once again, prayer held a high priority for me. Some of us students met for regular prayer meetings, which continued for years. Students and faculty members met early in the morning to pray for our college family, for each other, and for the salvation of members of the college community who had never had the joy of coming to personal faith in our Lord Jesus Christ. Once again, God answered our prayers. We saw significant numbers of young people and some faculty members come to Christ over the four years I was on campus. And the prayers of that faithful band of pray-ers made an impact on the campus in many other ways.

When I began full-time vocational ministry, prayer was a significant part of my life. In fact, virtually every blessing I have ever enjoyed in the ministry can be attributed to prayer.

I thank God for the great ventures of prayer in which He has allowed me to participate over the years. I have seen the Lord respond in wonderful and powerful ways to the prayers of His people. At the same time, I thank God for the many servants of Jesus Christ who have contributed to my growth in prayer. I thank Him for opportunities to invest in the lives of others as we have shared in the ministry of prayer.

One of the great models and encouragers for me in praying has been Jeannie, my faithful wife and partner in ministry for over thirty years. Although she has not been a prominent public teacher on the subject of prayer, she has been a quiet, effective practitioner. For example, she has established small prayer groups and prayer ministries in neighborhoods where we have lived, which have had incredible impact on numerous lives. She has been used of God to help our children learn to pray—and many others as well. I have learned much about prayer from her.

Early in my Christian life I thought that someday I would graduate from the school of prayer—or at least advance to "graduate school." I now realize that is not true. In the deepest sense none of us will ever "graduate" until we are face to face with our Lord Jesus Christ. Only then will our communication and communion with Him be all we long for it to be. But that should not discourage us. Instead, it should *encourage* us to press on and become more faithful in prayer. In a real sense that is what this book is about. I pray that it will be a source of great encouragement and help to all who read it.

It seems that many Christians have missed the joy of communing with Jesus Christ. Prayer is life's greatest joy, highest privilege, and most powerful venture. Nothing can compare with it.

And so I share this humble attempt at presenting the basics of prayer as I have experienced and understood them. It is my prayer that you will be encouraged, strengthened, and motivated to become a stronger and more effective pray-er. The church of Jesus Christ needs great men, women, and young people of prayer today.

One of my daily prayers continues to be, "Lord, teach me to pray!"

As I pray it for myself, I pray it for you

Lord, teach us to pray!

PART I

Considering a Life of Prayer

I

RECOGNIZING THE UNLIMITED
POTENTIAL OF PRAYER

❦

THE YOUNG PASTOR picked up the microphone. He looked out at the conference hall filled with ministers and other church leaders, many of them older than he. His lower lip quivered as he began to speak softly. "I would like to tell you why I believe in prayer."

He paused to gain his composure and then continued, "I graduated from seminary about two years ago. I was unable to find a church until someone told me of a little rural church that was dying. Nobody wanted to go there."

He then told how the area's farmland was being bought up by large corporations whose employees came in only to run the operations and lived elsewhere. On top of that, the small congregation had earned a reputation for not treating its pastors well. In fact, the two previous pastors had actually left the ministry after retreating from the little church wounded and bleeding.

The young pastor took a deep breath and continued, "They called me to be their pastor, and I accepted. The first months of my ministry actually went fairly well. Then a problem erupted. One of the elders started to criticize my preaching. Soon other church members began to complain about my wife and family. Before long, it seemed that we could do nothing right.

"Months passed slowly, and the attacks increased. Finally, after less than a year, I reached the same point as my two predecessors. I, too, was wounded and bleeding. I was ready to leave the church—and the ministry. Finally, in desperation, I cried out to God. 'Lord, what should I do? I don't want to fail You or Your church, but I cannot continue. Please, Lord, help me!'

"As I wept and prayed, I sensed the Lord saying to me, 'Ask the elders to pray with you.' 'But, Lord,' I protested, 'they are my most severe critics. They are my persecutors. Why should I pray with them?' Again and again I sensed the Lord encouraging me to pray with the elders. After several days of resisting, I finally surrendered.

"In fear and trembling, I approached the elders. I told them my story. Then I asked them if they would pray with me. Much to my surprise, they agreed. The little group began to meet every Tuesday morning, praying for each other, our families, and the church. Within just a few weeks God began to change hearts. Answers to prayer began to emerge.

"For example, after several months of praying together, an amazing thing happened. A visitor appeared in one of our morning services! That led to many exciting conversations the following week. Soon other visitors began to worship with us. The past few months our church attendance has nearly doubled."

At this point the young pastor began to weep openly. Finally he was able to continue.

"I have come to believe deeply in the power of prayer. There is no other way to explain what has happened in our little church. God has intervened. He has heard our prayers. He has brought hope and encouragement to an impossible situation."

That dramatic testimony from a young pastor took place just before I was to deliver the keynote address to that conference. I do not remember what I spoke about that evening, but I will never forget the words of the young pastor. I agreed with him then—and I agree with him now.

God does hear and answer the prayers of desperate Christians—including Christian leaders.

THE POTENTIAL OF PRAYER IN TIMES OF NEED

Jim Cymbala, pastor of the well-known Brooklyn Tabernacle, would agree. In his recent book, *Fresh Wind, Fresh Fire,* Jim tells an amazing story of his early ministry.

Twenty-five years ago, he became pastor of a dying church in a deteriorating neighborhood in Brooklyn, New York. Just a handful of people remained in the little congregation. In his first month as pastor, a major crisis developed: They could not meet the monthly $232 mortgage payment. Jim has related the story in this way.

I went upstairs, sat at my little desk, put my head down, and began to cry. "God," I sobbed, "what can I do? We can't even pay the mortgage."

That night was the midweek service, and I knew there wouldn't be more than three or four people attending. The offering would probably be less than ten dollars. How was I going to get through this?

I cried out to the Lord for a full hour or so. Eventually, I dried my tears—and a new thought came. *Wait a minute! Besides the mail slot in the front door, the church also has a post office box. I'll go across the street and see what's there. Surely God will answer my prayer!*

With renewed confidence I walked across the street, crossed the post office lobby, and twirled the knob on the little box. I peered inside.

Nothing.

As I stepped back into the sunshine, trucks roared down Atlantic Avenue. If one had flattened me just then, I wouldn't have felt any lower. Was God abandoning us? Was I doing something that displeased him? I trudged wearily back across the street to the little building.

As I unlocked the door, I was met with another surprise. There on the foyer floor was something that hadn't been there just three minutes earlier: a simple white envelope. No address, no stamp—nothing. Just a white envelope.

With trembling hands I opened it to find . . . *two $50 bills.*

I began shouting all by myself in the empty church. "God, you came through! You came through!" We had $160 in the bank, and with this $100 we could make the mortgage payment. My soul let out a deep "Hallelujah!" What a lesson for a disheartened young pastor!

To this day I don't know where that money came from. I only know it was a sign to me that God was near—and faithful.[1]

Jim Cymbala became a believer in prayer. In fact, before very long he declared to the little congregation, "From this day on, the prayer meeting will be the barometer of our church. What happens on Tuesday night will be the gauge by which we will judge success or failure, because that will be the measure by which God blesses us." He concluded, "This [prayer] will be the engine that will drive the church."[2]

Jim had discovered what Charles Haddon Spurgeon, the great British pulpiteer, declared long ago. "The condition of the church may be very accurately gauged by its prayer meetings. So is the prayer meeting a grace-ometer, and from it we may judge the amount of divine working among a people. If God be near a church, it must pray. And if he be not there, one of the first tokens of his absence will be a slothfulness in prayer."[3]

Many pastors and other Christian leaders have learned that principle. So have Christian parents, other adults, young people, and even children. Great churches, families, and spiritual lives are built on the foundation of prayer.

Prayer has awesome potential—not only for pastors and churches but also for Christians in every realm of life. God has asked us to pray. In fact, He has *commanded* us to pray.

And our Lord has promised to answer our prayers. Often we simply do not have because we do not ask (James 4:2). He is waiting for us to ask.

The apostle Paul wrote, "Now to him who is able to do immeasurably more than all we ask or imagine, according to his power that is at work within us" (Eph. 3:20). That is the kind of God we serve and with whom we can communicate. He is able to do more than we could ever ask or even imagine. God's invitation to the prophet Jeremiah should be a source of encouragement to all of us: "Call to me and I will answer you and tell you great and unsearchable things you do not know" (Jer. 33:3).

I remember hearing about that principle in operation a number of years ago from a Christian lay leader. I was conducting a seminar in the church where he was an elder. During my stay I came to know him well, along with his wife and five adult children.

They seemed to be a model Christian family. Each one of the children was a deeply committed Christian, involved in significant ministry. Since I, the father of three young children, was so impressed, I asked the secret of his success in being a husband and father. I wanted to learn from him.

To my surprise, he broke into tears. He shared with me that he had been anything but a model father. He said that during the formative years of his children's lives, he had focused primarily on making money and becoming successful in his business. He became a self-made millionaire. But he nearly lost his wife and children.

The Lord brought him to the end of himself. With little warning, his business failed. He lost virtually everything. In the midst of his despair, he cried out to God. And the Lord taught him how to pray. It became the foundation of his life. "Prayer," he said, "is the secret to our children walking with God. I cannot take credit for it. I failed—but the Lord has answered our prayers."

Perhaps you can identify with these stories. You have enjoyed similar experiences. Prayer has had a profound effect on your life and ministry. To others, such accounts may seem exaggerated or atypical—or even unimportant.

Most Christian leaders believe in prayer. However, many admit that they do not invest much time in praying. Somehow, with scores of things vying for our time and attention, prayer is often not a high priority. As John Munro observed, "Nothing reveals our spiritual condition so accurately as our private prayers. Most Christians, however, know that [their] prayer life is one of their weakest points."[4]

I believe one of Satan's most clever devices is to encourage us not to pray—and to do all he can to prevent us from praying. He does not mind if we believe in prayer so long as we do not do it. In that way he can weaken our ministries.

Samuel Chadwick said it well. "The one concern of the devil is to keep Christians from praying. He fears nothing from prayerless studies, prayerless work and prayerless religion. He laughs at our toil, mocks at our wisdom, but trembles when we pray."[5]

My grandfather was a man of prayer. During the latter years of his life, he spent hours each week in personal prayer. In addition, he loved to pray with his wife and other family members and friends. As a young child, I sometimes grew impatient with what seemed to be his very long prayers. As I grew older, however, I came to enjoy praying with him.

When I was a teenager, I told my grandfather I was sensing the call to serve God in full-time ministry. His first and fervent counsel to me was that if I was to be used of God in the ministry, I should be certain never to wear out my trousers in the seat but rather in the knees. In other words, I should spend more time kneeling in prayer that sitting down.

What wise counsel!

The Scriptures are filled with accounts of persons for whom prayer was a high priority. In fact, virtually every major victory in the lives of God's people came in response to the prayers of one or more servants of the Lord.

Gideon prayed to the Lord, and He gave him a great victory over the Midianites (Judg. 6–7).

Hannah, who was unable to have children, prayed fervently (1 Sam. 1:10, 27; 2:20), and God gave her a son, Samuel, who became a great prophet.

David, who is described in Scripture as a man after God's own heart (1 Sam. 13:14; Acts 13:22), lived a life of prayer, evidenced by his many psalms of deep devotion to God. God honored him and used him as a great king of Israel.

Nehemiah wept, fasted, prayed—and God used him to lead the difficult task of rebuilding the walls of Jerusalem, resulting in a great spiritual revival among the people of Israel. In fact, the Book of Nehemiah records twelve times Nehemiah prayed!

Threatened with death by lions, Daniel continued, as before, to pray three times a day (Dan. 6:10–13). And amazingly, God saved his life in the den of lions. Daniel was a man of prayer. And so were Elijah, Hezekiah, Ezra, Isaiah, Habakkuk, and Jeremiah—and many other men and women, young people, and children.

Each of these individuals faced "impossible situations"—but they believed in the potential of prayer. They did not merely speak about prayer or discuss its possibilities. They did it!

PRAYER AND THE WORD

The New Testament continues the chronicle of answered prayer. Awesome events took place as God's people humbled themselves and asked for His involvement. The Book of Acts is a commentary on the activity and results of prayer. The early church leaders were men and women of prayer—and the Word.

In our day many Christian leaders have given much attention to focusing on the Word but have often neglected prayer. The techniques of how to present the Word publicly receive a high priority in theological curricula. However, relatively few courses are taught on the subject of prayer. By contrast, the early church depended on leaders who were committed to both the Word *and* prayer. It is admirable to be men and women of the Word, but it is not enough. After three thousand Jews responded to Peter's preaching of the Word on the Day of Pentecost, they continued in prayer (Acts 2:42).

When Peter and John faced the first major crisis experienced by the early church after Jesus' ascension, they rushed to join their brothers and sisters in raising their voices together in prayer, asking for boldness to speak God's Word (4:24–31). And the Lord answered in a remarkable way.

Soon after that historic prayer meeting, when the Jerusalem elders became overburdened with ministry responsibilities, they appointed deacons to carry on some of the work so they could devote themselves "to prayer and the ministry of the Word" (6:4). It was not a matter of prayer *or* the Word. It took prayer *and* the Word.

Preaching and teaching the Word of God are essential; the exposition of the Scriptures is vital. But so is the ministry of prayer. We must not choose between the two; we must be committed to both. The church needs Christian leaders who are committed to the Word and prayer. To neglect the Word is to dilute our spiritual message; to neglect prayer is to dilute our spiritual power.

E. M. Bounds understood that principle when he wrote, "The preacher must be preeminently a man of prayer. . . . The character of our praying will determine the character of our preaching. . . . Prayer makes preaching strong, gives it unction and makes it stick." Then he concluded, "In every ministry weighty for good, prayer has always been a serious business."[6]

Preaching needs to be undergirded with prayer, and so must every kind of ministry carried on by God's people.

Bounds wrote, "How vast are the possibilities of prayer! How wide is its reach! What great things are accomplished by this divinely appointed means of grace! It lays its hand on Almighty God and moves him to do what he would not otherwise do if prayer was not offered. It brings things to pass which would never otherwise occur."[7]

Bounds continues:

> Prayer puts God in the matter with commanding force: "Ask of me things to come concerning my sons," says God, "and concerning the work of my hands command ye me" [Isa. 45:11].
>
> We are charged in God's Word "always to pray," "in everything by prayer," "continuing instant in prayer," to "pray everywhere," "praying always." The promise is as illimitable as the command is comprehensive. "All things whatsoever ye shall ask in prayer, believing, ye shall receive," "whatever ye shall ask," "if ye ask anything" . . . These statements are but samples of the all-comprehending possibilities of prayer under the promises of God to those who meet the conditions of right praying.
>
> [Those] who have done mighty things for God have always been mighty in prayer, have well understood the possibilities of prayer, and have made most of these possibilities. The Son of God . . . has shown us the all-potent and far-reaching possibilities of prayer. Paul was mighty for God because he knew how to use, and how to get others to use, the mighty spiritual forces of prayer.[8]

The Book of Acts records the powerful ministries of Peter and Paul as they preached and taught the Word, faithfully communicating God's truth. But why was their ministry of the Scriptures so effective? Because they prayed! Peter prayed for the believers in Samaria (Acts 8:15) and for dead Dorcas (9:40). And in Joppa he prayed at noon on the flat roof of a house (10:9; 11:5). Paul prayed in Damascus after his conversion (9:11); he and Barnabas committed elders to the Lord in prayer (13:2–3); he and Silas prayed when incarcerated in a Philippian jail (16:25); he prayed with Ephesian elders in Miletus (20:36); he prayed with believers on the beach at Tyre (21:5); he prayed at the Jerusalem temple (22:17); and he prayed for healing for Publius's father (28:8).

Paul repeatedly assured the readers of his epistles that he was praying for them (Rom. 1:10; 2 Cor. 13:7; Eph. 1:18; 3:16–19; Phil. 1:4; Col. 1:3, 9–10; 1 Thess. 1:2; 2 Thess. 1:11; 2 Tim. 1:3; Philem. 4, 6).

THE AWESOME POTENTIAL OF PRAYER

The potential in prayer is so immense it is almost indescribable. Prayer spells the difference between doing things for God in our own strength or carrying on His ministry by the power of the Holy Spirit.

Prayer made the difference between Peter denying his Lord and the same Peter preaching with great power and incredible results on the Day of Pentecost. Prayer was a factor in changing the fragmented, timid disciples, who fled for their lives when Jesus was arrested, into men of great spiritual boldness and unity on the streets of Jerusalem as Peter proclaimed the gospel on the Day of Pentecost.

Yet many are seemingly missing out on the power of prayer. As James wrote, "You want something but don't get it. You kill and covet, but you cannot have what you want. You quarrel and fight. You do not have, because you do not ask God" (James 4:2). Jesus has extended to us an incomparable invitation and promise, "Ask and it will be given to you" (Matt. 7:7).

In 1855 Joseph Scriven expressed the practical truth of ignoring that gracious invitation when he penned the words we have sung so frequently:

> O what peace we often forfeit,
> O what needless pain we bear,
> All because we do not carry
> Everything to God in prayer.[9]

That song is a commentary on my own life and ministry. Many times I have attempted to do things for God in my own strength rather than reaching out to Him in prayer, asking for His wisdom, power, and provision.

Learning to pray effectively is much more than an academic exercise. It requires a radical change for most of us. It translates us from focusing on ourselves and our own abilities to focusing on God and His unlimited resources.

Most of us have come to recognize our limitations. As a result, many Christian leaders find it more and more difficult to take risks—to venture out in faith. Many of us have adopted the ministry style of "playing it safe" and walking by sight rather than by faith.

Prayer moves us from the safe and comfortable to the impossible and even miraculous areas of life and ministry. A life of prayer is a life of great adventure and unlimited potential. I have found it to be so in my own life and ministry. And so have many others.

Early in my ministry I was pastoring a newly planted church. It was an exciting ministry. God was blessing us in so many ways. In fact, the growth was so remarkable that we had outgrown our temporary facilities. We were suffering from a severe case of numerical suffocation. It had become a very desperate situation.

At the same time, we had begun plans to build our first church building. But even with the best-case scenario, we would not be able to complete those new facilities for at least a year. Actually, two years was a more probable time line.

We attempted to find another temporary location, but to no avail. The situation became more and more difficult. There seemed to be no solution. The ministry of the church was beginning to be affected negatively.

Then when all else failed—when we had done everything we could think to do—we came up with the idea of calling the church together for special prayer. As we gathered together, the leaders and other members of the congregation cried out to the Lord. We reminded Him that it was His church, that we were His people, and that unless He provided a different place for us to meet, the whole ministry would be stifled.

How gracious was our Lord. He heard and answered our prayers within days. The facility He provided was ideal. During the months we rented that building, the congregation more than doubled in size.

Cultivating a life of prayer is not optional for those of us who are committed to loving and obeying Jesus Christ and who desire deeply to be used by Him to the maximum. Becoming a man or woman of prayer is imperative if the potential of our ministries is to be fulfilled.

Our Lord is ready to make Himself and all His resources available to us. He is waiting for us to pray. The potential of prayer is virtually unlimited—if we will only pray as Jesus encouraged us to pray.

Dear Lord,
help us to understand
more and more
who You are
and what prayer is all about.
And, Lord,
please give us a glimpse
of prayer's awesome potential.
Lord, teach us to pray!

2

Understanding the Purpose
of Prayer

❦

E. M. BOUNDS REMINDS US, "Prayer honors God; it dishonors self. It is man's plea of weakness, ignorance, want; a plea which heaven cannot disregard. God delights to have us pray."[1]

Phillips Brooks wrote, "The purpose of prayer is not to get man's will done in heaven, but to get God's will done on earth."[2]

Augustine asserted that God "could have bestowed these things on us even without our prayers; but He wished that by our prayers we should be taught from where these benefits come."[3]

Oswald Chambers stated, "When a person is born from above, the life of the Son of God is born in him, and he can either starve that life or nourish it. Prayer is the way the life of God is nourished." [4]

These are helpful statements on the purposes of prayer. None of them contradicts or eliminates the others. They represent the fact that the purpose of prayer is not singular but multiple.

Is prayer really necessary? Why should Christians pray? Unless we become more aware of *why* God wants us to pray, we tend to neglect prayer.

This chapter focuses on three major reasons why every Christian should cultivate a life of prayer: to obey God, to commune with God, and to align ourselves with God's agenda.

PRAYER IS OBEYING GOD

If there were no other reason to pray other than to obey our Lord's clear commands about praying, every sincere Christian should respond with full obedience.

In both civilian and military life those who do not follow their leaders' orders are in serious jeopardy. And those who continue to ignore such orders are disciplined severely. In fact, if they do not respond appropriately, they are ultimately fired or court-martialed. The same basic principle applies to disciples of Jesus Christ. Obedience is at the very heart of authentic Christian discipleship.

We need to heed the Lord's words to Saul through His servant Samuel: "Does the LORD delight in burnt offerings and sacrifices as much as in obeying the voice of the LORD? To obey is better than sacrifice, and to heed is better than the fat of rams. For rebellion is like the sin of divination, and arrogance like the evil of idolatry" (1 Sam. 15:22–23).

In one sense, failing to spend time in prayer with our Lord is a form of rebellion. It communicates that we do not need Him very much, that we can carry on our ministries and leadership responsibilities in our own strength.

The Bible is filled with God's instructions for His people to pray. Sometimes He invites us to come to Him in prayer. Other times, He firmly commands us to pray. But these are not merely top-down statements. Our Lord loves us deeply. He has created us to live in wonderful fellowship with Him. He longs to "walk in the garden" with us as He did with Adam—to communicate with us.

Here are some of God's loving invitations:

"Therefore let everyone who is godly pray to you while you may be found" (Ps. 32:6).

"Seek the LORD while he may be found; call on him while he is near" (Isa. 55:6).

"Ask and it will be given to you" (Matt. 7:7).

"Then Jesus told his disciples a parable to show them that they should always pray" (Luke 18:1).

"Ask and you will receive" (John 16:24).

"Pray in the Spirit on all occasions with all kinds of prayers and requests" (Eph. 6:18).

"Do not be anxious about anything, but in everything, by prayer and petition, with thanksgiving, present your requests to God" (Phil. 4:6).

"Pray continually" (1 Thess. 5:17).

"Is any one of you in trouble? He should pray" (James 5:13).

"Pray for each other" (James 5:16).

"Pray in the Holy Spirit" (Jude 20).

Our Lord's invitations are tender and loving; His commands are multiple and explicit. We are to pray on all occasions, in all kinds of situations—even continually! And we are to pray "in the Spirit," as both Paul and Jude wrote (Eph. 6:18; Jude 20). This means to pray by means of the Holy Spirit's power, that is, with His enabling which is made possible as we are filled and controlled by the Holy Spirit.

Prayer is essential to the Christian life and it is an imperative for Christian leadership. It is virtually impossible to be effective disciples of Jesus Christ without cultivating and practicing the life of prayer.

However, prayer is more than an obligation. Martin Luther stated it well: "To be a Christian without prayer is no more possible than to be alive without breathing."[5] It is no mere religious duty. Through prayer, all God's resources become available to us, including the unspeakable resource of Himself. This is not to suggest that most Christian leaders openly rebel against cultivating and developing their prayer lives. Few if any leaders make a conscious decision that prayer will not be an important factor in their lives and ministries.

The challenge most clergy and lay leaders have faced at some time is simply that ministry is so demanding and the responsibilities so consuming that they have not found or taken time to give prayer a high priority. It is possible to become enslaved to our ministry schedules.

The "tyranny of the urgent" becomes our plight as we attempt to tend to all our ministry responsibilities. Without realizing it, many Christian leaders have become like an old car that might run for a while on diluted fuel but is not very powerful or effective. We need the power and high spiritual performance that can be activated only by prayer.

Our Lord has invited us—and commanded us—to pray. It is not distasteful, like drinking cod liver oil. Rather, prayer is like a cool drink to a dry and thirsty throat, a soothing ointment to an aching back, a refreshing oasis in a hot, dry desert. Prayer stands as a privilege reserved for those who would return the Father's love.

PRAYER IS COMMUNING WITH GOD

The greatest privilege of prayer is that of coming into the actual presence of God to enjoy loving conversation and communion with Him. We are to pray frequently (1 Thess. 5:17) and openly (Rev. 3:20) and even "with confidence so that we may receive mercy and find grace to help us in our time of need" (Heb. 4:16).

What an invitation! There is none other like it.

Bill Hybels has described certain responses to this wonderful invitation in this way:

> By intuition or experience we understand that the most intimate communication with God comes only through prayer.
>
> Ask people who have faced tragedy or trial, heartbreak or grief, failure and defeat, loneliness or discrimination. Ask what happened in their souls when they finally fell on their knees and poured out their hearts to the Lord.
>
> Such people have told me, "I can't explain it, but I felt like God understood me."
>
> Others have said, "I felt surrounded by His presence."
>
> Or, "I felt comfort and peace I'd never felt before."[6]

Such a sense of God's presence or of intimate communion with Him does not have to be reserved for times of crisis or for infrequent occasions of "spiritual highs." To the contrary, communion with Him can be frequent and regular.

As a college student I was first introduced to a wonderful concept of prayer through a remarkable book, one which has become a classic. Simply entitled *Prayer*, it was written during the early part of the twentieth century by a Norwegian bishop, O. H. Hallesby, who was also a professor at the Independent Theological Seminary of Oslo. Hallesby's simple contention was that prayer is communion with God. He defined it in this simple way: "To pray is to invite Jesus into our hearts."

This practical theology of prayer was based on the invitation of Jesus recorded in Revelation 3:20: "Here I am! I stand at the door and knock. If anyone hears my voice and opens the door, I will come in and eat with him, and he with me." Hallesby wrote:

> This teaches us in the first place, that it is not our prayer which moves the Lord Jesus. It is Jesus who moves us to pray. He knocks.
>
> Prayer is the breath of the soul, the organ by which we receive Christ into our parched and withered hearts. . . . All He needs is access. . . . As air enters in quietly when we breathe, and does its normal work in our lungs, so Jesus enters quietly into our hearts and does His blessed work there.
>
> He calls it to *"sup" with us.*
>
> This affords a new glimpse into the nature of prayer, showing us that God has designed prayer as a means of intimate and joyous fellowship between God and man.[7]

Unfortunately many Christians do not enjoy this dimension of prayer. I myself did not begin to appreciate this aspect of praying until I had been a Christian for a number of years. My introduction to the writings of Hallesby opened my life to what some would call "dialogical praying." But it was not until a number of years later when I was working on my doctoral dissertation that I came to a more serious understanding of this kind of praying. For the past twenty or more years I have continued to experience this wonderful dimension of prayer. I have found that my early morning times of fellowship with God in the Word and in prayer prepare me to continue throughout the day in an ongoing communion with God.

Praying "without ceasing" (1 Thess. 5:17, KJV) means communing with our Lord throughout the day.

Not long ago a young seminarian asked to see me. He had taken a seminary course from me that focused on the spiritual disciplines and in which prayer was one of the major subjects we considered. The idea of communing with God in prayer was a radical concept to him. He was a brilliant young man who had trained to be an engineer. His life was ordered and logical. However, he had not been successful in building meaningful relationships with others.

This young man's concept of prayer was telling God what he wanted and expecting God to answer accordingly. He was frustrated by the fact that his prayer life was not productive. In fact, he had developed a theology that is popular today with many Christians. He had concluded that God had given him a good mind and generous resources so he could figure things out for himself most of the time. He had decided he would not bother God with the "little" things of life. Instead, he would approach God in prayer only when he needed something "big" or when he was facing a major crisis. As a result, he did not pray very much.

When taking the Spiritual Disciplines course, he decided he would try the communing or dialogical kind of prayer. He later said it had transformed his life. It opened up for him a new and wonderful relationship with the Lord. For the first time in his Christian life, this young minister began to experience a sense of the presence of God. He was no longer talking *at* God. He was now communing *with* God. He said it was "more wonderful than I can express."

Our Lord has invited each of us to share in that kind of intimate, joyous fellowship and communion with Him in prayer—at any time or any place. He knocks on the door of our lives and waits for us to respond—to commune with Him, to *sup* with Him (as the King James Version puts it)—and He with us.

PRAYER MOVES US TO GOD'S AGENDA

That kind of intimate fellowship with God will help us focus more on Him and less on ourselves. Communing with God in prayer encourages us to see situations as our Lord sees them, to become more concerned about God's will than our own, to pray earnestly and authentically for His will to be done rather than our own.

Jesus has given us the model for that kind of praying. He prayed this way in the Garden of Gethsemane, at one of His greatest times of need. Judas, one of His trusted disciples, was about to betray Him, and Peter, one of His most devoted followers, was about to deny Him three times. The remainder of the Twelve would soon desert Him. The cross lay before Him. And soon, in a mysterious way no one can fully understand, even His Father would "forsake" Him. Jesus was to become the sacrificial Lamb of God who would take away the sins of the world. Only He could do it. There was no other.

This was the reason for which Jesus had been born. All His earthly life had been preparation for this awesome moment. This was the focus of His miraculous incarnation. The time had come.

Humanly speaking, Jesus was alone. He had just completed the Passover meal with His disciples. He had attempted to prepare them for this hour. But they were so preoccupied with themselves that they did not understand what their Master was talking about. Their major concern was about which of them would become the greatest in the kingdom of God.

And so, at His great time of need, Jesus found that His disciples were not much help or encouragement. He asked them to pray with Him, but they fell asleep.

There was only One to whom He could go, One with whom He could communicate openly and intimately. As Jesus prayed, He opened His heart to His Father.

That He prayed was not surprising. It was *what* He prayed that was astonishing. He asked His Father to rescue Him from His imminent suffering and death. His humanity was fully exposed. He did not want to die so savagely; He dreaded carrying the incomprehensible burden of the sins of the entire world. He prayed, "My Father, if it is possible, may this cup be taken from me" (Matt. 26:39).

That is the human kind of praying with which most of us can readily identify. It is wonderful to know God receives that kind of praying graciously from any of His children in all kinds of circumstances. The basic focus of Jesus' prayer was, "Father, if there is any way to get Me out of this situation, please do it."

Few of us, if any, need to be taught that kind of prayer. It is natural for all of us. It is common. I have prayed that prayer many times in my life, and no doubt most believers have done the same. And because of God's love and grace, such praying is often productive.

How many times has the Lord answered that kind of prayer for us? If we had perfect recall, many of us could spend hours testifying how God has answered our prayers in times of great need and desperation.

But the example of Jesus in His Gethsemane experience is an entirely different kind of praying. It is uncommon, infrequent, unnatural. It is truly remarkable. It is the way God wants us always to pray. For in His Gethsemane prayer Jesus added, "Yet not as I will, but as you will. . . . May your will be done" (Matt. 26:39, 42).

Of course, on earlier occasions Jesus had taught His disciples to pray that way. One day they had asked Jesus to teach them to pray, and He did. He taught them, among other things, to pray, "Your will be done on earth as it is in heaven" (6:10).

But they did not understand what that meant. It was too radical for them. Only after Pentecost did they begin to pray that kind of prayer. And what an incredible difference it made in their lives and ministries. The apostle John stated that in "approaching God" we are to ask "according to his will" (1 John 5:14). That is, we are to submit our desires to His, wanting what He wants even if it conflicts with our wishes. Praying in the will of God means our prayers are in harmony with God's character and with what He has revealed in His Word. When we pray this way, then He answers us. "This is the confidence we have in approaching God: that if we ask anything according to his will, he hears us. And if we know that he hears us—whatever we ask—we know that we have what we asked of him" (5:14–15).

Praying according to God's agenda also means we pray in Jesus' name. "And I will do whatever you ask in my name, so that the Son may bring glory to the Father. You may ask me for anything in my name, and I will do it" (John 14:13–14). "My Father will give you whatever you ask in my name" (16:23). This means to pray as if Jesus were praying. That is, our requests should conform to His requests; our petitions should be in accord with what we sense from the Scriptures that *He* would ask for.

Perhaps without even realizing it, many of us are self-centered in our praying, thinking God exists to help us fulfill our own desires. By our very nature, we tend to focus on ourselves. It is common for us to be much more concerned about our will being done than His will.

Several years ago I was invited to preach at a large evangelical church. The pastor was a dynamic Christian leader whose reputation had spread throughout the world. He had heard that I would be ministering in the city where he pastored, and he graciously invited me to preach at his morning service.

I enjoyed the service very much. After greeting many of the saints, I was invited to the pastor's home. His wife had prepared a wonderful dinner. We sat down to eat together. Then it happened. I was totally unprepared for what took place. The pastor thanked me for my message and the ministry to the church family. Then his entire mood changed. He became very emotional. He lashed out at me with great anger.

The reason for his unhappiness was not my preaching. Instead, it was my prayer just before the message. Within that context, I had prayed Jesus' words in Gethsemane, "May Your will be done." The pastor told me I should never pray that way. He said it was wrong to pray according to the will of God.

I was astonished. I confess that I was young and was not accustomed to that kind of criticism. I was hurt and confused. But finally I meekly asked, "Why should I not pray that God's will be done when Jesus prayed that way?" His immediate and hostile reply was that it was a cop-out. It let God off the hook. The pastor said we should not let God "get out" of His responsibility of answering our prayers as we pray them. This is what I would call an inverted concept of prayer. According to this theology God exists for us rather than we for Him. God has an obligation to do whatever we ask or tell Him to do.

That pastor is not alone in subscribing to that kind of theology. Many Christians believe prayer is a device to secure whatever they want at a given moment. They may neglect God much of the time, but whenever they want something, they believe He is bound to give it to them when they ask.

But James would disagree. He declared that Christians often do not receive what they pray for simply because they ask with the wrong motive or they ask for things they would like (James 4:1–3). But God says no to those kinds of requests. Why? Because He loves us too much to give us things that would ultimately harm us or others.

As someone has said, God is not a cosmic bellboy for whom we can press a button to get things. Rosalind Rinker has shared that truth clearly: "I have discovered that the real purpose of prayer is to put God at the center of our attention, and forget ourselves and the impression we are making on others."[8] Catherine Marshall put it in slightly different words: "The purpose of prayer is to find God's will and to make that will our prayer."[9]

Prayer includes giving God our requests, but it is far more than that. Walter Liefeld wrote that "if we conceive of prayer basically as a means of acquiring things from God, we trivialize prayer."[10] Prayer helps us live and minister with utter dependency on God. Proper praying focuses on seeking to do the will of God, not on fulfilling our own needs.

Rowland Hogben, a teacher in the China Inland Mission Training Centre during the early part of the twentieth century, summarized this truth well when he said, "Prayer is an interruption of personal ambition."[11]

Of that profound statement, one of his students, David Adeney, later wrote:

> I have often thought of these words of my teacher at the China Inland Mission Training Centre in London, where I was studying shortly before sailing for China in 1934. They remind me that a busy life is no excuse for lack of prayer. I would never admit that I considered prayer less important than my other activities, but in practice I have so often found myself postponing or hurrying through a time of prayer because other things need to be done.
>
> I was in effect demonstrating that I regarded my efforts as being more important than waiting upon God. A time spent in prayer is an expression of my faith and dependence on God, and a recognition of the fact that I cannot fulfill His will apart from the grace of the Lord Jesus and the power of the Holy Spirit.[12]

People naturally tend to be self-reliant. Even for Christian leaders it is easy to establish our measurable goals and to embark on our strategic plans without giving much thought to prayer, except sometimes to ask

God to bless our efforts. Often we do not give much attention to prayer unless and until we encounter some problem in fulfilling our plans.

I met such a young pastor a few years ago shortly after I had become the president of an evangelical denomination in the United States. During a break at a conference where I was speaking, this young man introduced himself to me and related a remarkable story. He said, "A few months ago, when you assumed your leadership position, you immediately began to call us to prayer.

"I was quite unimpressed," he continued. "I was serving a church that was doing very well. Attendance was growing by about 10 to 15 percent a year. I thought I had learned all the necessary principles of church growth, and from my point of view I was successful in putting them into practice.

"In fact, I had worked out a computer program that helped me predict not only that growth would take place, but when it would take place. Therefore, when you began to talk about prayer, I honestly thought I didn't need it—nor did our church. We were doing very well without it.

"Then, about Christmastime, three older ladies from our church asked if they could meet each week to pray for me and the church. I didn't know how to answer except to say yes. I thought, *It certainly won't hurt if these sincere ladies want to pray.* I promptly forgot about it and continued with my ministry during the busy Advent season.

"When January arrived, I expected our attendance to drop, as it usually did during the cold winter season. But it didn't. In fact, it increased. I couldn't figure it out. Then we entered February, and significant growth began to take place. I was astounded—and troubled. I went to my computer again and again but was not able to solve the puzzle. Finally, I went to the elders of the church to ask if they thought I was preaching better than usual. They told me I was not!

"I was sitting in my study one day with my head in my hands trying to understand what was taking place. Without realizing it, I began to pray. I cried out, 'Lord, what is going on? Please help me understand.'

"The Lord brought those three little ladies to mind. I had forgotten all about them. I began to wonder if their prayers had anything to do with this unexplainable growth. And so I went looking for them. I discovered that not only were they meeting regularly to pray for me and the church, but they had enlisted others to pray with them.

"There is no doubt that their prayers were the key to the growth taking place. God was answering their prayers for the church and for me. My ministry has been radically changed. I have come not only to believe in prayer but also to practice it. We have become a praying church, and God is doing wondrous things in response to our prayers."

Although most pastors are not opposed to prayer as this man was, the principle of prayerlessness exists in the lives of many Christian leaders. For many, it is simply a matter of busyness or the priorities of time and resources. But the results are still the same.

Bill Hybels has expressed it this way: "*Prayer is an unnatural activity. From birth we have been learning the rules of self-reliance as we strain and struggle to achieve self-sufficiency. Prayer flies in the face of those deep-seated values. It is an assault on human autonomy, an indictment of independent living. To people in the fast lane, determined to make it on their own, prayer is an embarrassing interruption.*"[13]

Without doubt, one of the greatest contributions of prayer is to help us move to our Lord's agenda from our own agenda, to move to God-dependence from self-reliance, to understand that the purpose of prayer is for us to surrender to His lordship and to submit to His sovereign will—not to convince God to bless our self-initiated goals and plans.

Lord, we surrender!
We raise the white flag to You.
Help us to understand Your purposes for prayer
so that we can pray more frequently
and effectively!
Help us to obey You in all things
and to enjoy communion with You
day by day.
We long to seek You and Your will
and not our own.
May Your kingdom come
and Your will be done
on earth
as it is in heaven.

3

SURVEYING THE AWESOME POWER OF PRAYER

❦

Although most of us have heard it many times, it is important for us to consider it once again. It provides some important insights concerning prayer and the power of God.

Several times I have enjoyed visiting the location where it took place. Each time, I have been overcome with a sense of awe at the power of God displayed on that very mountaintop.

The location was Mount Carmel. The event took place when Elijah, a prophet of the Lord, went up against King Ahab, 450 prophets of Baal, and 400 prophets of Asherah (1 Kings 18).

Elijah shouted to the people, "How long will you waver between two opinions? If the LORD is God, follow him; but if Baal is God, follow him" (18:21). Then Elijah summoned the prophets of Baal to a "prayer challenge." The contest rules were simple. "Get two bulls for us. Let them [the prophets of Baal] choose one for themselves, and let them cut it into pieces and put it on the wood but not set fire to it. I will prepare the other bull and put it on the wood but not set fire to it. Then you call on the name of your god, and I will call on the name of the LORD. The god who answers by fire—he is God" (18:23–24).

What a challenge!

All the people agreed it was a good idea, and so the contest proceeded.

The prophets of Baal went first. After they had prepared the bull and the wood, they called on Baal from morning till noon. But there was no response.

At noon Elijah began to taunt them. They continued through the afternoon. They danced around the altar and slashed themselves with swords and spears until their blood flowed; they shouted and continued their frantic praying until it was time for the evening sacrifice. "But there was no response, no one answered, no one paid attention" (18:29).

Then it was Elijah's turn to pray. He repaired the altar of the Lord and prepared his bull. He dug a trench around the altar and asked that four large jars of water be poured on it. Then he asked that the same dousing be done again, and again a third time. "The water ran down around the altar and even filled the trench" (18:35).

Then Elijah prayed. It was a simple and direct prayer. "O Lord, God of Abraham, Isaac and Israel, let it be known today that you are God in Israel and that I am your servant and have done all these things at your command. Answer me, O Lord, answer me, so these people will know that you, O Lord, are God, and that you are turning their hearts back again" (18:36–37).

Then immediately "the fire of the Lord fell." In fact, it "burned up the sacrifice, the wood, the stones and the soil, and also licked up the water in the trench" (18:38).

Hundreds of years later, the apostle James wrote about that remarkable display of God's power. "Elijah was a man just like us. He prayed earnestly that it would not rain, and it did not rain on the land for three and a half years. Again he prayed, and the heavens gave rain, and the earth produced its crops" (James 5:17–18). Thus he contended, "The prayer of a righteous man is *powerful* and *effective*" (5:16, italics added).

When is the last time we saw God's power unleashed in response to our prayers? When were any of us last involved in a "prayer challenge" with evil rulers in our community or nation? When has the Lord's power been evident in our churches, in our prayer meetings, in our lives?

God's power released in answer to the prayer of His servant Elijah was indeed remarkable. And of course we are not called to duplicate what happened that day on Mount Carmel. In fact, we must be careful not to yield to the temptation of attempting to imitate or even "franchise" whatever God does in a given situation. He does not honor such an approach. It does not work.

Yet the story of Elijah on Mount Carmel is not merely an isolated story of the unleashing of the power of God in response to prayer. The Bible reports a number of such occasions. The power of God was unleashed in response to the prayers of many of God's servants throughout the Old and New Testaments, including Abraham, Moses, Hannah, Samuel, David, Hezekiah, Ezra, Nehemiah, Daniel, Peter, John, Paul, and James.

In addition, the pages of church history contain more of the same. Seldom do we see God moving in such an unusual way except in response to the prayers of His people. That principle of prayer prompted John Wesley to say, "God does nothing but in answer to prayer."[1]

The great Reformer, Martin Luther, agreed. He declared, "Prayer is a powerful thing, for God has bound and tied Himself thereto."[2]

Charles Finney later wrote, "John Knox was a man famous for his power in prayer, so that Queen Mary used to say that she feared his prayers more than all the armies of Europe."[3]

And in this regard Luther added, "None can believe how powerful prayer is, and what it is able to effect, but those who have learned it by personal experience."[4]

Down through the ages God has answered the prayers of His people. Frequently He has displayed His power. However, God does not do so for show or simply to be spectacular. He manifests His power when it is appropriate to accomplish His will.

Again the important question may be asked: When is the last time we saw God's power unleashed in response to our prayers? And we would do well to consider a second question: Where is the power of God in our ministries?

THE POWER OF GOD MADE AVAILABLE

The awesome power of God is available to believers today. Jesus promised such power to His disciples (and to us) in the prophetic statement He made just before He ascended to be with His Father in heaven. Jesus said, "But you will receive power when the Holy Spirit comes on you; and you will be my witnesses in Jerusalem, and in all Judea and Samaria, and to the ends of the earth" (Acts 1:8).

S. D. Gordon wrote about this power in his classic book *Quiet Talks on Prayer*.

> There is one inlet of power in life—anybody's life—any kind of power: just one inlet—the Holy Spirit. He is power. He is in everyone who opens his door to God. He eagerly enters every open door. He comes in by our invitation and consent. His presence within is the vital thing.
>
> But with many of us while He is in, He is not in control: in as guest; not as host. That is to say He is hindered in His natural movement; tied up, so that He cannot do what He would. And so we are not conscious or only partially conscious of His presence. And others are still less so. But to yield to His mastery, to cultivate His friendship, to give Him full swing—that will result in what is called power. One inlet of power—the Holy Spirit in control.[5]

There is great potential power in prayer. The early church discovered this basic truth right away. In fact, the church was born in the midst of a powerful prayer meeting (1:13–14). Jesus' prophetic statement in Acts 1:8 was fulfilled. His followers were filled with the Holy Spirit and began to display unnatural power—the power of the Holy Spirit (Acts 2).

Just a few weeks before this, Peter had failed his Lord miserably when he trusted in his own strength. Now he stood unafraid before a crowd of thousands gathered in Jerusalem. He preached a simple message on the life, death, and resurrection of Jesus, and he did so with great boldness and power. The results were truly remarkable.

But that was only the beginning. Believers in the early church continued the work of Pentecost on their knees. In fact the Book of Acts, as discussed in chapter 1, records many instances of prayer. The power of God was unleashed in appropriate ways as the people of God prayed.

Thomas Constable has summarized the prayer ministry of the early church as follows:

> In Acts we see the disciples giving prayer a prominent place in their personal and corporate lives. The early Christians expressed their great

dependence on God that they felt by praying frequently and fervently. The apostles considered prayer one of their primary duties along with the ministry of the Word (Acts 6:1–4). It was as the believers in Antioch of Syria were praying and fasting that God directed them to send Barnabas and Paul farther west into the Roman Empire. The missionaries prayed before they appointed elders in the new churches that they established. They realized the need for God's guidance and enablement for these new leaders. The church's expansion from Jerusalem to the uttermost parts of the earth was a result of prayer. The apostles obtained strength and encouragement from God in prison through prayer many times.[6]

This display of power was not glitzy or spectacular. Instead, though it was displayed in various ways, it was always practical. It focused on the source of power, the Lord Himself. So the power was not an end in itself. It did not call attention to itself. People did not worship the power; they worshiped the Source of the power. It was used in day-by-day ministry. It brought glory to God and advancement to His mission.

For example, shortly after the significant Pentecost event, Peter and John had joined with other believers for prayer about three o'clock in the afternoon in the temple courts. On their way to the prayer meeting they were interrupted by a man, crippled from birth, who asked them for money. Peter looked straight at the beggar and shared with him something far better than money. He said, "'Silver or gold I do not have, but what I have I give you. In the name of Jesus Christ of Nazareth, walk.' Taking him by the right hand, he helped him up" (3:6–7).

The results were immediate and remarkable. "Instantly the man's feet and ankles became strong. He jumped to his feet and began to walk. Then he went with them into the temple courts, walking and jumping, and praising God" (3:7–8). Recognizing that this man had been crippled for over forty years, the people were filled with amazement, astonishment, and wonder. They went running to Peter and John.

Peter responded to them, "Why does this surprise you? Why do you stare at us as if by our own *power* or godliness we had made this man walk?" (3:12, italics added). Peter acknowledged immediately that it was not his power that had healed this man. It was the power of Jesus Christ, the one His enemies thought they had gotten rid of when they crucified Him. But Jesus was indeed alive, and His power was being manifested through the Holy Spirit.

Peter concluded, "By faith in the name of Jesus, this man whom you see and know was made strong. It is Jesus' name and the faith that comes through him that has given this complete healing to him, as you can all see" (3:16).

Then the priests, the captain of the temple guard, and the Sadducees put Peter and John in jail (4:1–3). The next day the two apostles were brought before the high priest, Annas, and the rulers, elders, and teachers of the law, who asked them a most insightful question. Instead of rejoicing and praising God for His miraculous healing of the crippled man, they asked, "By what *power* or what name did you do this?" (4:7, italics added).

Peter replied, "It is by the name of Jesus Christ of Nazareth, whom you crucified but whom God raised from the dead, that this man stands before you healed." Then Peter added, "Salvation is found in no one else, for there is no other name under heaven given to men by which we must be saved" (4:10, 12).

Jesus Christ was the source of the power Peter and John needed. And He is the source of the spiritual power all Christian leaders desperately need.

Interestingly, after Peter and John had been intimidated, warned, and commanded not to mention the name of Jesus again, they returned to their own people—the church. And they engaged in another powerful prayer meeting.

When "they raised their voices together in prayer to God" (4:24), the results were immediate. "After they prayed, the place where they were meeting was shaken. And they were all filled with the Holy Spirit and spoke the word of God boldly" (4:31). God answered their prayer. They had prayed for great boldness (4:29), and the Lord answered them.

The benefits of that prayer meeting were many. One of the positive results is described this way: "With great *power* the apostles continued to testify to the resurrection of the Lord Jesus, and much grace was upon them all" (4:33, italics added).

Concerning this kind of power Corrie ten Boom wrote, "Prayer is powerful. The devil smiles when we make plans. He laughs when we get too busy. But he trembles when we pray—especially when we pray together. Remember, though, that it is God who answers, and He always answers in a way that He knows is best for everyone."[7]

GOD'S POWER MADE PERFECT IN WEAKNESS

Christians must be careful never to mistake our power for God's. Some Christians seem to be obsessed with the matter of power. They seem to love the sensational. They constantly try to be spectacular. They face the temptation of trying to "make things happen," to produce or manufacture divine power. Others, however, seem to ignore God's power altogether. They have so overreacted to what they consider the misuse of power that they virtually deny the availability of God's power.

Because of these two extremes, many non-Christians observe Christians either as powerless and irrelevant, or else as preoccupied with a superficial, exaggerated, fabricated kind of power.

The disciples of Jesus struggled with this power issue. John Guest describes it this way.

> Try to imagine the anguish of the disciples as they confront the terrifying demonic power gripping the young boy who has been brought to them (Mark 9:18, 22). . . . The disciples are no strangers to the power of the evil one as it manifests itself in such unfortunate people. They have seen the spectacular deliverance of the man of the Gerasenes, in whom the demons were so numerous that they named themselves, corporately, "Legion" (Mark 5:1–20).
>
> But they had not yet encountered a case as terrifying as the one now before them. How long they tried in vain to drive out the evil spirit, we do not know. We do know that the father of the possessed boy lost confidence in their efforts. Imagine their frustration and embarrassment when he brought his son to Jesus and explained, "I asked your disciples to cast it out and they were not able" (Mark 9:18).
>
> Jesus, of course, succeeds where his followers have failed: with a word of command and a touch of healing, he banishes the evil spirit and restores the boy to full health. The chastened disciples wait until Jesus has entered the house, and then ask him privately, "Why could we not cast it out?" (9:28).

His response is startling . . . "This kind cannot be driven out by anything but prayer" (Mark 9:29).

That is all.

The disciples' failure stems not from lack of divine prerogatives, but from lack of prayer. Had they prayed more, been more "men of prayer," Jesus seems to suggest (some versions of the account also mention fasting as an important element which gave evidence of sincerity and intensity in prayer) they would have succeeded here as in so many previous instances.[8]

Guest then shares how this account relates to spiritual power in our lives. "This word of Jesus is both comforting and troubling, and for precisely the same reason: because it locates the effective exercise of spiritual power squarely within the province of each one of us. Our humanity need no longer limit our ability to overcome spiritual opposition: the *power of prayer* is, after all, available to us.

"But at the same time, we may no longer hide behind our humanity, no longer use it to excuse our spiritual impotence: the *power of prayer* is available to us—if only we will learn to take advantage of it."[9]

How much *personal power* do we need to receive and use the power of God in our ministry? The answer is "None!"

The apostle Paul came to realize that simple and profound truth. He reached the place in his life where he declared, "I will not boast about myself, except about my weaknesses" (2 Cor. 12:5).

Then he related that he had been given a "thorn in the flesh" as a messenger of Satan to keep him from becoming conceited. He said, "Three times I pleaded with the Lord to take it away from me. But he said to me, 'My grace is sufficient for you, for *my power* is made perfect in weakness'" (12:8–9, italics added). He added, "Therefore, I will boast all the more gladly about my weaknesses, so that *Christ's power* may rest on me. That is why, for Christ's sake, I delight in weaknesses, in insults, in hardships, in persecutions, in difficulties. For when I am weak, then I am strong" (12:9–10, italics added).

Paul needed the power that only Christ can give. And so do we!

I remember well one of the first times I experienced this principle. As a young evangelist I was invited to preach at a youth rally in a small city in eastern South Dakota. Most of the churches in that little community had joined together to host an outreach rally for young people.

Because a boyhood friend of mine was hosting the event, I was especially looking forward to sharing in the ministry. In addition, I loved young people and enjoyed greatly the opportunity to share the Good News of Jesus Christ with them.

As my wife, Jeannie, and I arrived in town on a Saturday afternoon, I began to feel ill. We had dinner with our friend and then proceeded to the local high school gymnasium, where the rally was to take place. By the time I was being introduced to preach, I had become very sick. I was running a high fever and as a result I was trembling.

I knew I would be unable to preach unless the Lord gave me strength. In the meantime the opening part of the service did not go very well. A youth choir that was supposed to sing did not arrive, and as a result, the musical portion of the rally was weak. In addition, although they expected several hundred young people, a crowd of less than two hundred showed up. The mood of the meeting was disconnected and lifeless.

Finally it was time for me to preach. I literally staggered to the pulpit. I held on for dear life; I was not certain how long I could stand or if I could even speak. I shared my situation with those assembled and asked them to pray for me. Then I led in a public prayer. I prayed the prayer of the apostle Paul: I acknowledged my weakness and asked for the Lord's power to be made manifest in my weakness.

The Lord answered in a remarkable way. Seldom have I preached with more power. The young people listened in rapt attention. The moving of the Holy Spirit was obvious.

When I completed my simple gospel message and extended the invitation, I was not prepared for the response. Virtually every non-Christian young person in the auditorium came forward to receive Christ. By God's grace there were enough Christian adults and young people present to counsel personally with every one of the inquirers. Not one person remained seated. Everyone had gone to the front to seek Christ or to pray with those who had come to receive Him into their lives.

It was a memorable evening. The power of God was made manifest in weakness; His strength was made perfect in my weakness.

I am not suggesting that our best and most effective preaching can take place only when we are sick or physically weak. I am saying, however, that the Lord wants us to acknowledge to Him our weakness and insufficiency whenever we are involved in any kind of ministry so that His power can be released in us and through us. He is waiting for us to pray, to ask for the release of His power.

God's power shows up best in weak people.

Lord, we acknowledge that You alone
can supply the spiritual power we need.
We long to be like Elijah—
to be known by our righteousness—
and our effectual, powerful praying.
We rejoice that You have said that
Your power
shows up best in weak people.
We are weak, Lord.
Grant us Your power to accomplish Your will,
and we will give You the glory!

4

Enjoying the Intimate Privacy of Prayer

⚬━✦━⚬

W HEN YOU PRAY, go into your room, close the door and pray to your Father, who is unseen. Then your Father, who sees what is done in secret, will reward you" (Matt. 6:6).

At first glance, this verse may seem to say the Lord is instructing us to go into our room and close the door. That may remind us of an angry parent punishing a child. If so, it does not bring back pleasant memories to many of us. For others the verse may seem more like an encouragement to take refuge from our busy, demanding lifestyles. Going to our room and closing the door may be one of the few opportunities to find a place of quiet and solitude.

In actuality, these words of Jesus do not fit either scenario. Instead, Jesus has invited us to go to a place where we can be alone with Him, a place where we can talk to Him and share our concerns, burdens, and needs.

This is an invitation for us to commune with Jesus, to be in His presence, to draw near, to enjoy His company. It is an opportunity to rest in His love and care, to sense His presence, to be still and know He is God, to cast our anxieties on Him. It is a time to be assured that He loves us and that He enjoys caring for us.

Some call such a place a prayer closet. But whatever we may call it, all of us need a place where we can be alone with God. For some it is a bedroom, a study, or even a corner of a backyard. For others, always on the move, it may be a hotel room, an office, or even an automobile. Wherever the place, the focus is always the same: to retreat from our busy, demanding, hectic, overscheduled lives and find intimacy with God.

As noted in a previous chapter, Jesus found such times and places in His personal life to be alone with His Father. He frequently withdrew from His disciples, the crowds, and the rigors of ministry to pray. When ministering in Galilee, Jesus got up early in the morning, while it was still dark, to go off to a solitary place to pray alone (Mark 1:35). In fact, within the heavy demands of His personal and public ministry, Jesus chose to withdraw frequently to private places to pray to God His Father (Luke 5:16).

Although He surely needed as much sleep as we do, the Bible records an occasion when Jesus went out to a mountainside to spend the entire night praying to His Father before selecting His twelve disciples (6:12). No doubt He prayed that way frequently. Just before He walked on the water He went to the hills to pray (Matt. 14:23; Mark 6:46), and when He went up on the mount of Transfiguration, He went for the purpose of prayer (Luke 9:28). Luke 9:18 also refers to His "praying in private."

THE INVITATION OF JESUS

Perhaps the most memorable occasion on which Jesus withdrew to pray was the night of His betrayal. He took the eleven disciples (Judas had already departed to carry out his dastardly deed) to the Garden of Gethsemane on the Mount of Olives, just across the Kidron Valley from the place where they had gathered for the Passover supper.

After arriving, Jesus invited Peter, James, and John to join Him in an intimate place of prayer. He asked them to watch and pray with Him. He explained that His soul was overwhelmed with sorrow to the point of death (Matt. 26:36–46).

Unfortunately His disciples did not respond as needed. In fact, they missed an opportunity of a lifetime. Jesus had asked them to share in a most intimate time of communication between God the Father and God the Son. But they missed it. They chose to sleep. How sad.

We must be careful not to repeat their behavior. Our Lord urges us, like the disciples, to come to Him, to commune with Him in prayer, to fellowship with Him. We dare not miss the opportunity, for our own sakes, yes, but also for the sake of Christ and the advancement of His ministry.

Charles Swindoll has stated our challenge well: "The One who instructed us to 'be still and know that I am God' must hurt when He witnesses our frantic, compulsive, agitated motions. In place of a quiet, responsive spirit we offer Him an inner washing machine—churning with anxiety, clogged with too much activity, and spilling over with resentment and impatience. Sometimes He must watch our convulsions with an inner sigh."[1]

Praying in secret places is not the only kind of prayer to which our Lord calls us. But it is a great place to begin. We are not well prepared for other kinds of praying until we become faithful in practicing personal, intimate times of prayer with our Lord.

And, like Jesus, this may require us to give up some sleep from time to time, or to turn off the television set, or to give up a sporting event. Such times of intimate communion with God do not just happen. We need to take the initiative. Otherwise, we may end up like the disciples, missing a priceless opportunity for fellowship with God.

David Brainerd, a young missionary to the American Indians of a past generation, stated this truth when he wrote in his journal, "I have found that the more I do in secret prayer, the more I have delighted to do, and the more I have enjoyed the spirit of prayer."[2]

Prayer is the vehicle that enables us to enjoy God in the deepest expression of intimacy available to us. Words cannot describe such times.

We do well to return to the writings of O. H. Hallesby, who addressed this subject with deep spiritual insight.

> Prayer is the breath of the soul, the organ by which we receive Christ into our parched and withered hearts. He says, If any man open the door, I will come in to him. . . . God has designed prayer as a means of intimate and joyous fellowship between God and man. . . .
>
> To pray is nothing more involved than to let Jesus into our needs. To

pray is to give Jesus permission to employ his power in the alleviation of our distress. To pray is to let Jesus glorify His name in the midst of our needs. . . .

Prayer should be the means by which I, at all times, receive all that I need, and, for this reason, be my daily refuge, my daily consolation, my daily joy, my source of rich and inexhaustible joy in life.[3]

Devoted praying is not a religious duty or even a mere religious experience. It is profound, deep, and inexpressible. It is experiencing God in the ultimate sense.

PRAYER AND OUR RELATIONSHIP WITH GOD

From a slightly different perspective, John Guest has communicated great insight about intimate prayer.

Prayer is first and foremost an expression of an intimate relationship with God.

Prayer includes discipline, but it is not merely a discipline. It involves setting aside a regular time and place, but it is not merely an item on our schedule. It includes asking for things we need, but it is not merely a shopping list of requests and rejoicings. It involves speaking to God and God speaking to us, but it is not merely an exchange of memoranda.

More than anything else, prayer is a relationship. When we reduce it to a regimen, we deprive ourselves of what all who knew God throughout the scriptures expressed in their prayers: that God is alive, and that He knows us and lets Himself be known by us, that we can enjoy a deep and intimate personal relationship with Him in prayer.[4]

Prayer moves us from the mere rational to the relational. It transports us from talking about God to talking with God. As Edmund Clowney put it, "Prayer is not a magical formula to be repeated, but the personal communication, awed and adoring, of the redeemed creature who stands in the presence of the Saviour God."[5]

Prayer is to be more than an occasional event. It should be part of our lifestyle. We have the privilege of cultivating the remarkable experience of learning to pray without ceasing. And our times of intimate, personal, private prayer equip and prepare us for continuous praying.

It assures us of the fact that our relationship with God is not merely casual or occasional. Rather, we have the privilege of living in a close, intimate, loving relationship with Him day by day, even moment by moment.

Love is at the very heart of our intimate prayer communication with our Lord. Rosalind Rinker said it well: "After all, it isn't the words we say nor how we say them. It is the open heart attitude which God looks for. . . . Prayer is the expression of the human heart in conversation with God. The more natural the prayers, the more real He becomes. It has all been simplified for me to this extent: prayer is a dialogue between two persons who love each other."[6]

Love is at the core of every authentically deep, intimate relationship. That is God's design. The most meaningful intimate relationship between two persons—a husband and a wife—takes place within the context of a Christian marriage. And the deepest, most intimate expression of spiritual communication takes place when a true follower of Jesus Christ opens his or her heart to Him—with love—in prayer.

Thomas Constable expresses this truth in a wonderful way.

God presents Himself in the Bible as being open and interested in hearing whatever concerns His children (James 5:13; 1 Peter 5:7). He wants to hear whatever interests us, even the smallest details of our lives. Consequently we should feel free to unburden our hearts and tell God anything and everything. He is the friend who sticks closer than a brother. We can converse with Him casually and comfortably as we would with our most intimate acquaintance.

Even though God already knows whatever we might tell Him before we tell Him, He still wants us to tell Him. This proves that God desires fellowship with us. Fellowship with God is one of the primary purposes of prayer. Family members who do not talk to each other enough develop problems in their relationship. Keeping the lines of communication open with God is also essential to a healthy spiritual relationship. In marriage, communication is usually informal and unrehearsed, and it can be that way with our heavenly bridegroom too.[7]

Margaret Magdalen says this about Jesus' praying: "The first thing, then, that Jesus taught His disciples about prayer was that it involved relationship. In doing so, He opened a window for them on to the secret of His own prayer life. The solitude and silence which He needed so much (why else would He have sought them so regularly?) were spent rapt in intimate communion with the God whom He loved and personally addressed as Father. This joy of intimacy is now extended to the disciples and later, among early Christians, would be the supreme privilege given to converts immediately after baptism, when they would be taught the Lord's Prayer."[8]

Love in that kind of context is more than a mere feeling, an infatuation, or a human emotion. As the apostle John expressed it, "Let us not love with words or tongue but with actions and in truth" (1 John 3:18).

In other words, authentic love involves action. It is an act of the will. It requires a conscious decision. And it calls for commitment. To "love the Lord your God with all your heart and with all your soul and with all your mind and with all your strength" (Mark 12:30) requires more than merely a warm, fuzzy feeling. It requires action!

And one of the action steps we need to take is to spend time with God—focusing on Him, expressing our love to Him, communing with Him. Prayer enables us to know God personally. Only people of prayer have that joy and privilege. There is no other way. W. Bingham Hunter addresses this important truth with biblical and theological clarity. "The fact of God's personalness means that knowing *about* Him is different than knowing Him. Most of what the Bible says about prayer assumes this distinction. But we forget this. We tend to view prayer as a process of gathering information about God and practicing certain techniques. But prayer is interpersonal communication between two individuals. In Scripture, it matters far, far less *how, when* and *what* you say than how well you know *Him* to whom you pray."[9]

God is not hiding behind a tree making it difficult for us to communicate with Him in prayer. Instead, the Bible teaches clearly that God takes the initiative in prayer.

He comes to seek us.

He invites—even commands—us to pray.

He longs to commune with us.

He knocks at the door of our spiritual hearts.

He waits for us to respond in prayer.

He offers us an intimate relationship with Him that defies human description. In fact, He invites us to experience the kind of relationship He enjoyed with Adam and Eve before the Fall.

We can walk with Him every moment of every day. We can talk with Him about anything and everything. We can enter His presence at any time.

THE PRESENCE OF GOD

"'Should you not fear me?' declares the LORD. 'Should you not tremble in my presence?'" (Jer. 5:22). Those were the questions the Lord asked His people through His prophet Jeremiah. And they are two questions He would ask us. Do we fear God? Do we tremble when we are in His presence?

Shortly before Jesus ascended to heaven He gave His disciples the Great Commission. He told them to go and make disciples of all nations. In that same context He assured them of His presence: "And surely I am with you always, to the very end of the age" (Matt. 28:20).

Although Jesus was departing from them physically, He promised to be with them all the time, to the very end of the age. This fulfilled a promise He had made to them (and us) several days before His crucifixion: "But I tell you the truth: It is for your good that I am going away. Unless I go away, the Counselor will not come to you; but if I go, I will send him to you" (John 16:7).

Earlier Jesus had said to them, "And I will ask the Father, and he will give you another Counselor to be with you forever—the Spirit of truth. The world cannot accept him, because it neither sees him nor knows him. But you know him, for he lives with you and will be in you. I will not leave you as orphans; I will come to you. . . . On that day you will realize that I am in my Father, and you are in me, and I am in you" (14:16–18, 20).

Though He would soon be leaving them, His departure would actually be good for them. Though He would no longer be with them physically, He would be present with them in the person of the Holy Spirit. In other words, though He would no longer live *with* them, He would now live *in* them.

And that is His promise to us. Each day we can experience the presence of Jesus Christ in our lives by means of the indwelling Holy Spirit. Practicing the presence of God is not reserved for a few spiritually elite Christians; it is available to every believer.

Jesus reinforced that teaching with repeated statements about abiding in them. "Remain in me, and I will remain in you. . . . I am the vine; you are the branches. If a man remains in me and I in him, he will bear much fruit; apart from me you can do nothing" (15:4–5). "If you obey my commands, you will remain in my love" (15:10).

Sometime later, the apostle Paul spoke of that same truth when he referred to "Christ in you, the hope of glory" (Col. 1:27).

Jesus Christ indeed did not leave His disciples or us as orphans. He did not desert or abandon them or us when He ascended to the Father. Instead, He provided Someone for them and us who exceeds His being with us physically!

The change in the lives of the apostles and other early Christians as a result of being filled with the Holy Spirit was dramatic. For example, the apostle Peter and the others began to do things they had never before been able to do. It was their praying that unleashed the presence and power of the Holy Spirit in their lives.

Over the years I have had the privilege of visiting and ministering in hundreds of churches throughout the United States and in the world. One of my deepest concerns is how relatively few churches seem to experience the presence of Jesus Christ.

Many local churches have become merely human organizations. They are frequently led by gifted pastors who seem to do little in the power of the Holy Spirit. Frequently when I am in that kind of environment, I am prompted by the Holy Spirit to ask the disturbing question, "How long has it been since you have sensed the presence of Jesus Christ in this church?" Or, "What would happen if Jesus showed up in your worship service next Sunday?"

Many of our Lord's servants are missing the greatest privilege of Christian life and ministry; they are not living and ministering with the presence and power of the Holy Spirit. I believe we should expect to experience the presence of Christ when we gather for worship on the Lord's Day or at any other gathering of believers. Our Lord has promised His presence when we gather in His name (Matt. 18:20). It is tragic when we do not even expect it.

The early Christians expected it. They not only believed in the resurrection of Jesus Christ theologically; they also lived and ministered as though He was actually alive and in their presence. They did everything in the name of Jesus.

It is enlightening to note the frequent occurrence of the phrase "in the name of Jesus" in the Book of Acts. They met in His name; they prayed in His name; they worshiped in His name; they ministered in His name; they preached in His name; they witnessed in His name. (See Acts 4:10, 17–18, 30; 5:40–41; 8:12; 9:15, 27; 10:43, 48; 15:26; 16:18; 19:5, 13, 17; 21:13; 22:16.) And in so doing, they were referring to the presence of Jesus. In other words, using the name of Jesus represented His presence.

Brother Lawrence was not the first follower of Jesus to practice the presence of God. The apostles and the early believers led the way. And that wonderful lifestyle is available to every one of us. John Baillie truly grasped that truth when he penned the following verse in his diary of private prayer:

> Almighty and eternal God,
> You are hidden from my sight:
> You are beyond the understanding of my mind:
> Your thoughts are not as my thoughts:
> Your ways are past finding out.
> Yet You have breathed Your Spirit into my life:
> Yet You have formed my mind to seek You:
> Yet You have inclined my heart to love You:
> Yet You have made me restless for the rest that is in You:
> Yet You have planted within me a hunger and thirst
> that makes me dissatisfied with all the joys of earth.
> O You who alone know what lies before me this day, grant
> that in every hour of it I may stay close to You. Let me be in the

world, yet not of it. Let me use this world without abusing it. If I buy, let me be as though I possessed not. If I have nothing, let me be as though possessing all things. Let me today embark on no undertaking that is not in line with Your will for my life, nor shrink from any sacrifice which Your will may demand. Suggest, direct, control every movement of my mind; for my Lord Christ's sake. Amen.[10]

THE WHY AND HOW OF PRAYER

Prayer benefits us, our families and loved ones, our church families, our places of study and employment, our communities and cities, our nation, and the world.

Prayer benefits every person, institution, and ministry for which we pray. In these first four chapters of this book we have explored some of the reasons *why* we should pray. Here is a summary of several of them:

- We should pray because our Lord has asked us—even commanded us—to pray without ceasing.

- We should pray because our Lord invites us to fellowship with Him, to enjoy intimate and deep communion with Him.

- We should pray because prayer helps transport us from our own agenda to God's agenda, from our will to His will.

- We should pray because it helps us grow in our relationship to God.

- We should pray because it allows us to be used by God to advance His work.

- We should pray because God delights in answering our prayers.

- We should pray because it provides the spiritual power we need, power that can come only from God.

- We should pray because prayer and the Word are the means by which to defeat our enemy Satan and to live victoriously.

- We should pray because there is no higher privilege in life than to communicate with the living God, the Creator and Sustainer of all.

- We should pray because prayer ushers us into the very presence of God!

But how do we cultivate this life of prayer? How do we experience such an intimate relationship with God? And how can we fulfill the great potential of prayer our Lord has offered us? How do we appropriate God's provision and protection? Where do we begin, and how do we proceed? These are some of the practical subjects discussed in the next chapters. Our Lord stands ready to teach us if we are ready to learn.

Thank You, dear Lord,
for inviting us to Your intimate place of prayer.
We are in awe at the privilege of
coming into Your presence
to commune with You
in prayer.
Thank You for Your love which is incomprehensible.
We would love You with all of our hearts
and souls
and minds
and strength.
Lord, teach us to pray!

PART 2

Cultivating a Life of Prayer

5

DETERMINING THE PROPER POSTURE OF PRAYER

◦━━◦

P RAYER REQUIRES the proper posture.

That may sound like a strange statement. In our busy culture, posture and its relationship to prayer may seem a totally unnecessary subject, or a secondary subject at best. But the posture we assume when we pray is extremely significant.

Why should God care about our posture when we pray? Isn't the main thing simply that we talk to Him, regardless of our pose or demeanor?

Our minds naturally tend toward the various possibilities for physical posture when we pray. Should we kneel, stand, sit, or even lie prostrate on the floor before our holy God?

These are legitimate considerations. But this is not where we should begin our consideration of the proper posture for prayer. We need to begin with discussing the *spiritual* posture of prayer. When our spiritual posture is correct, the appropriate physical posture will follow.

THE POSTURE OF THE HEART

Physical appearances can be deceptive. Samuel found that to be true when the Lord sent him to Jesse's family to anoint the next king of Israel. When he met Jesse's first son, Eliab, he was very impressed. He thought, "Surely

51

the Lord's anointed stands here before the LORD'" (1 Sam. 16:6). But the Lord had other plans. His criteria for leadership do not always conform to ours, or to that of our culture.

"But the LORD said to Samuel, 'Do not consider his appearance or his height, for I have rejected him. The LORD does not look at the things man looks at. Man looks at the outward appearance, but the LORD looks at the heart'" (16:7).

God knows our hearts (Ps. 44:21), searches our hearts (1 Chron. 28:9), and He ponders and understands the thoughts of our hearts (Ps. 139:2). He is not impressed with our attempts to impress Him. But He does receive those who come to Him with broken and contrite hearts. David understood that. He wrote, "You do not delight in sacrifice, or I would bring it; you do not take pleasure in burnt offerings." Then he added, "The sacrifices of God are a broken spirit; a broken and contrite heart, O God, you will not despise" (51:16–17).

The proper posture in which to approach God is the opposite of pride, arrogance, pretense, and self-reliance. Warren Wiersbe has summarized well this matter of the posture of the heart.

> Many different prayer postures are recorded in the Bible and all of them are acceptable. Some people bowed their knees when they prayed (Gen. 24:52; 2 Chron. 20:18; Eph. 3:14). When Jesus prayed in Gethsemane, He began by bowing His knees (Luke 22:41); He then fell on His face as He talked to the Father (Matt. 26:39). It was Daniel's practice to kneel when he prayed (Dan. 6:10), but King David sat when he talked to God about the promised kingdom (2 Sam. 7:18). Abraham stood when he interceded for Sodom (Gen. 18:22). So there are many postures for prayer.
>
> The important thing is *the posture of the heart*. It is much easier to bow the knees than to bow the heart in submission to God. While the outward posture can be evidence of the inward spiritual attitude, it is not always so. Again, the important thing is *the posture of the heart*.[1]

Our Lord said, "Whoever has haughty eyes and a proud heart, him will I not endure" (Ps. 101:5). As we know, pride is often so subtle. It is quite easy to detect in the lives of others but much more difficult to recognize in ourselves.

Jesus, teaching in the Sermon on the Mount, spoke clearly to this important issue. "Why do you look at the speck of sawdust in your brother's eye and pay no attention to the plank in your own eye? How can you say to your brother, 'Let me take the speck out of your eye,' when all the time there is a plank in your own eye? You hypocrite, first take the plank out of your own eye, and then you will see clearly to remove the speck from your brother's eye" (Matt. 7:3–5).

When we come to God in prayer, we need to come to Him with broken and contrite hearts. It is foolish to attempt to come into His presence with a proud heart. Writing about the life of prayer, James quoted from Proverbs 3:34, "God opposes the proud but gives grace to the humble" (James 4:6). When we go to God in prayer, we do not need His opposition. We need His grace.

THE POSTURE OF HUMILITY

The Lord has promised grace to those who approach Him in prayer with the spirit of humility.

After telling a parable about the Pharisee and the tax collector, who both went to the temple to pray, Jesus concluded with this application: "For everyone who exalts himself will be humbled, and he who humbles himself will be exalted" (Luke 18:14). That is God's design.

Andrew Murray described the kind of humility we need to bring to our times of prayer. "Humility is perfect quietness of heart. It is to have no trouble. It is never to be fretted or irritated or sore or disappointed. It is to expect nothing, to wonder at nothing that is done to me. It is to be at rest when nobody praises me and when I am blamed or despised. It is to have a blessed home in the Lord, where I can go in and shut the door and kneel to my Father in secret, and am at peace as in the deep sea of calmness when all around and above is trouble."[2]

Our immediate response to that description might be defensive. Many would realize they do not bring that kind of humility to God. But the proper solution is simply to bring ourselves to God as we are, and then to humble ourselves before Him. Dwight L. Moody wrote, "God has nothing to say to the self-righteous. Unless you humble yourself before him in the dust, and confess before him your iniquities and sins, the gate of heaven, which is open only for *sinners*, saved by *grace*, must be shut against you forever."[3]

God puts a great price on humility of heart, as E. M. Bounds wrote.

> It is good to be clothed with humility as a garment. It is written, God resisteth the proud, but giveth grace to the humble. That which brings the praying soul near to God is humility of heart. That which gives wings to prayer is lowliness of mind. That which gives ready access to the throne of grace is self-depreciation. Pride, self-esteem, and self-praise effectually shut the door of prayer.
>
> He who would come to God must approach him with self hid from his own eyes. He must not be puffed-up with self-conceit, nor be possessed with an over-estimate of his virtues and good works. Humility is a rare Christian grace, of great price in the courts of heaven, entering into and being an inseparable condition of effectual praying. It gives access to God when other qualities fail. . . . Our prayers must have much of the dust on them before they can ever have much of the glory of the skies in them.[4]

THE POSTURE OF HELPLESSNESS

Without realizing it, Christians often come to God with preconceived plans and agendas. Frequently we do not ask God anything in our prayers. Instead, we tell Him what to do, how to do it, and when to do it. Many of us are especially adept at telling the Lord when He should act on our behalf. But prayer that is focused on *helping God* is bound to fail.

Little children readily learn how to manipulate their parents to get what they want. They know when and how to approach them. Children easily discover which parent is more likely to grant their desires. That kind of behavior is carried over into praying. Some have never known the joy of simply coming to the Lord with empty hands and asking Him to fill them, without their help.

A number of years ago I read a book on group problem-solving. As a college textbook, it had nothing to do with the life of prayer. However, as I was reading it the Holy Spirit interrupted me and taught me a helpful principle that dramatically affected my prayer life.

The authors contended that the major challenge of most group problem-solving sessions is that the group seldom focuses on the problem. Instead, they tend to begin their group discussion by talking about possible solutions. Seldom do they ever clarify or define the problem. Nor do they even agree on what the real problem might be.

In most problem-solving gatherings many of the participants bring to the discussion their preconceived opinions about what the solution should be. Rather than using the group to solve the problem, the members of the group engage in arguing about who has the best solution. As a result, they seldom agree on an appropriate and workable solution.

As I read that book, the Lord began to speak to me about my prayer life. I had never realized it, but I seldom if ever had come to the Lord with my problems. Instead, I brought my preconceived solutions and asked Him to fulfill them. Without realizing it, I was not asking God for what I needed. I was telling God what to do.

Jesus taught us, "Apart from me you can do nothing" (John 15:5). But He added, "If you remain in me and my words remain in you, *ask* whatever you wish, and it will be given you" (15:7, italics added). Asking contrasts sharply with telling Him what to do.

Without Him we can do nothing. But with Him, we can ask for anything, and it will be given to us.

In a real sense we can never truly pray without a sense of helplessness. We must come to our Lord with the understanding that we cannot control the situation, that we cannot supply what is needed, that we cannot demand our own way with God.

Coming to Him humbly and openly, we need to recognize the fact that unless God does it, it will not be done. Prayer and helplessness are inseparable. As O. H. Hallesby noted, "Only he who is helpless can truly pray."[5] Then he added,

> My helpless friend, your helplessness is the most powerful plea which rises up to the tender father heart of God. He has heard your prayer from the very first moment that you honestly cried to him in your need, and night and day He inclines His ear toward earth in order to ascertain if any of the helpless children of men are turning to Him in their distress....

Be not anxious because of your helplessness. Above all, do not let it
prevent you from praying. Helplessness is the real secret and the impelling
power of prayer. You should therefore rather try to thank God for the feeling of helplessness which He has given you. It is one of the greatest gifts
which God can impart to us. For it is only when we are helpless that we
open our hearts to Jesus and let Him help us in our distress, according to
His grace and mercy.[6]

This incredible truth stands so contrary to our I-can-do-it myself culture! We need to realize just how helpless we are and how hopeless are many
of the situations we face without His loving intervention and provision.

God's children have frequently been in "hopeless" situations. Abraham
faced one of them on Mount Moriah when his son Isaac lay bound to the
altar of sacrifice. So did Moses and the people of Israel when the Red Sea
was before them and the armies of Pharaoh were advancing behind them.
Hannah desperately wanted a child. David went out to meet Goliath.
Daniel was cast into a lions' den. Peter was thrown into prison. The list
could go on and on.

I have found myself in those kinds of helpless, hopeless situations
on a number of occasions. One of the most memorable situations occurred early in my ministry. I was riding on the crest of the wave of
success in the ministry. The Lord had been so good to me. Virtually
everything I had done had been successful according to our culture's
standards. The congregation I served was growing rapidly; everything
was going exceedingly well.

Then the Lord interrupted our lives. We sensed that He was calling us
to establish a new ministry that would primarily serve pastors and local
churches. As we called the church together to pray, they agreed and even
commissioned us to assume the new ministry.

But after a few months things were not going well. Although I felt I
was being led of the Lord and was being obedient to Him, the ministry
was not being marked by success. I went weeks without being paid. There
seemed to be relatively few measurable results.

Then on a rainy Southern California evening things came to the
breaking point. As I was driving in my car to an appointment, I was

carrying on a prayer conversation with God. I was rehearsing all I had tried to do in obedience to Him and how helpless I was feeling and how hopeless the situation looked. Suddenly in the depth of my frustration and deep hurt I cried out, "Lord, why don't you just take my life? I'm ready to come to heaven and be with you!" It was one of the awesome times when I sensed the Lord speaking back to me. I did not see a vision or hear an audible voice, but I clearly sensed He was saying to me, with great tenderness and love, "Son, I already have taken your life."

The Lord was reminding me that He was my Lord—that years before I had given Him my life unreservedly. It was no longer mine. My life was His.

I pulled the car over to the side of the busy street and began to weep openly. As I sobbed, I cried out to God. I confessed my desire to be successful and my tendency to control situations. I released everything to Him.

I remember telling the Lord that if He really wanted me to be a failure, I was willing. If somehow my failure in the ministry would bring more glory to IHm than success, I was available. Up to that point in my life I had never felt so utterly helpless. But in my deep helplessness that night, the Lord came to me to bring hope, encouragement, and strength, and He rescued me.

David found himself in that kind of situation several times. On one of those occasions, he wrote, "In my distress I called to the LORD; I cried to my God for help. From his temple he heard my voice; my cry came before him, into his ears. . . . The LORD thundered from heaven; the voice of the Most High resounded. . . . He reached down from on high and took hold of me; he drew me out of deep waters. He rescued me from my powerful enemy. . . . He brought me out into a spacious place; he rescued me because he delighted in me" (Ps. 18: 6, 13, 16–17, 19).

When we acknowledge our helplessness and cry to God for His help, He can rescue us, protect us, and provide for us.

THE POSTURE OF AWE

One of the dangers of our frenzied culture is that we tend to hurry into the presence of God, share our list of wants with Him, then rush back to our hectic lives and overcrowded schedules for the rest of the day. What a sad thing that is, and how foolish. David wrote, "The LORD reigns, let the nations tremble; he sits enthroned between the cherubim, let the earth shake. Great is the LORD in Zion; he is exalted over all the nations. Let them praise your great and awesome name—he is holy.... Exalt the LORD our God and worship at his holy mountain, for the LORD our God is holy" (Ps. 99:1–3, 9).

There is no one like the Lord—awesome in holiness, power, and love. No wonder He is to be worshiped and exalted!

In our humanness we frequently enter His presence with words we speak or sing. But sometimes, when we sense the presence of God, it is good to be silent before the Lord. It is not easy for most of us to be silent. But God has encouraged it. He has said, "Be still, and know that I am God; I will be exalted among the nations, I will be exalted in the earth" (46:10).

I believe it is an insult to come into God's presence, verbalize what is on our minds in an attempt to get what we want, and then rush back to our busy lives expecting God to take care of our requests. I need not point my finger at others. That has been my own experience at times—and I have discovered that God is not pleased with that approach.

That truth has been illustrated to me a number of times over the years as I have been involved in pastoral counseling. I have found that people would get entangled in major problems and crises through their own sin and disobedience. Then, when they could no longer endure the situation, they would make an appointment to see their pastor. They would often come to the counseling situation expecting me to straighten things out within an hour so they could return to their lives as normal. Seldom would a husband or wife come with a mind open to resolving failure in their own lives. Inevitably, they came so I could help straighten out the weaknesses and failures of their mate.

Often without realizing it, we tend to do the same thing with God. Many of us come to Him in prayer to resolve a situation or straighten out another person so we can enjoy life once again in the comfort zone.

Several years ago a Christian leader from Africa was visiting the church I was pastoring. He was impressed with how much time I spent counseling. It was difficult for him to understand, since such counseling was not offered in his church. With simple and uncritical logic, he concluded, "I think I see the difference between our churches. In America, you counsel Christians who are having problems. In Africa, we ask them to repent."

He was not suggesting that there was not a place for legitimate pastoral counseling. Nor am I. In fact, I have given much of my life to that important ministry. However, without fully realizing it he was being used of God to remind me of the great need for authentic and deep repentance in the lives of Christians from every culture of the world. Prayers of repentance can bring us into the awesome presence of God.

In short, self-centered prayers focus on ourselves. God-centered prayers bring us into the very presence of God. We would do well to approach God with a deep sense of awe. This is where meaningful prayer begins. Only then are we prepared to consider our physical posture as it relates to our praying. When the posture of our hearts is what it should be, when we come to God with a spirit of humility and the recognition of our utter helplessness, then we are ready to employ the most meaningful and appropriate physical posture for our times of prayer.

THE PHYSICAL POSTURE OF PRAYER

I have never been in the presence of an earthly king. But on various occasions I have had the privilege of meeting political and business leaders whom our culture would regard as important individuals. I have found myself always wanting to be on my best behavior—to be respectful and appropriate in what I do and say.

If that is a legitimate concern for times when we are with important people, how much more should we pay attention to the times when we approach God in prayer. Nothing can compare to the privilege of being in the presence of the King of kings and the Lord of lords.

Napoleon Bonaparte declared, "If Socrates would enter the room we should rise and do him honor. But if Jesus Christ came into the room we should fall down on our knees and worship Him."[7]

That's a good place to begin our prayers—on our knees!

Dean Merrill, referring to the 1991 National Prayer Breakfast in Washington, D.C., related how Charles Stanley closed his message on that occasion by asking the two thousand attendees to kneel with him in prayer. Merrill then posed the question, "Who can deny that over the past 25 years we have been kneeling less and less?" He continued, "Certain formal occasions still require it, of course: weddings, ordinations, commissioning services for overseas ministry, and the Eucharist in some traditions. Otherwise, we don't kneel before a holy God much anymore. Instead, we face one another and join hands. Kneeling is being replaced by our more interactive, let's-share approach to spiritual matters."

He then concluded:

Modern sophisms notwithstanding, I still find myself wondering if kneeling doesn't hold some value. When I get down on my knees to pray, the quality of my interaction with God is somehow changed. And I don't think it's just the nostalgic memory of boyhood days when, as a preacher's kid in the Midwest, I knelt on a plank floor with the rest of the congregation at our Wednesday night prayer meetings. I benefit from the practice now.

The biggest benefit is that kneeling reminds us who's who in the dialogue. Prayer is not a couple of fellows chatting about the Dallas Cowboys. It is a human being coming face to face with his or her Supreme Authority, the ineffable God who is approachable but still the One in charge.

Thus, kneeling is a way of saying: "I fully understand who's Boss here. Far be it from me to try to manipulate you or play games with you. I'm well aware of my status in this relationship, and I deeply appreciate your taking time to interact with me."[8]

Kneeling is not the only posture for prayer. But it is a wonderful place to begin as we approach God in prayer. Kneeling when we pray is a habit worth developing. It is a posture that enhances our sense of coming into the presence of God, of humbling ourselves before Him. Kneeling can remind us vividly of who God is and who we are. Of course, some individuals cannot kneel because of physical limitations. However, all of us can adopt a kneeling attitude in the presence of God.

Scripture refers to a number of other appropriate postures in praying.

Standing. Moses stood on holy ground—without his sandals—as God conversed with him. God said, "Take off your sandals, for the place where you are standing is holy ground" (Exod. 3:5). It is good for us to recognize that whenever we pray, we, like Moses, are standing in the very presence of God.

Abraham stood before the Lord as he pleaded in prayer for God to deliver Sodom. "The men turned away and went toward Sodom, but Abraham remained standing before the LORD" (Gen. 18:22). God heard the prayers of Abraham and made an opportunity for Sodom to be spared.

Lying prostrate. As Ezra praised the Lord, the people bowed down and worshiped the Lord with their faces to the ground. "Ezra praised the LORD, the great God; and all the people lifted their hands and responded, 'Amen! Amen!' Then they bowed down and worshiped the LORD with their faces to the ground" (Neh. 8:6).

Jesus Himself fell on His face in prayer to His Father in the Garden of Gethsemane. "Going a little farther, he fell to the ground and prayed that if possible the hour might pass from him" (Mark 14:35).

Heads down. From the time of Abraham, servants of the Lord have bowed down in prayer to Him. "When Abraham's servant heard what they said, he bowed down to the ground before the LORD" (Gen. 24:52).

Faces up. Isaiah lifted up his head to see the Lord seated on a throne, high and exalted in the temple. "In the year that King Uzziah died, I saw the Lord seated on a throne, high and exalted, and the train of his robe filled the temple" (Isa. 6:1).

Walking. Before the Fall, Adam walked and talked with God in the Garden of Eden (Gen. 2:8; 3:8–9). Many Christians today are enjoying that same kind of opportunity to commune with God as they walk, often praying for those who live in the houses or apartments they are passing.

Hands folded. Although the Bible does not teach us to fold our hands in prayer, it is a meaningful act for many.

Hands raised. The psalmist wrote about raising his hands to God, both in times of need and in times of praise and worship. "Hear my cry for mercy as I call to you for help, as I lift up my hands toward your Most Holy Place" (Ps. 28:2). "I have seen you in the sanctuary and beheld your power and your glory. Because your love is better than life, my lips will glorify you. I will praise you as long as I live, and in your name I will lift up my hands" (63:2–4). "O LORD, I call to you; come quickly to me. Hear my voice when I call to you. May my prayer be set before you like incense; may the lifting up of my hands be like the evening sacrifice" (141:1–2).

Lying down. The psalmist also wrote about praying when lying in bed. "On my bed I remember you; I think of you through the watches of the night" (63:6). While lying in bed, he communed with God. " I call with all my heart; answer me, O LORD, and I will obey your decrees. I call out to you; save me and I will keep your statutes. I rise before dawn and cry for help; I have put my hope in your word. My eyes stay open through the watches of the night, that I may meditate on your promises" (119:145–148).

Sitting. We can pray when we are sitting, as David did when he prayed for his family and their descendants (2 Sam. 7:18–29).

Our posture helps determine the quality of our prayer times. How we act in the presence of our holy God can enhance or detract from our times of prayer.

The posture of prayer begins with the posture of the heart. Its companions are the posture of humility, the posture of helplessness, and the posture of coming before God with a sense of awe.

Lord, we would bow
both our heads and our hearts
as we come to You in prayer.
We would come to You with deep humility
and with a healthy sense of helplessness.
We are utterly dependent on You, dear Lord.
We bow before You in awe
as we seek You and Your will
in all we do!

6

CHERISHING THE
PURITY OF PRAYER

~⊶⊷~

M ANY CHRISTIANS, even some Christian leaders, complain that prayer does not work. They say that God seems far away, that they have little or no sense of His presence, that He does not seem to answer their prayers.

This problem may be related to something Jesus said in the Sermon on the Mount. "Blessed are the pure in heart, for they will see God" (Matt. 5:8). If we are to "see God," that is, communicate effectively with Him in prayer, we must approach Him with clean hearts and hands.

Jesus taught His disciples to pray, "Forgive us our sins, for we also forgive everyone who sins against us" (Luke 11:4). Praying this prayer should not become a meaningless ritual. It needs to flow from the heart with sincerity and fervency. "Lord Jesus, forgive my sins, as I forgive others."

APPROACHING GOD WITH A PURE HEART

Mastering the basics of a golf swing requires understanding and practice. Similarly in praying we need to understand and then practice the basic ingredients of prayer. Confessing our sins is one of the basics. It must not be ignored.

The writer of Proverbs asked, "Who can say, 'I have kept my heart pure; I am clean and without sin'?" (Prov. 20:9). The truth is, none of us can.

Although there are many challenges to sincere prayer, nothing will hinder our prayers more effectively than sin. The psalmist expressed it this way: "If I had cherished sin in my heart, the Lord would not have listened" (Ps. 66:18). And because of Judah's disobedience, her prayers were blocked (Jer. 11:11; Zech. 7:13). Unconfessed sin is one of the major reasons the prayers of many professing Christians seem not to be answered. An unforgiving spirit can hinder our prayers as well (Mark 11:25).

Bill Hybels has addressed this important subject.

> *Unconfessed sin* cuts off our communication with the Father. . . . The prophet Malachi spoke out against *cheating God.* Despite God's clear instructions to offer only the best animals as sacrifices to the Lord, the Israelites were taking their prize animals to market where they could get top dollar for them. Then they took the worthless animals—the blind, the lame, the ready to die—and brought them to God's altar.
>
> Besides attempting to cheat God, Israelite leaders were *cheating the poor.* They were paying absurdly low wages, making life economically impossible for single mothers and treating illegal immigrants unjustly (Mal. 3:5).
>
> In addition, men were *cheating their wives,* and divorce was rampant. "You weep and wail because [the LORD] no longer pays attention to your offerings or accepts them with pleasure from your hands. You ask, Why? It is because the LORD is acting as the witness between you and the wife of your youth, because you have broken faith with her, though she is your partner, the wife of your marriage covenant" (Mal. 2:13–14).
>
> Through Malachi God exclaimed, "After cheating me, the oppressed among you, and even your own wives, you have the audacity to ask for my favor! You mock me, and then you expect me to grant your requests! But why should I honor your requests when you don't honor mine?"
>
> If you're tolerating sin in your life, don't waste your breath praying unless it's a prayer of confession. Receive the Lord's forgiveness, and then he will listen when you pour out your heart to him.[1]

We need our Lord's forgiveness and cleansing each day and each moment. We cannot provide a clean heart for ourselves, but our Lord can. As we confess our sins, God has promised to "*forgive* us our sins and *purify* us from all unrighteousness" (1 John 1:9, italics added).

Sammy Tippit has written:

> The principle of forgiveness is a response to the holiness and grace of God. . . . Holiness produces humility of heart. Grace is then applied to the heart of humility. The depth of our confession is only as great as the clarity of our view of the holiness of God. Too much confession is rooted in comparison to other people. We can always justify our attitudes and actions by thinking we are not as bad as some other Christians. Such comparison only produces pride in our hearts.
>
> However, when we focus on the holy God, we must cry out with Isaiah, "Woe is me! . . . I am ruined! For I am a man of unclean lips, and I live among a people of unclean lips, and my eyes have seen the King, the LORD Almighty" (Isa. 6:5).[7]

Confession of our sins provides the key to purity of heart. Only when we confess our sins can we be forgiven and purified. And that is essential for effectiveness in prayer.

This is a subject we all know well. We have talked about it, and many of us have preached about it. Without realizing it, most of us believe we have mastered it. But we must be careful not to be deceived by the evil one. We must never take sin, confession, and forgiveness lightly.

A wonderful prayer has been given to us by David. We would do well to pray it daily as we follow the Lord. "Cleanse me with hyssop, and I will be clean; wash me, and I will be whiter than snow. Let me hear joy and gladness; let the bones you have crushed rejoice. Hide your face from my sins and blot out all my iniquity. Create in me a pure heart, O God, and renew a steadfast spirit within me" (Ps. 51:7–10).

Only our gracious Lord can give us pure hearts. We cannot produce purity by ourselves, nor do we merit the purity only God can provide, not even those of us who are Christian leaders.

Confession and asking for forgiveness and cleansing is not the only prayer we should pray, but it must be the first. It ushers us into the presence of God. Isaiah declared that important truth when he wrote, "Surely the arm of the LORD is not too short to save, nor his ear too dull to hear. But your iniquities have separated you from your God; your sins have hidden his face from you, so that he will not hear" (Isa. 59:1–2).

For our communication lines to be open with God, we need to be cleansed of sin—in the present tense. Yesterday's purity is not sufficient for today. Nor is any expression of self-righteousness appropriate. We can enjoy the presence of God only when we are clean.

In his classic book *Quiet Talks on Prayer*, S. D. Gordon has written, "And the fact to put down plainly in blackest ink once for all is this—*sin hinders prayer*. There is nothing surprising about this. That we think the reverse is the surprising thing. Prayer is transacting business with God. Sin is *breaking with God*."[3]

If we are not ready to deal with sin, we are not ready to pray. Only when we allow our Lord to forgive our sins and to cleanse us are we able to communicate meaningfully with Him.

A term used in communications theory is "noise," which describes anything and everything that hinders or obstructs the communication process. It can be anything from static on a telephone line to poor lighting in a room, or even the nervous gestures of a speaker that distract the audience from what he or she is saying.

Sin is the "noise" that blocks communication between God and the one who is praying. Although a sin may seem small or unimportant, it will always affect the spiritual communication process. We cannot pray effectively when we are tolerating sin in any form.

David asked the question, "Who may ascend the hill of the LORD? Who may stand in his holy place?" And then he answered, "He who has clean hands and a pure heart" (Ps. 24:3–4).

Christian leaders—in fact, all believers—must have pure hearts if they are to overcome the major hindrance to our prayers, namely, sin. David prayed, "Search me, O God, and *know my heart*; test me and know my anxious thoughts. See if there is any offensive way in me, and lead me in the way everlasting" (139:23–24, italics added). As the apostle John wrote, "If we claim to be without sin, we deceive ourselves and the truth is not in us.

If we confess our sins, he is faithful and just and will *forgive us* our sins and *purify us* from all unrighteousness" (1 John 1:8–9, italics added).

The Greek word rendered "confess" means literally "to say the same thing." That is, confession entails having the same attitude toward sin God has, namely, hatred. Genuine confession, then, acknowledges that sin is undesirable, and disdains and hates it, recognizing that it is incompatible with God's character and with victorious Christian living.

Is it really necessary, however, for believers to confess their sin and ask forgiveness? Christians received forgiveness of sins the moment they trusted Christ as their Savior (Eph. 1:7). But 1 John 1:9 refers not to one's position in Christ, but to what one writer calls "familial" forgiveness.[4] "It is perfectly understandable how a son may need to ask his father to forgive him for his faults while at the same time his position within the family is not in jeopardy. A Christian who never asks his heavenly Father for forgiveness for his sin can hardly have much sensitivity to the ways in which he grieves his Father."[5]

APPROACHING GOD WITH PURE HANDS

If confession is the means for us to receive clean hearts, then repentance is the way God provides for His children to approach Him with clean hands.

If we are willing to turn from sin, God is willing to listen to us. Through Isaiah the Lord said, "Stop bringing meaningless offerings! Your incense is detestable to me. New Moons, Sabbaths and convocations—I cannot bear your evil assemblies. . . . When you spread out *your hands* in prayer, I will hide my eyes from you; even if you offer many prayers, I will not listen. *Your hands* are full of blood; wash and make yourselves clean. Take your evil deeds out of my sight! Stop doing wrong; learn to do right!" (Isa. 1:13–17, italics added).

By God's grace, we can live with both pure hearts and pure hands, cleansed not by our efforts or by attempting to create our own righteousness, but cleansed by the very blood of Jesus Christ (1 John 1:7).

The Book of Proverbs declares this truth: "He who conceals his sins does not prosper, but whoever *confesses* and *renounces* them finds mercy"

(Prov. 28:13, italics added). The Hebrew word translated "renounce" means "to forsake." That is what repentance means: to turn around, to turn from sin to God, to forsake our sins.

No wonder James wrote so emphatically on this subject. "*Wash your hands*, you sinners, and *purify your hearts*, you double-minded. Grieve, mourn, and wail. Change your laughter to mourning and your joy to gloom. Humble yourselves before the Lord, and he will lift you up" (James 4:8–10, italics added).

Washing our hands and having hearts made pure go together. We must allow the Lord to purify our hearts through the confession of our sins, and then we must "wash our hands," that is, have pure conduct.

Though addressed to the nation of Israel, 2 Chronicles 7:14 includes a principle that is applicable to all believers: "If my people, who are called by my name, will humble themselves and pray and seek my face and turn from their wicked ways, then will I hear from heaven and will forgive their sin and will heal their land." In the next verse God gives another promise to those who will humble themselves, pray, and *turn* from their wicked ways: "Now my eyes will be open and my ears attentive to the prayers offered in this place" (7:15). If we humbly turn from sin, our gracious Lord will forgive us and will be attentive to our prayers.

At the same time, confession of our sins will be shallow and ineffective if we do not *turn*. I experienced that truth in a graphic and painful way early in my ministry. I was involved in youth ministry and was asked by a juvenile judge to come into court for a preliminary hearing for a young man accused of stealing a car with two other high school boys.

In the judge's chambers I sat to the right of the teenager, while his parents were seated on his left. The judge sat directly across a huge courtroom table and asked the young man some very thoughtful questions. In response the young man contended that he had never stolen anything in his entire life and that he was unaware the other boys were stealing the car until it was actually happening.

He then confessed his responsibility and begged for forgiveness. The judge asked him directly, "Are you sorry for what you have done?" With that, the young man broke into tears. He sobbed and sobbed. He assured the judge that he was very sorry and that he would never again be part of such a thing.

The seasoned judge looked at the teenager with compassion and said, "I believe you are sorry for what you have done. I could place you in a juvenile correctional facility for the rest of your teenage years, but I am going to give you another chance. But if you ever come back to my court again, I will throw the book at you."

The young man, his parents, and I went out into the hallway. We had a prayer circle of rejoicing and thanking God. The young man had confessed his sin and had apparently wept tears of remorse. And the judge had forgiven him.

Unfortunately, just a few days later that same young man suddenly went on a car-stealing spree that took him hundreds of miles across the state. He was personally responsible for stealing three more cars. As a result, he was sentenced to prison for a number of years.

The point is clear. It is important for us to confess our sins, and it is good to do so with tears and outward remorse, but ultimately it will be in vain if we do not turn from our sins and follow Jesus Christ with purity of devotion.

Calling Israel to repentance was one of the major messages of the Old Testament prophets. For example, Jeremiah wrote, "Return, faithless Israel" (Jer. 3:12), "Return, faithless people" (3:14, 22), and "Let us return to the Lord" (Lam. 3:40). Ezekiel challenged the nation, "Repent! Turn away from all your offenses" (Ezek. 18:30), and "Repent and live" (18:32). Hosea said, "Return, O Israel, to the Lord your God. Your sins have been your downfall" (Hos. 14:1). And Joel wrote, " 'Even now,' declares the Lord, 'return to me with all your heart, with fasting and weeping and mourning. Rend your heart and not your garments. Return to the Lord your God, for he is gracious and compassionate, slow to anger and abounding in love, and he relents from sending calamity'" (Joel 2:12–13).

In five of the seven church messages in Revelation 2–3 Jesus called on believers to repent: Ephesus (Rev. 2:5), Pergamum (2:16), Thyatira (2:22), Sardis (3:3), and Laodicea (3:19).

To turn to the Lord with all our hearts and to follow Him in obedience is basic to authentic Christian discipleship. This is not a matter of earning God's favor or displaying the kinds of good works about which the scribes and the Pharisees boasted. Instead, it is a matter of living in a loving relationship with our Lord. Repeatedly Jesus stated that if we love Him, we will obey His commands (e.g., John 14:15, 21, 23). And He concluded, "He who loves me will be loved by my Father, and I too will love him and show myself to him" (14:21).

Confession of our sins to God and turning from sin opens the door for enjoying life at its best. We can walk in a deep and loving relationship with our heavenly Father, His Son—our Lord and Savior—and the Holy Spirit. Also it allows us to "approach the throne of grace with confidence, so that we may receive mercy and find grace to help us in our time of need" (Heb. 4:16).

APPROACHING GOD WITH PURE RELATIONSHIPS

The apostle John addressed the matter of enjoying life at its best when he wrote, "But if we walk in the light, as he is in the light, we have fellowship with one another, and the blood of Jesus, his Son, purifies us from all sin" (1 John 1:7).

The Christian life is lived in relationships—with God and with others. And prayer enables us to enjoy a wonderful, loving relationship with Him.

Brother Lawrence described the privilege of that relationship as follows.

> I consider myself as the most wretched of men, full of sores and corruption, and who has committed all sorts of crimes against his King. Touched with sensible regret, I confess to Him all my wickedness, I ask His forgiveness, I abandon myself in His hands that He may do what He pleases with me. The King, full of mercy and goodness, very far from chastising me, embraces me with love, makes me eat at His table, serves me with His own hand, gives me the key of His treasures; He converses and delights Himself with me incessantly, in a thousand ways, and treats me in all respect as His favorite. It is thus I consider myself from time to time in His holy presence.[6]

It is certainly possible to be a Christian leader in today's world and not enjoy a deep, loving, intimate relationship with the Lord. The Christian ministry can become predictable and routine. In fact, I believe many

Christian leaders who seem to have success in ministry are not living in a joyous relationship with Jesus Christ.

It is possible—even easy—to become enamored with ourselves and to be deceived by the devil into believing that somehow we are responsible for praise that should really be directed to God. To put it in the vernacular of a journalist, "Foolish is the Christian leader who begins to believe his own press clippings."

Bill Hybels expresses this matter as follows: "God expects us to maintain strict personal integrity. He expects us to show thoughtfulness and love toward others and to maintain a relationship with him. 'What does the Lord require of you? To act justly and to love mercy and to walk humbly with your God' (Micah 6:8). If we refuse to do these things, we are presumptuous to expect God to answer our prayers."[7]

Hallesby wrote, "To pray is to let Jesus come into our hearts."[8] And he continued, "Prayer is the breath of the soul, the organ by which we receive Christ into our parched and withered hearts. . . . God has designed prayer as a means of intimate and joyous fellowship between God and man."[9]

Leith Anderson has written the following in his remarkable book on prayer, *When God Says No.*

> Everything about prayer is based on relationship. Without a relationship with God we're just talking to ourselves. That relationship may be good or bad, new or old, close or distant, warm or cold. But some relationship is a prerequisite to prayer. . . .
>
> The better the relationship, the better the prayer. If we are alienated from God because of neglect or sin, our channels of communication will be weak or cluttered. If our prayer is frequent and our relationship strong, then prayer will be direct, intimate and effective.
>
> Fortunately, God constantly desires and works to make his relationship with us strong. For our part we have a responsibility to press on to God with a right motivation. We don't seek friendship with God for what we can get from God, but for God himself. The relationship should be the end as well as the means. We should be satisfied with God even if he never grants a single request we make. It's when we know and love God for himself that we develop the intimacy that results in prayers heard and requests granted.[10]

Love is at the center of any deep, authentic, fulfilling relationship with God. Jesus urged, "Love the Lord your God with all your heart and with all your soul and with all your mind and with all your strength" (Mark 12:30). We can live in a loving, intimate relationship with Him each day, assured that nothing can "separate us from the love of God that is in Christ Jesus our Lord" (Rom. 8:39).

ENJOYING A LOVING RELATIONSHIP WITH OTHERS

Just as our Lord invites us to pray to Him within the context of a loving, intimate relationship, He also calls for us to live in a loving relationship with others. In fact, Jesus taught that "if you are offering your gift at the altar and there remember that your brother has something against you, leave your gift there in front of the altar. First go and be reconciled to your brother; then come and offer your gift" (Matt. 5:23–24).

One sin Satan seems to use to block our communication with God more effectively than any other is that of unforgiveness.

After Jesus taught His disciples how to pray, He continued, "For if you forgive men when they sin against you, your heavenly Father will also forgive you. But if you do not forgive men their sins, your Father will not forgive your sins" (6:14-15). To be forgiven by our Lord, to be able to approach Him with clean hands and a clean heart, we must forgive others. Only then will our Lord forgive us. Only then will our communication flow freely as we pray. Only then will God hear our prayers.

As we deal with the sin of unforgiveness in general, the Bible addresses some related sins that will hinder our prayers specifically. For example, Peter warned husbands to "be considerate as you live with your wives, and treat them with respect as the weaker partner and as heirs with you of the gracious gift of life, so that nothing will hinder your prayers" (1 Pet. 3:7).

Broken or fractured relationships with others can hinder our prayers significantly, beginning with our spouse and family members and extending to others. Loving our Lord and loving others is essential. "Love must be sincere. . . . Be devoted to one another in brotherly love. Honor one another above yourselves. . . . Live in harmony with one another. Do not be proud, but be willing to associate with people of low position" (Rom. 12:9–10, 16).

Authentic Christian love begins with our families and the Christian family, but it goes far beyond that. Quoting from Proverbs 25:21–22, Paul wrote, "If your enemy is hungry, feed him; if he is thirsty, give him something to drink" (Rom. 12:20). He concluded, "Let no debt remain outstanding, except the continuing debt to love one another, for he who loves his fellowman has fulfilled the law. [All the commandments] are summed up in this one rule: 'Love your neighbor as yourself.' Love does no harm to its neighbor. Therefore love is the fulfillment of the law" (13:8–10).

In summary, one of the major reasons prayers go unanswered is that the pray-er is harboring sin. Dealing with sin and expressing genuine love open up the channels of God's blessings. As we approach God in prayer, we need to do so with hearts of purity, holiness, love, forgiveness, and consideration.

Then He will hear us and respond to our prayers.

⸻

Dear heavenly Father, we come to You humbly.
Please cleanse our hearts,
and our hands,
and our relationships
with You and with others.
We would turn from sin
to pursue You
and to commune with You
in the great privilege of prayer!

7

DELIGHTING IN THE PRAISE AND WORSHIP OF PRAYER

━━◆━━

AFTER PRAYERS OF CONFESSION the first and most appropriate thing for us to do in the presence of God is to offer Him praise. David declared, "It is good to praise the LORD and make music to your name, O Most High, to proclaim your love in the morning and your faithfulness at night" (Ps. 92:1–2).

If we have dealt with sin, if we have turned from our own agendas to focus on Him, what else is appropriate except to worship Him? What else can we say in such a holy and wonderful moment except to express our praise and worship to Him?

Most Christian leaders are under tremendous time pressures. Often we do not pray fervently until we are facing a major need or crisis. Not that there is anything wrong with crisis praying. In fact, it is wise to pray at such times. But there is something inherently wrong with the way we pray if we regularly and consistently rush into God's presence, tell Him what we think we need, and then rush back to lives filled to overflowing with frenzied schedules. Meaningful prayer must be more than that.

Years ago Malcom Boyd wrote a book about prayer entitled *Are You Running with Me, Jesus?* Unfortunately, to me, that title seems rather irreverent and is a commentary on the prayer lives of many Christian leaders.

The thought of coming quietly and deliberately into the presence of

God is somewhat curious or even rare in our culture. Most of us are too busy doing good things for God to set aside valuable time for a quality experience in prayer. I confess I have been guilty of that at various times in my ministry.

Sammy Tippit has put into perspective this matter of praise. "Jesus taught that when we come into the presence of God, we enter the presence of purity. We can come into His presence only by the blood of the Lamb with clean hands and a pure heart. We must enter His presence with a sense of reverence and awe, for God is holy.

"We must open the door of prayer with our focus on God. We acknowledge His goodness, greatness, and purity with praise and thanksgiving. Something supernatural transpires when we offer to Him the sacrifice of praise from our hearts. God dwells in the midst of the praises of His people. And praise quickly becomes worship."[1]

Praise and worship are at the center of what it means to be a true disciple of Jesus Christ. Whenever we encounter the living Christ, praise and worship are appropriate. That was the response of Mary Magdalene and the other Mary when they went to the tomb of Jesus after His burial. "Suddenly Jesus met them. 'Greetings,' he said. They came to him, clasped his feet and worshiped him" (Matt. 28:9). I find it difficult to read that passage without being deeply moved. I long for that kind of response whenever I sense I am in the presence of Jesus—to fall before Him in awe and worship Him.

Several days later, in Galilee, the eleven disciples met Jesus. Their response was the same as that of the two Marys. The biblical account reports, "When they saw him, they worshiped him" (28:17). As we come regularly into the presence of our Lord Jesus, we, like the disciples and the women, must fall before Him and worship Him.

David said it well. "Come, let us sing for joy to the LORD; let us shout aloud to the Rock of our salvation. Let us come before him with thanksgiving and extol him with music and song. For the LORD is the great God, the great King above all gods. In his hand are the depths of the earth, and the mountain peaks belong to him. The sea is his, for he made it, and his hands formed the dry land. Come, let us bow down in worship, let us kneel before the LORD our Maker; for he is our God and we are the people of his pasture, and the flock under his care" (Ps. 95:1–7).

ENTERING INTO PRAYER

When Jesus taught His disciples to pray, He told them to begin with the words, "Our Father in heaven, hallowed be your name" (Matt. 6:9). These words suggest three important principles for our praying.

First, we need to begin by approaching God reverently as our Father. Meaningful prayer begins with our acknowledging who God really is, namely, our heavenly Father who has created us and who loves us more than we can begin to imagine. Sensing His position as our Father encourages us to recognize His love and care for us, and His desire to fellowship with us, His children.

Again, Hallesby's comments are helpful in describing this situation. "Prayer is the breath of the soul, the organ by which we receive Christ into our parched and withered hearts. He says, 'if any man open the door, I will come in to him' . . . He calls us to sup with Him.

"In Biblical language the common meal is symbolical of intimate and joyous fellowship. This affords a new glimpse into the nature of prayer, showing us that God has designed prayer as a means of intimate and joyous fellowship between God and man."[2]

Wouldn't it be helpful if at least once a day we chose to enter the presence of God to share a delightful spiritual meal with Him rather than just throwing some words at Him on the run? In this scenario we would sit down at His table to share some nourishing food from His Word and to converse with Him in prayer rather than hurriedly going though a fast-food drive-through prayer lane. Praying "on the run" may have a legitimate place at times. But such praying can never replace our need for prolonged times of intimate communion with God.

Just think, the God of the universe—"our Father in heaven"—has invited us for dinner. How can we ignore or neglect His invitation to eat with Him? Can we do anything less than respond with joy and expectation by setting aside an uninterrupted time for prayer every day? This is not an easy or natural thing to do. In fact, for a number of reasons most of us find it difficult.

Years ago my life was controlled to a significant extent by my datebook. Often my schedule was determined literally months in advance. Then one day, as I was praying over my schedule for the day, the obvious suddenly hit me.

I had been establishing appointments for every person and every event that was important in my life except for the two most important categories. First, there was no scheduled time for my wife and family. I was basically giving them the "leftovers" from my other appointments. As a result, some days hardly any time remained for the individuals who were the most important and deeply loved people in my life.

Second, even more astonishingly, I realized that I rarely if ever scheduled an appointment with God. That recognition transformed my schedule and my prayer life. I began to schedule time alone with God every day. In fact, whenever I buy a new datebook now, I always set my regular appointments with God first and my appointments with my wife and family second.

I have found that in my demanding schedule, there is no other way to be assured of quality time with God. And of course, I must not only write the dates into my calendar; I must also honor those time commitments. Alan Redpath described this challenge.

> How hard it is to get right through into the very presence of God when we pray! How difficult it is to force our way through the crowd of distracting thoughts, of worldly cares, even of sinful desires. For any of us who know anything at all of the school of prayer will know from experience that a man's holiest moments—at least the moments which should be his holiest—are the moments which are beset more than any others by the onslaught of the enemy upon his mind and thoughts.
>
> How hard it is to realize when we pray that God is, and that He is the rewarder of them that diligently seek Him! How seldom do we get through the clouds that seem to exist beneath His feet in order that we might, in prayer, see His face![3]

Second, we should acknowledge where our Father is—in heaven. When we pray we do well to acknowledge the presence of Christ in the person of the Holy Spirit. At the same time, although we pray in the name of Jesus, we usually address our prayers to our heavenly Father. Interestingly Jesus taught us to begin our prayers by acknowledging that our Father God is in heaven.

One significant reason for doing so is that it helps to envision the Lord as Isaiah saw Him, "seated on a throne, high and exalted, and the train of his robe filled the temple. Above him were seraphs, each with six wings: With two wings they covered their faces, with two they covered their feet, and with two they were flying" (Isa. 6:1–2).

That view of God transports me quickly from any casual or disrespectful tendencies I may have as I approach Him in prayer. It helps me enter His presence in a worshipful attitude.

In addition, the Word of God instructs us to focus on the heavenly as opposed to the temporal things of this world. For example, Jesus spoke often about the kingdom of heaven and how we should be involved in the priorities of God's rule.

In the Sermon on the Mount Jesus told us we need not worry about the things that usually occupy the attention of the unsaved, such as food, clothing, and shelter. He assured us that our Father in heaven takes care of those things. Jesus said, "But seek first his kingdom and his righteousness, and all these things will be given to you as well" (Matt. 6:33).

Earlier Jesus talked about prayer and fasting. Then, addressing the subject of heaven, He said, "Do not store up for yourselves treasures on earth, where moth and rust destroy, and where thieves break in and steal. But store up for yourselves treasures in heaven, where moth and rust do not destroy, and where thieves do not break in and steal. For where your treasure is, there your heart will be also" (6:19–21).

I have found it helpful not only to envision God the Father on His throne in heaven, but also to focus on the Son and the Holy Spirit. Ascended to heaven, Jesus is sitting at the right hand of God the Father. Paul wrote to the Colossians, "Since, then, you have been raised with Christ, set your hearts on things above, where Christ is seated at the right hand of God. Set your minds on things above, not on earthly things" (Col. 3:1–2). The writer of Hebrews has encouraged us, "Let us fix our eyes on Jesus, the author and perfecter of our faith, who for the joy set before him endured the cross, scorning its shame, and sat down at the right hand of the throne of God" (Heb. 12:2).

The apostle Paul reported not only where Jesus is at the present time, but also what Jesus is doing. In his letter to the Roman Christians, Paul spoke of "Christ Jesus, who died . . . and is at the right hand of God and is also interceding for us" (Rom. 8:34). And then he continued, "Who can separate us from the love of Christ? Shall trouble or hardship or persecution or famine or nakedness or danger or sword? As it is written: 'For your sake we face death all day long; we are considered as sheep to be slaughtered.' No, in all these things we are more than conquerors through him who loved us" (8:35–37). What a gift of love that our Lord Jesus Christ intercedes for us to God the Father!

The writer of Hebrews shared this remarkable truth in a slightly different way: "But because Jesus lives forever, he has a permanent priesthood. Therefore he is able to save completely those who come to God through him, because he always lives to intercede for them" (Heb. 7:24–25). Whenever we feel alone in our praying, we are being deceived by Satan. We need to remember that the Father is seated on His throne ready to listen to our prayers. And His Son, Jesus Christ, is seated next to Him, deeply engaged in interceding for us. Could any situation be more conducive to our praying? Our Father is waiting for us to take time from our busy schedules to come into His presence to communicate with Him.

And if that were not enough, the prayer ministry of the Holy Spirit is also provided for us. "In the same way, the Spirit helps us in our weakness. We do not know what we ought to pray for, but the Spirit himself intercedes for us with groans that words cannot express. And he who searches our hearts knows the mind of the Spirit, because the Spirit intercedes for the saints in accordance with God's will" (Rom. 8:26–27). When we do not know how to express our concerns or our needs in words, the Holy Spirit interprets our cries for help to the Father.

The more I mature in my prayer life, the more—not less, but more—I depend on the Holy Spirit for help in my praying. The reasons are obvious. When we pray self-centered prayers, it is usually easy for us to figure out what we want and when we want it. But when we begin more earnestly to seek God's will and to desire God's agenda for our lives, we often do not know just what to ask for. Increasingly our prayers become more focused on surrendering to the Lord and making ourselves available to be used by Him in any way He desires.

I am convinced that the Father, the Son, and the Holy Spirit are all waiting for our prayer visits. God is not hiding from us, nor is He attempting to make prayer difficult. Instead, He is waiting for us to come to Him like trusting little children so that we can enjoy His company and ask Him for anything and everything we need to fulfill His will. We are to ask and then leave the results with God.

Third, we should hallow the name of God as we come to Him in prayer. Marcus Dods has written, "Of the petitions which are included in this prayer, none has been less prayed than this which our Lord sets first. Many a man has cried earnestly and sincerely enough, Give me this day my daily bread; many with deeper earnestness and out of a more appalling helplessness, have cried, Deliver us from evil; but few have learnt to have this petition deepest in the heart and readiest on the lip, Hallowed be thy name."[4]

What does it mean to hallow the name of God? How is it done? William Hendriksen gives this answer: "*To hallow God's name* means to hold it in reverence; hence, to hold *him* in reverence, to honor, glorify, and exalt him. To do this, far more than a merely intellectual knowledge of the meaning of the divine names is required. Humility of spirit, gratitude of heart, earnest study of God's works until observation changes into rapturous astonishment and worship is certainly implied."[5]

Hendriksen continued, "*Hallowed be thy name* means, therefore, that the one who has been brought into fellowship with this tenderly loving Father now calls upon everyone to share this experience with him, and to exalt this glorious God. This means far more than that the petitioner is doing his utmost to fight profanity. It has a positive context. The supplicant calls upon the entire creation and especially upon the world of men to praise his God. He exclaims, as it were, 'O magnify Jehovah *with me*, and let us exalt his name *together*'" (Ps. 34:3).[6]

Why did Jesus instruct us to hallow or revere God's *name*? Does this mean we should focus on His name rather than His person? Once again, Hendriksen has some helpful insights. "In ancient times the name was not generally regarded as a mere appellation to distinguish one person from another, but often rather as an expression of the very nature of the person so indicated, or of his position, etc. This was true to such an extent that frequently when in some important respect the facts concerning a man had undergone a change, he was given a new name. . . . The name was to some extent identified with the person. This is especially true with respect to the names of God. God's name is *God himself as revealed in all his works.*"[7]

In other words, when we hallow the name of God, we are speaking to Him and about Him. It is not merely the *name* of God we are hallowing; it is the *person* of God. Therefore it is both helpful and meaningful for us to know the various biblical names for God and what they mean.

> In the Old Testament the Supreme Being is called *'El,* that is, God, viewed as the Mighty One. This name occurs in various combinations. *'El-Shaddai* is God Almighty, the source of salvation for his people (Gen. 17:1; Exod. 6:3). *'Elohim* (Gen. 1:1) is a plural, and refers to God in the fulness of his power. *'Elyon* indicates the Most High (Num. 24:16). *'Adonai* points to God as Master (properly "my Master") or Lord; cf. "O Lord, I am not a man of words" (Exod. 4:10). The meaning of the name *Jehovah* is to some extent explained in Exodus 3:13, 14; cf. 6:2, 3. It is a form of the verb *to be,* and has been interpreted to mean "I am that I am," or "I shall be what I shall be. . . ."
>
> Various combinations occur in connection with this name. Probably most familiar are the designations "Jehovah of hosts" (Ps. 46:7, 11) and "Jehovah our righteousness" (Jer. 23:6). Other combinations are "Jehovah will provide"(Gen. 22:14), "Jehovah [is] my banner" (Exod. 17:15), "Jehovah heals you" (Exod. 15:26), "Jehovah [is] peace" (Judg. 6:24), and "Jehovah [is] my shepherd" (Ps. 23:1).[8]

To know and revere the name of God is where we need to begin. But how do we utilize that knowledge to hallow the name of God?

Many have written on this subject, but perhaps no one more helpfully than William Barclay.

> "Hallowed be Thy name"—it is probably true to say that of all the petitions of the Lord's Prayer this is the one the meaning for which we would find it most difficult to express. If we were asked, what does this petition actually mean? not a few of us would find some difficulty in answering.

First, then, let us concentrate on the actual meaning of the words.

The word which is translated *hallowed* is a part of the Greek verb *hagiazesthai*. The Greek verb *hagiazesthai* is connected with the adjective *hagios*, and means *to treat a person or a thing as hagios. Hagios* is the word which is usually translated *holy*; but the basic meaning of *hagios* is *different* or *separate*. A thing that is *hagios* is *different* from other things. A person who is *hagios* is *separate* from other people.

So a temple is *hagios* because it is *different* from other things. An altar is *hagios* because it exists for a purpose *different* from the purpose of ordinary things. God's day is *hagios* because it is *different* from other days. A priest is *hagios* because he is *separate* from other men. So, then, this petition means, "Let God's name be treated differently from all other names; let God's name be given a position which is absolutely unique."[9]

And so, as we begin to pray, we acknowledge that His name is different from all others; that God alone is holy—set apart—and that by His love and grace He invites us to enter His presence to praise and worship Him and to present our needs to Him.

We are much like the Magi who came to worship the baby Jesus. "On coming to the house, they saw the child with his mother Mary, and they bowed down and worshiped him" (Matt. 2:11). That is where prayer begins. We bow before our God and *worship* Him!

The Magi continued in their worship by presenting gifts to Jesus. "Then they opened their treasures and presented him with gifts of gold and of incense and of myrrh" (2:11). For us it is fitting to give the Lord the gifts of worship, praise, and thanksgiving.

The psalms are filled with exhortations and encouragements for us to praise God. Among those exhortations, the psalmist declared, "It is fitting for the upright to praise him" (Ps. 33:1). The psalms conclude with a great crescendo by sharing this final statement: "Praise the Lord. Praise God in his sanctuary; praise him in his mighty heavens. Praise him for his acts of power; praise him for his surpassing greatness. Praise him with the sounding of the trumpet, praise him with the harp and lyre, praise him with tambourine and dancing, praise him with the strings and flute, praise him with the clash of cymbals, praise him with resounding cymbals. Let everything that has breath praise the Lord. Praise the Lord" (Ps. 150:1–6).

The writer of Hebrews stated that the Mosaic Covenant had regulations for worship and also an earthly sanctuary (Heb. 9:1). He continued, "Through Jesus, therefore, let us continually offer to God a *sacrifice of praise*—the fruit of lips that confess his name" (13:15, italics added). That is consistent with the testimony of David in Psalm 34:1, "I will extol the Lord at all times; his *praise* will always be on my lips" (italics added).

Offering God praise—having His praise on our lips continually—transports us from our natural tendencies to complain and criticize. It becomes a strategic part of fulfilling our Lord's injunction for us to "pray continually" (1 Thess. 5:17). Beginning each day with a time of worship and praise prepares us for continuing to offer the Lord expressions of praise the rest of the day.

In Psalm 100:4 our Lord encouraged that kind of praying. "Enter his gates with thanksgiving and his courts with praise; give thanks to him and praise his name." That wonderful verse is preceded by the invitation, "Shout for joy to the Lord, all the earth. Worship the Lord with gladness; come before him with joyful songs" (100:1–2).

Singing, a significant element of corporate worship, can be a helpful ingredient in our personal worship. I always include a time of singing hymns and/or praise songs in my prayer times. In fact, I have taken a number of pages from various hymnals and songbooks to include in my prayer notebook.

Just as singing psalms, hymns, and spiritual songs has become a part of most Christian worship services, so can the singing of hymns be meaningful in our personal and family times of worship. I would suggest songs and hymns that focus specifically on praise and worship. It is especially meaningful when those songs are sung directly to the Lord.

The same is true of the psalms and other scriptural passages we can use in our times of praise and worship. David taught us this truth in some of his writing: "Sing joyfully to the Lord, you righteous; it is fitting for the upright to praise him. Sing to him a new song; play skillfully, and shout for joy" (Ps. 33:1, 3). "It is good to praise the Lord and make music to your name, O Most High, to proclaim your love in the morning and your faithfulness at night" (92:1–2).

Charles H. Spurgeon put the matter of singing and expressing praise verbally into practical perspective. "With the earliest birds I will make one more singer in the great concert-hall of God. I will not want more rest, or a longer time to myself to consider all my troubles, I will give my best time, the first hour of the day, to the praise of my God."[10]

How then can we follow the Lord's instruction to pray, "Our Father in heaven, hallowed be your name"? These are some suggestions, based on the comments in this chapter.

1. Meditate on our relationship with God as our Father.
2. Thank Him for making us His children by salvation and for being a loving, caring, providing Father.
3. Think of His position in heaven, where He is seated as the sovereign Lord over the universe.
4. Contemplate Jesus' role as our interceding High Priest.
5. Thank God the Father that His Son and the Holy Spirit are interceding on our behalf.
6. Hold the Lord's name in high reverence in recognition of His sovereign authority.
7. Study and meditate on His many names, and what they tell us about His character and His work.
8. Tell the Lord why His name is so wonderful.
9. Sing praises to the Lord.
10. Reflect on these points throughout the day.

Following these steps can enrich the life of the Christian with meaningful worship.

⊶✦⊷

Our Father,
We acknowledge You as our heavenly Father
and we thank You for making Yourself available to us.
We hallow your name, dear Father,
and we would joyfully bring to You our heartfelt praise.
May our mouths be filled with Your praise and glory
all the day!

8

CLAIMING GOD'S PROMISES
THROUGH PRAYER

∘━━✦━━∘

ΠEHEMIAH WAS FACING an incredible challenge.

His brother, Hanani, and some other men had just returned from Jerusalem with a sobering report. "Those who survived the exile and are back in the province are in great trouble and disgrace. The wall of Jerusalem is broken down, and its gates have been burned with fire" (Neh. 1:3).

After sharing the bad news, Hanani and his friends returned to life as usual. Like many contemporary Christians, they were good at analyzing the problem but did little or nothing to resolve it.

Nehemiah was of a different stripe. He was a man of both faith and prayer. He was grieved deeply by the situation. But instead of merely shedding tears or complaining or passing off the responsibility to those back in Jerusalem, he took aggressive action. He began to pray. "When I heard these things, I sat down and wept. For some days I mourned and fasted and prayed before the God of heaven" (1:4).

That he mourned, fasted, and prayed for some four months is impressive. But *what* Nehemiah prayed made a significant difference. Nehemiah began his prayer with praise and adoration for God, not with his request; he entered into the Lord's presence and worshiped Him. He acknowledged the greatness of God and affirmed the wonderful covenant of love God had made with His people. He asked the Lord to listen to his prayer.

"O Lord, God of heaven, the great and awesome God, who keeps his covenant of love with those who love him and obey his commands, let your ear be attentive and your eyes open to hear the prayer your servant is praying before you day and night for your servants, the people of Israel" (1:5–6).

Before sharing his specific prayer request, Nehemiah presented a prayer of confession to the Lord. "I confess the sins we Israelites, including myself and my father's house, have committed against you. We have acted very wickedly toward you. We have not obeyed the commands, decrees and laws you gave your servant Moses" (1:6–7). Nehemiah confessed not only his own sin, but also the sins of his people. As a man of prayer, he knew that confession needed to take place before he made his petition.

Nehemiah then cried out to the Lord with his request. And he did it by praying in response to the covenant God had made with His people. Nehemiah identified promises to His children and then humbly and sensitively claimed those promises. "Remember the instruction you gave your servant Moses, saying, 'If you are unfaithful, I will scatter you among the nations, but if you return to me and obey my commands, then even if your exiled people are at the farthest horizon, I will gather them from there and bring them to the place I have chosen as a dwelling for my Name.' They are your servants and your people, whom you redeemed by your great strength and your mighty hand" (1:8–10).

Nehemiah and the people of Israel were in exile because God's covenant people had sinned against Him. Over and over the Lord had urged them to return to Him in repentance, but they would not respond. And so the Lord brought judgment on them, allowing them to be conquered by their enemies and taken into exile.

Within that context Nehemiah claimed the promise the Lord made to His people through Moses just before they entered the Promised Land. The promise was this: "When all these blessings and curses I have set before you come upon you and you take them to heart wherever the Lord your God disperses you among the nations, and when you and your children return to the Lord your God and obey him with all your heart and with all your soul . . . then the Lord your God will restore your fortunes and have compassion on you and gather you again from all the nations where he scattered you. Even if you have been banished to the most distant land under the heavens, from there the LORD your God will gather you and bring you back" (Deut. 30:1–4).

Nehemiah claimed that promise in his prayer. He knew the promises of God, and he believed that God would honor His promises. Only after worshiping the Lord, confessing his sin and the sins of his people, and identifying the covenant promises God had given to them did Nehemiah share his personal request. His petition was brief and specific. "O Lord, let your ear be attentive to the prayer of this your servant and to the prayer of your servants who delight in revering your name. Give your servant success today by granting him favor in the presence of this man" (Neh. 1:11).

God answered Nehemiah's prayer. He gave him great favor with the king (2:1–10). Then the Lord used him to lead the people of Judah to rebuild the walls of Jerusalem in just fifty-two days (6:15). Even more importantly, the people of God returned to Him in a great spiritual renewal and revival (chaps. 7–13). Nehemiah was a man of both prayer *and* the Word of God.

PRAYER AND THE WORD

Like Nehemiah, Abraham was a man of prayer and a man of the Word. He believed the promises of God. "Against all hope, Abraham in hope believed and so became the father of many nations" (Rom. 4:18), and he "believed God and it was credited to him as righteousness" (4:3).

Abraham demonstrated great faith in God. He believed God would keep His promise to make him the father of a great nation, even though he and his wife, Sarah, were beyond the years of childbearing—and had no children.

Paul summarized that kind of faith in God and in His promises as follows: "Yet he [Abraham] did not waver through unbelief regarding the promise of God, but was strengthened in his faith and gave glory to God, being fully persuaded that God had power to do what he had promised. This is why 'it was credited to him as righteousness'" (4:20–22).

Daniel, too, believed the promises of God and prayed accordingly, claiming God's promises in His Word. Aware that Judah's seventy-year exile in Babylon was almost up, as prophesied by Jeremiah (in Jer. 25:11–12;

29:10–11), Daniel prayed and fasted (Dan. 9:3). His marvelous prayer recorded in Daniel 9:4–19 began with praise, addressing the Lord as "the great and awesome God, who keeps his covenant of love with all who love him and obey his commands" (9:4), and included several references to God's character: "you are righteous" (9:7); "the LORD our God is righteous in everything he does" (9:14); "your great mercy" (9:18). Then Daniel repeatedly confessed his people's sins (9:5–6, 9–16). Claiming God's promise to Jeremiah, Daniel then prayed that the Lord would restore His people to their city Jerusalem.

Enoch, Noah, Isaac, Joseph, Moses, Rahab, Gideon, Barak, Samson, Jephthah, David, Samuel, the prophets, and many others down through the pages of history were servants of the Lord who believed in Him and took His promises seriously as they claimed God's promises in prayer and then sought His guidance and provision. We need to do the same. The promises God has shared with us through His Word are vitally linked to a life of prayer. If we are to be effective in our praying, we must know what our Lord has promised us and then humbly pray that His promises be fulfilled in our lives.

That was the way the early church leaders prayed. They believed God and claimed His promises in prayer. That is why they gathered in a room to pray after the ascension of Jesus (Acts 1:13–14). They prayed together as they awaited the fulfillment of the promise Jesus had given them concerning the coming of the Holy Spirit.

A few days after being filled with the Holy Spirit on the Day of Pentecost, the early Christians faced their first major crisis. Peter and John were arrested and imprisoned, and then were commanded by the Jewish leaders not to speak or teach at all in the name of Jesus (4:18). But as soon as they were released, Peter and John returned to the church family and told them what had happened. In response to their report, the people of God joined in corporate prayer, raising their voices together in prayer to God (4:24).

And how did they pray? They followed the same pattern of prayer our Lord Jesus taught His disciples, the same pattern Nehemiah employed. That is, they began their prayers with praise and adoration. "Sovereign Lord," they said, "You made the heaven and the earth and the sea and everything in them" (4:24).

Then they quoted a wonderful promise from the Word of God that the Lord had made through David in Psalm 2. They prayed, "You spoke by the Holy Spirit through the mouth of your servant, our father David: 'Why do the nations rage and the peoples plot in vain? The kings of the earth take their stand and the rulers gather together against the Lord and against His Anointed One'" (Acts 4:25–26).

Next, they applied that portion of Scripture to their own situation. They acknowledged that God was greater than their enemies. They prayed, "Indeed Herod and Pontius Pilate met together with the Gentiles and the people of Israel in this city to conspire against your holy servant Jesus, whom you anointed. They did what your power and will had decided beforehand should happen" (4:27–28).

They affirmed who God was, who they were, and who Herod, Pilate, and the other leaders were. They acknowledged that God was in charge of all the events that had taken place—even the crucifixion of Jesus—and that He was well aware of the intimidation and threats the Jewish religious leaders had just made against Peter and John. And so they prayed, "Now, Lord, consider their threats and enable your servants to speak your word with great boldness. Stretch out your hand to heal and perform miraculous signs and wonders through the name of your holy servant Jesus" (4:29–30).

God heard and answered their prayers in a wonderfully powerful way. The Bible reports, "After they prayed, the place where they were meeting was shaken. And they were all filled with the Holy Spirit and spoke the word of God boldly" (4:31).

As we enter the presence of God in prayer, we need to acknowledge who He is. Then, after we offer Him appropriate worship and praise, it is wise to pray back to Him specific promises from His Word that apply to the requests we are bringing to Him.

The Lord gives us some wonderful promises concerning His Word in the Book of Proverbs: "My son, if you accept my words and store up my commands within you, turning your ear to wisdom and applying your heart to understanding . . . and if you look for it as for silver and search for it as for hidden treasure, then you will understand the fear of the LORD and find the knowledge of God. For the LORD gives wisdom, and from his mouth come knowledge and understanding. He holds victory in store for the upright, he is a shield to those whose walk is blameless, for he guards the course of the just and protects the way of his faithful ones" (Prov. 2:1–2, 4–8).

R. Kelso Carter's hymn, "Standing on the Promises," expresses graphically the value of claiming His promises. Two of the stanzas and the chorus strongly convey the importance of appropriating His promises.

> Standing on the promises that cannot fail,
> When the howling storms of doubt and fear assail,
> By the living Word of God I shall prevail,
> Standing on the promises of God.

> Standing on the promises of Christ the Lord,
> Bound to Him eternally by love's strong cord,
> Overcoming daily with the Spirit's sword,
> Standing on the promises of God.

> Standing, standing,
> Standing on the promises of God my Savior;
> Standing, standing,
> I'm standing on the promises of God.[1]

We do well to spend time in the Word when we pray. And it is helpful to ask the Holy Spirit to guide us in our study of the Bible for passages and promises that relate to the problems, concerns, or needs we are facing in our lives and therefore are bringing to the Lord in prayer.

Thomas Benton Brooks put it this way: "If you would have God hear you when you pray, you must hear him when He speaks."[2] And the main way God speaks to us today is through His Word. "The Word of God is living and active. Sharper than any double-edged sword, it penetrates even to dividing soul and spirit, joints and marrow; it judges the thoughts and attitudes of the heart" (Heb. 4:12).

An added dimension of confidence and faith is added to our prayers when we "pray" the promises of God.

PRAYING THE WORD OF GOD

One of the marvelous ways to blend prayer and the Word is to "pray" Scripture. In other words, when the Holy Spirit leads you to a given Scripture passage in your study and/or in your praying, you can pray that

Scripture back to God. I have found this to be especially helpful in the several major areas of prayer we are considering in this book.

Praying Prayers of Praise and Worship

First, it is wonderful to pray the psalms or other expressions of praise and worship in the Bible. Following are some brief excerpts from some wonderful psalms and other biblical passages that can be used in our praise and worship of God. I find it especially helpful to personalize the psalms as I use them in prayer. I have given some examples below by placing my personalized version in brackets.

"Praise the LORD, O my soul; all my inmost being, praise his holy name. Praise the LORD, O my soul, and forget not all his benefits—who forgives all [my] sins and heals all [my] diseases, who redeems [my] life from the pit and crowns [me] with love and compassion, who satisfies [my] desires with good things so that [my] youth is renewed like the eagle's" (Ps. 103:1 5).

"My heart is steadfast, O God; I will sing and make music with all my soul. Awake, harp and lyre! I will awaken the dawn. I will praise you, O LORD, among the nations; I will sing of you among the peoples. For great is your love, higher than the heavens; your faithfulness reaches to the skies. Be exalted, O God, above the heavens, and let your glory be over all the earth" (108:1–5).

"Praise the LORD. I will extol [You] with all my heart in the council of the upright and in the assembly. Great are [Your] works . . . they are pondered by all who delight in them. Glorious and majestic are [Your] deeds, and [Your] righteousness endures forever. [You have] caused [Your] wonders to be remembered; [You are] gracious and compassionate" (111:1–4).

"Praise be to you, O LORD, God of our father Israel, from everlasting to everlasting. Yours, O LORD, is the greatness and the power and the glory and the majesty and the splendor, for everything in heaven and earth is yours. Yours, O LORD, is the kingdom; you are exalted as head over all. Wealth and honor come from you; you are the ruler of all things. In your hands are strength and power to exalt and give strength to all. Now, our God, we give you thanks, and praise your glorious name" (1 Chron. 29:10–13).

"Holy, holy, holy is the Lord God Almighty, who was, and is, and is to come. . . . You are worthy, our Lord and God, to receive glory and honor and power, for you created all things, and by your will they were created and have their being" (Rev. 4:8, 11).

In addition to using these wonderful portions of Scripture, along with so many other appropriate biblical expressions of praise, I find it helpful and meaningful, as I mentioned in the previous chapter, to sing passages of the Word. I enjoy including some of the psalms that have been set to music, some of the great hymns of the church, and some of the more contemporary Scripture songs such as "Be Exalted, O God," "Great Is the Lord," and "How Majestic Is Your Name."

Praying the Promises of God

As mentioned, claiming God's promises in prayer is a biblical model established by a number of servants of the Lord in both the Old and New Testaments. Following are some of the promises the Lord has led me to claim—and to pray—at various times.

When I have assumed leadership roles to which God has called me and the church in some way has confirmed, either by calling me to pastor a church or to lead a Christian ministry, I have found the Lord leading me to the following passage again and again. In fact, I pray through this passage quite often. "Be strong and very courageous. Be careful to obey all the law my servant Moses gave you; do not turn from it to the right or to the left, that you may be successful wherever you go. Do not let this Book of the Law depart from your mouth; meditate on it day and night, so that you may be careful to do everything written in it. Then you will be prosperous and successful. Have I not commanded you? Be strong and courageous. Do not be terrified; do not be discouraged, for the LORD your God will be with you wherever you go" (Josh. 1:7–9).

Another passage I often use in prayer is well known to many of us. Yet it has deep meaning to those who are concerned about the need for revival in the church and for a spiritual awakening in our nation. "If my people, who are called by my name, will humble themselves and pray and seek my face and turn from their wicked ways, then I will hear from heaven and will forgive their sin and will heal their land" (2 Chron. 7:14). Though addressed to the nation of Israel, this promise can be applied today.

Still another passage that means a lot to me is from Psalm 92: "The righteous will flourish like a palm tree, they will grow like a cedar of Lebanon; planted in the house of the LORD, they will flourish in the courts of our God. They will still bear fruit in old age, they will stay fresh and green, proclaiming, 'The LORD is upright; he is my Rock, and there is no wickedness in him'" (92:12–15).

When facing a need for finances or some other resource, it is appropriate to claim the simple and clear promise of our Lord in Philippians 4:19: "And my God will meet all your needs according to his glorious riches in Christ Jesus."

In the battles of life, when we begin to lose perspective or when God seems far away, it is helpful to affirm in prayer who He is. This is one of those passages that a mentor of mine, Charlie Riggs, refers to as a "plumb line." It is a passage we should claim again and again in prayer. "The one who calls you is faithful and he will do it" (1 Thess. 5:24).

Matthew 18:19–20 is a passage I often find appropriate when I gather with other Christians to pray. It is good to acknowledge the presence of Jesus when we pray together and to claim His promise regarding praying together in agreement. "Again, I tell you that if two of you on earth agree about anything you ask for, it will be done for you by my Father in heaven. For where two or three come together in my name, there am I with them."

My "life verse" is Matthew 6:33: "But seek first his kingdom and his righteousness, and all these things will be given to you as well." As a teenager, I sensed the Holy Spirit guiding me to claim that verse as a major focus of my Christian life. It has been a source of great blessing as I have "prayed" and "claimed" the promise over and over again.

I am not suggesting that we can arbitrarily claim every promise God made to every person in the Bible. In fact, some of His promises are negative judgments, which we would not want to claim! However, God has made many promises to us who trust and obey Him. And sometimes the Holy Spirit will guide us to a specific promise He has made and will affirm in our hearts that He is extending that promise to us.

Praying for Our Own Needs or Interceding for Others

Once again, the Word of God provides many promises that are appropriate when we are in need or even in distress—or as we intercede for others facing major needs. Following are some wonderful examples. "Answer me when I call to you, O my righteous God. Give me relief from my distress; be merciful to me and hear my prayer" (Ps. 4:1).

"Give ear to my words, O Lord, consider my sighing. Listen to my cry for help, my King and my God, for to you I pray. In the morning, O Lord, you hear my voice; in the morning I lay my requests before you and wait in expectation" (5:1–3).

"To you, O Lord, I lift up my soul; in you I trust, O my God. Do not let me be put to shame, nor let my enemies triumph over me. No one whose hope is in you will ever be put to shame, but they will be put to shame who are treacherous without excuse. Show me your ways, O Lord, teach me your paths; guide me in your truth and teach me, for you are God my Savior, and my hope is in you all day long" (25:1–5).

"In you, O Lord, I have taken refuge; let me never be put to shame; deliver me in your righteousness. Turn your ear to me, come quickly to my rescue; be my rock of refuge, a strong fortress to save me. Since you are my rock and my fortress, for the sake of your name lead and guide me" (31:1–3).

Using the Word of God in our praying is both meaningful and beneficial. Sadly these two wonderful spiritual disciplines—the discipline of prayer and the discipline of the Word—are often separated. As mentioned previously, the early church leaders were men and women of the Word *and* prayer. For some reason, in this generation many Christian leaders have given a great deal of attention to the Word but have often neglected the ministry of prayer.

Richard Trench said, "Prayer is not overcoming God's reluctance; it is laying hold of His highest willingness."[3] And His willingness is most clearly and helpfully communicated in His Word.

Lord, help us to be persons of Your Word,
who not only read it,
but pray it
and obey it!
Like Abraham of old,
we would claim Your promises by faith.

9

RECEIVING GOD'S
PROVISION THROUGH PRAYER

J ESUS TAUGHT His disciples to pray, "Give us today our daily bread" (Matt. 6.11). He also encouraged them (and us) to "ask and it will be given to you; seek and you will find; knock and the door will be opened to you. For everyone who asks receives; he who seeks finds; and to him who knocks, the door will be opened" (7:7–8).

His application of this simple, yet profound, teaching is unmistakable. "Which of you, if his son asks for bread, will give him a stone? Or if he asks for a fish, will give him a snake?" (7:9–10). Then He concluded, "If you, then, though you are evil, know how to give good gifts to your children, how much more will your Father in heaven give good gifts to those who ask him?" (7: 11).

That teaching is at the very core of our praying.

Satan attempts to convince us that God does not hear us or does not care about us. Satan seeks to deceive us. When he succeeds in misleading and deceiving us, we may be deprived of God's best for us.

In contrast, our Lord Jesus teaches us that God loves us and that He longs to give good and profitable gifts to His children who will ask Him. Like an earthly father who loves to provide for his children, so God delights in providing for His own. His gifts are always "good and perfect," as James wrote (James 1:17). Yet we often do not have what we need simply because we "do not ask God" for what we need (4:2).

GOD'S PROMISE TO PROVIDE

Often our needs in a given situation seem so big, and the pressures in our lives can be so strong. It is easy to lose perspective regarding how small our problems actually are in comparison with the greatness of God and the vastness of His resources.

The resources of God are immeasurable. The apostle Paul acknowledged that fact when he wrote, "Now to him who is able to do immeasurably more than all we ask or imagine, according to his power that is at work within us, to him be glory in the church and in Christ Jesus throughout all generations, for ever and ever! Amen" (Eph. 3:20–21). The real question, then, is not whether God's resources are adequate, nor whether God is able to channel those resources so our needs will be met. The bottom-line question pertains to us—and to our asking.

A number of years ago I arrived home one evening just in time for dinner after a full day at my office. Our son, Daniel, who was four years old at the time, greeted me at the door. He was very excited about something. He could hardly wait to tell me about it.

"Dad, guess what?" he exclaimed. "I learned to swim today."

"That's great, Dan," I said. "Where did you learn? Did Mom take you to the swimming pool?"

"Oh no," he said excitedly. "She took me to the library. I got this book on how to swim—and I got the directions—and now I can swim. Let me show you." Dan then got down on the living room floor, and kicked his feet and paddled his arms. He thought he knew how to swim.

However, when I took him to the pool a couple days later, he could not swim. He needed more than to know the directions. He needed to get into the water and learn by doing!

That same principle relates to the life of prayer. It is one thing to read books on prayer and "get the directions." It is quite another to become a person of prayer. Prayer does not just happen. It requires action and time.

Many Christians tend to make praying either too complicated or too simple. Both can effectively lead us astray. To become effective in praying, we need to understand the biblical teaching of prayer in applicable terms. A number of Bible passages could be considered, but one that outlines three practical aspects of prayer is James 4:1–10. Let's consider this passage.

ASKING GOD FOR WHAT WE NEED

From the time we were children, we have learned to ask others for what we feel we need. Unfortunately many Christians tend to share their needs or problems with everyone around them but are often uncertain about going to God in prayer and asking Him to meet their needs.

Thomas Constable speaks to this point. "Some sincere Christians believe that it is selfish and not very trusting to ask God to give us anything. Some Christians believe that praying for personal needs is more a mark of unbelief than of trust in God. After all, since God loves us perfectly, will he not do what is best for us?

"Such an attitude may superficially sound spiritual. However, it contradicts Jesus' clear teaching that God's children should ask him for their needs (Matt. 6:9–13; Luke 11:1–4). . . . God not only encourages us to ask him for what we need, but also commands us to do so. He does so to teach us to look to him for our needs because he is our provider."[1]

The Book of James describes the natural way human beings attempt to secure what they want. James asked a couple of very important questions: "What causes fights and quarrels among you? Don't they come from your desires that battle within you? You want something but don't get it. You kill and covet, but you cannot have what you want. You quarrel and fight" (James 4:1–2).

This is a dilemma all of us have faced either knowingly or unknowingly. We have wanted something and were unable to get it, so we followed our natural tendency to covet, quarrel, or fight to try to secure what we wanted. But often our activity has failed to secure what we wanted to gain or achieve. Many people learn subtle and even polite ways to fulfill their wants, such as scheming, deceiving, or manipulating. Yet they often do not get what they want, so they fret and strive, but to no avail. The solution to this common dilemma is quite simple. James wrote, "You do not have, because you do not ask God" (4:2).

Interestingly Martin Luther presented the simple solution to this problem in the second stanza of his great hymn, "A Mighty Fortress Is Our God."

> Did we in our own strength confide,
> Our striving would be losing,
> Were not the right man on our side,
> The man of God's own choosing.
> Dost ask who that may be?
> Christ Jesus, it is He—
> Lord Sabaoth His name,
> From age to age the same—
> And He must win the battle.[2]

We often lose the battle because of our own striving. We try to fight the battle ourselves. We rely on our own strength instead of asking the Lord for His help. By depending on ourselves and not asking the Lord, we deprive ourselves of good things our gracious Lord would gladly provide for us—if we would just ask Him.

Jesus shared this basic truth repeatedly. Some of His statements may seem rather radical or even unbelievable when we first consider them. For example, He said, "I will do whatever you ask in my name, so that the Son may bring glory to the Father" (John 14:13). Then He repeated that point to make it perfectly clear to those who may have been astonished by His teaching. He said, "You may ask me for anything in my name, and I will do it" (14:14). The principle seems clear. If we ask "in His name," He will give us anything and everything we ask for.

Yet it sounds too good to be true. Most of us have tried doing this. We have gone to God in prayer and simply asked Him for something we wanted. Sometimes it has worked. And many of us have been astonished at how simple and practical that kind of prayer can be. Admittedly, however, it does not always work. Virtually every Christian has been disappointed with that kind of praying at one time or another. We asked God for something in the name of Jesus, and we did not get it. We tried to be as sincere as we could. We asked with as much faith as we could muster. But regardless of what we did or how many times we prayed or how many different approaches we attempted, we did not receive what we asked for. As a result, many Christians conclude that prayer simply does not work and that God does not always keep His promise to give when we ask. There are times when we ask but do not receive, when we seek but do not find, and when we knock but no doors seem to open.

When I was in first grade, our reading book was about a boy and girl named Billy and Jane. They had a pet monkey named Winky. Now my father was a pastor of a rural church in South Dakota. My mother taught in the local high school. I had a brother and three sisters and a dog named Pep, but I did not have a monkey. It was quite easy to conclude that I needed one. And so I began to pray for a monkey. Every night when my father or mother would pray with me before I went to bed, I would pray earnestly and fervently for a monkey. But I never received one. Though I prayed with childlike faith and deep conviction, my prayers were not answered. Why didn't Jesus keep the promise He made when He said, "You may ask for anything in my name, and I will do it"?

Fortunately my godly parents taught me the answer: When we ask God for something, there is a second step in prayer that must go with the first. We often do not receive what we ask God for simply because we have ignored or failed to understand the second step.

ASKING GOD WITH THE RIGHT MOTIVES

We need to pray for the right things in the right way. James stated this truth clearly. "When you ask, you do not receive, because you ask with wrong motives, that you may spend what you get on your pleasures" (James 4:3). The King James Version translates this verse vividly: "Ye ask, and receive not, because ye ask amiss, that ye may consume it upon your lusts."

The basic guidelines for Christian discipleship are consistent throughout the Bible. The first steps of following Jesus as His authentic disciple are three, as He stated in Mark 8:34. "If anyone would come after me, he must deny himself and take up his cross and follow me." Jesus then added, "For whoever wants to save his life will lose it, but whoever loses his life for me and for the gospel will save it" (8:35).

In other words, when we decide to follow Jesus, we must first "deny" ourselves and move from our own agenda to His. We need to turn from our own desires and preferences to follow Him in all we do. The apostle Paul stated this truth in forthright terms: "For Christ's love compels us, because we are convinced that one died for all, and therefore all died. And he died for all, that those who live should no longer live for themselves, but for him who died for them and was raised again" (2 Cor. 5:14–15).

Paul did not just write about this kind of radical lifestyle. He lived it—and he modeled it. Paul wrote, "I have been crucified with Christ [in other words, I have died] and I no longer live, but Christ lives in me. The life I live in the body, I live by faith in the Son of God, who loved me and gave himself for me" (Gal. 2:20). And in his profound theological treatise on the resurrection of Jesus Christ, Paul testified, "I die every day" (1 Cor. 15:31).

That is practical discipleship. And it is a prerequisite to an effective prayer life. Prayer is not merely asking Jesus for what we think we want for ourselves or others. Even if our motives are sincere and our desires are noble, our prayers need to be more than that. We need to pray for God's will to be done. We need to ask for things that will strengthen our faith in Christ and will advance His work.

This is true not only for praying about monkeys or other temporal things. This is a basic principle for all biblical praying. Rosalind Goforth, who served as a pioneer missionary in China with her husband, Jonathan, wrote about this principle, remembering an anguishing situation that deeply tested her faith in God.

> During our fourth year in China, when we were spending the hot season at the coast, our little son, eighteen months old, was taken very ill with dysentery. After several days' fight for the child's life, there came the realization one evening that the angel of death was at hand.
>
> My whole soul rebelled; I actually seemed to hate God; I could see nothing but cruel injustice in it all; and the child seemed to be going fast. My husband and I knelt down beside the little one's bedside, and he [God] pleaded earnestly with me to yield my will and my child to God. After a long and bitter struggle, God gained the victory, and I told my husband I

would give my child to the Lord. Then my husband prayed, committing the precious soul into the Lord's keeping.

While he was praying, I noticed that the rapid hard breathing of the child had ceased. Thinking my darling was gone, I hastened for a light, for it was dark; but on examining the child's face I found that he had sunk into a deep, sound, natural sleep, which lasted most of the night. The following day he was practically well of the dysentery.

To me it has always seemed that the Lord tested me to almost the last moment; then, when I yielded my dearest treasure to him and put my Lord first, He gave back the child.[3]

In this heart-wrenching situation God was lovingly teaching His servant to trust Him in all things. He was teaching her that the basic principles of prayer are quite simple. But they cannot be compromised. We must surrender our will to God; we must surrender all we are and have, even our loved ones.

Many professing Christians, even leaders, seem to violate this basic principle of prayer. Often they pray for their own will to be done rather than God's, and then they wonder why their prayers are not answered. As a result, many become frustrated, angry, and even bitter because they contend that God has not answered their prayers. They simply do not seem to understand that the Lord has not forsaken them. He loves us deeply and wants to supply all we need.

In truth, the Lord has answered their prayers. He has said no to their request. In essence He has said, "My child, I love you, and I want what is best for you. I cannot grant your request because it would be harmful to you or to others or to the advancement of My work."

James 4:3 prompts us to think about the *why* of our praying. For example, why does a pastor pray for increased attendance in his church? Is it so he will have a reputation for being "successful," or is it so more people will be reached with the gospel and ministered to by the Word? Why do church elders pray for increased giving by believers in the congregation? Is it so they can have funds to build a facility larger than other churches in the community, or is it so people will learn the joy of giving and of being wise stewards of God's resources? Why does a Sunday school teacher pray that her lesson will "go over" well? Is it so she will have the reputation of being the best teacher in that Sunday school, or is it so her students will learn and apply the Word? The basic concern in our praying should always be for God's glory and not ours (John 14:13).

If we are to be effective in prayer and Christian discipleship, we, like Rosalind Goforth and the apostle Paul, must come to the place of surrender to our Lord. The goal of our lives must no longer be to live for our pleasures or even to live in a "comfort zone."

Dwight L. Moody expressed that truth with this practical advice about how we should pray: "Spread out your petition before God, and then say, 'Thy will, not mine, be done.' The sweetest lesson I have learned in God's school is to let the Lord choose for me."[4]

That is where God wants us to be. That is where He meets us. He will always respond to that kind of praying.

It is freeing and fulfilling to release our wills totally to Jesus Christ. We need to come to the place where we acknowledge that our lives are no longer our own. They have been bought with an indescribably precious price, the blood of our Lord Jesus Christ (1 Cor. 6:20).

God sometimes allows us to look back at a given situation and understand why He answered our prayers in the way He did rather than the way we thought we wanted Him to. This kind of reflection often leads to a time of great thanksgiving to God. He is so much wiser than we are. Our thanksgiving to God is sometimes joined with great and joyous laughter as we recognize our foolishness in comparison to His great insight and wisdom.

The apostle John expressed this second principle of prayer in graphic terms: "This is the confidence we have in approaching God: that if we ask anything according to his will, he hears us. And if we know that he hears us—whatever we ask—we know that we have what we asked of him" (1 John 5:14–15). When we follow Him as Lord, asking according to His will, we will receive whatever we ask.

SUBMITTING OURSELVES TO GOD

Besides expressing our needs to God and asking with the right motives, a third principle for effective praying is to submit ourselves to the Lord without reservation. James wrote, "Submit yourselves, then, to God" (James 4:7), and "Come near to God and he will come near to you" (4:8). Our Lord invites us to come near to Him with the promise that as we do, He will draw near to us. This is another invitation to the intimate life of communion and fellowship with God.

It is important to realize, however, that in order to enjoy that wonderful and indescribably joyful lifestyle of drawing near to God and communing regularly with Him, three specific steps must be taken. First, we must resist the devil (4:7). Fellowship with God and with the devil are mutually exclusive. In the deepest sense, every time we engage in prayer, it inevitably begins with a battle.

Our enemy opposes our attempts to communicate and commune with our Lord. We should not be surprised if, when we are attempting to pray, our phone rings, our children cry, or our minds wander. The evil one will use any clever device he can employ to prevent us from praying effectively or even praying at all. It is basic to understand that prayer is contrary to the enemy of our souls. I love John Piper's description of this reality: "If you do not know that life is war, you will not know what prayer is for."[5]

Every time we commit ourselves to follow Jesus, our enemy will oppose us. And every time we approach our Lord in prayer, the devil will try to distract us or lead us astray. The Christian life is a battle. We constantly need to submit ourselves to God and to draw near to Him so He can draw near to us.

As we resist Satan volitionally, our Lord has promised that the devil "will flee from you" (4:7). In other words, as we submit to God and draw near to Him in prayer and aggressively resist the devil, our Lord will give us victory.

Peter shared much the same counsel when he wrote, "Be self-controlled and alert. Your enemy the devil prowls around like a roaring lion looking for someone to devour. Resist him, standing firm in the faith, because you know that your brothers throughout the world are undergoing the same kind of sufferings" (1 Pet. 5:8–9). God has not promised that our lives will always be easy or even that they will always make sense. But He has promised us His presence, His provision, His protection. He will give us victory through our Lord Jesus Christ.

In recent years, as I have been under increasing attack from our enemy, I have repeatedly experienced the victory that only our Lord can give. Like John Piper, I have come to understand that authentic Christian discipleship moves us away from the Christian country club to the spiritual battlefield.

As soon as we become serious about following Jesus, we find ourselves out of sync with the world. Jesus said it would be so. Peter referred to us as "aliens and strangers in the world," and he urged us to "abstain from sinful desires, which war against your soul" (2:11). We need to do that in our day-to-day living, and also in our praying. Victory is assured if we will only follow Jesus. Paul shared this reality in a wonderful way when he wrote, "But thanks be to God, who always leads us in triumphal procession in Christ" (2 Cor. 2:14).

Second, we must lead clean lives. James admonished us, "Wash your hands, you sinners, and purify your hearts, you double-minded. Grieve, mourn and wail. Change your laughter to mourning and your joy to gloom" (James 4:8–9). As discussed in chapter 6, our Lord wants us to approach Him in prayer with hearts made pure by the confession of our sin, lives made clean by our repentance, and relationships made pure by our forgiveness of others. This passage reminds us that the Christian life is not always fun and games. Like Nehemiah, there are times when we need to be so overcome with a sense of our sins, needs, and failures that we enter God's presence with weeping, mourning, and fasting.

Third, we must humble ourselves before the Lord (4:10). He promised to do two things when we are humble before Him: to lift us up (4:10) and to give us grace (4:6). Most of us need to be lifted up at various times from discouragement, from a sense of failure, from weariness, from frustration, from attacks by our enemy. We would do well to pray, "Lord Jesus, I need to be lifted up by You." However, we need to recognize that the prerequisite for this prayer is for us genuinely to humble ourselves before Him.

As we humble ourselves before the Lord, He will pour out His grace on us. "God opposes the proud but gives grace to the humble" (4:6). It is by God's grace that we have been saved, and we need to appropriate His grace as we follow Jesus as our Lord. We can never earn or merit His grace. It is a free and generous gift from a loving and forgiving God. Grace is God's unmerited favor. From James's point of view, humbling ourselves before the Lord can be the means to opening a wonderful channel to divine grace.

The apostle Paul put the matter in a similar perspective when he wrote, "And God is able to make all grace abound to you, so that in all things, at all times, having all that you need, you will abound in every good work" (2 Cor. 9:8). He then continued, "As it is written: 'He has scattered abroad his gifts to the poor; his righteousness endures forever.' Now he who supplies seed to the sower and bread for food will also supply and increase your store of seed and will enlarge the harvest of your righteousness. You will be made rich in every way so that you can be generous on every occasion, and through us your generosity will result in thanksgiving to God" (9:9–11).

Grace is not an end in itself. God does not pour out His grace on His humble servants merely for our benefit and pleasure. He wants His grace to flow into our lives and then to flow out in ministry to others. He delights in supplying His grace in generous portions so we can generously share His grace with others. "Each one should use whatever gift [lit., grace-gift] he has received to serve others, faithfully administering God's grace in its various forms" (1 Pet. 4:10).

In one sense, that is who and what we are as Christians: dispensers of God's grace in the various ways He has poured out His grace on us. He gives to us so that we can lovingly share His grace with others. And that is a significant principle of prayer. Prayer is not to be self-centered. In fact, most of us will discover that as we grow and mature in our prayer lives, we will spend less and less time praying for ourselves and more and more time praying for others.

RECEIVING GOD'S GRACIOUS PROVISION

Our Lord loves to provide for His children. His promises are many. Here are a few of them from the Book of Psalms. "Taste and see that the LORD is good; blessed is the man who takes refuge in him. Fear the LORD, you his saints, for those who fear him lack nothing. The lions may grow weak and hungry, but those who seek the LORD lack no good thing" (Ps. 34:8–10).

"Cast your cares on the LORD and he will sustain you; he will never let the righteous fall" (55:22). "For the LORD God is a sun and shield; the LORD bestows favor and honor; no good thing does he withhold from those whose walk is blameless. O LORD Almighty, blessed is the man who trusts in you" (84:11–12).

Our God is a loving God. He is gracious and generous. And the Lord Jesus is the personification of the grace and provision of God. He has said, "I am the good shepherd; I know my sheep and my sheep know me—just as the Father knows me and I know the Father—and I lay down my life for the sheep" (John 10:14–15).

That is the spirit of our Lord. It is the spirit we are to bring to Him as we pray and seek His answers. His way is not always our way, nor will we always understand what He is doing. But He is to be trusted. He is waiting for us to ask, to seek, to knock.

Begin by simply asking God in childlike faith for what you think you need. Ask humbly, gently, reverently.

Ask the Lord to search your heart to make certain your motives are right—that you are not asking for something merely to gratify your appetites or desires, but that you are seeking for His will to be done. Surrender to Him unconditionally, without any terms or requirements. Simply release yourself to His love and His grace. Believe that He is listening to you, that He will hear—and that He will answer by His grace, in His time, according to His will.

Rest in Him. Bask in His love and His grace.

Lord, we come to You humbly to ask for our needs.
We come with open hearts—
and open hands.
We surrender to You
and Your will.
We long for Your love and grace
to be poured out upon us
so that we may receive what we need
and may be able to share freely with others.
We pray as You taught us to pray,
Lord, please give us today our daily bread.
Thank You!

10

Realizing God's
Protection through Prayer

My parents loved the Book of Psalms. Early in their marriage they selected a "family psalm." It was Psalm 91. They read and quoted it so often that it became a significant part of the spiritual fabric of my life.

Psalm 91 is filled with wonderful promises of God's protection. It begins, "He who dwells in the shelter of the Most High will rest in the shadow of the Almighty. I will say of the LORD, 'He is my refuge and my fortress, my God, in whom I trust'" (Ps. 91:1–2).

Our Lord has promised not only to supply all our needs (as discussed in chapter 9), but also to protect us. In fact, many of the psalms are filled with references to God's protection for those who dwell in Him, that is, who live in fellowship with Him. Besides being our refuge and our fortress (91:2), the Lord has promised to save His own from life's difficulties, "the fowler's snare" and "the deadly pestilence" (91:3). Like a caring mother hen, He will cover us with His feathers, and under His wings we can find refuge (91:4). His faithfulness will be our "shield and rampart" (91:4).

As a result, we need not "fear the terror of night, nor the arrow that flies by day, nor the pestilence that stalks in the darkness, nor the plague that destroys at midday" (91:5–6). Because He is our Protector, we can trust Him fully.

Frances Havergal has captured the essence of the protection our Lord has promised in a beautiful hymn, "Like a River Glorious." I sing it frequently in my personal devotional times.

> Hidden in the hollow of His blessed hand,
> Never foe can follow, never traitor stand;
> Not a surge of worry, not a shade of care,
> Not a blast of hurry touch the spirit there. . . .
> We may trust Him fully all for us to do;
> They who trust Him wholly find Him wholly true.[1]

These words express the experience of much of my own life and ministry. I have had the privilege of following Jesus Christ since I was seven years old. Coming under deep conviction of sin, I received Christ as my personal Savior. Then I committed my life to follow Him. In the ensuing years I have had the privilege of knowing Christ as a child, as a teenager, as a young adult, and now as an older adult. I have sought to love, obey, and serve Him.

And I have always found our Lord to be faithful. I have failed Him many times and in many ways, but He has never failed me. He has been my Protector throughout my life. Psalm 91 has not been merely an external source of comfort and encouragement for me. It has been the experience—the testimony—of my life. Indeed, God is my refuge and my fortress.

Jesus spoke about this important subject when He taught us to pray, "And lead us not into temptation, but deliver us from the evil one" (Matt. 6:13). There are at least four major ways by which our Lord offers His protection to us. First, He has promised to lead us. Second, He has promised to deliver us from the evil one. Third, He has promised to be our shelter at all times in every situation. Fourth, He has promised to provide His angels to guard us in all our ways. Each of these wonderful provisions is available to us. Prayer is the means by which we can appropriate God's promises to protect us.

ASKING OUR LORD TO LEAD US

In Psalm 23 David wrote the wonderful words that have blessed so many believers. "The LORD is my shepherd. . . . He leads me beside quiet waters, he restores my soul. He guides me in paths of righteousness, for His name's sake" (23:1–3).

As I begin each day, I pray first that the Lord will not lead me into temptation. Next I pray that instead of leading me into temptation, He will graciously lead me in paths of righteousness for His name's sake. The prayer that our Lord not lead us into temptation is actually a prayer for His protection and deliverance. At first thought this request may seem to contradict the biblical teaching that declares, "When tempted, no one should say, 'God is tempting me.' For God cannot be tempted by evil, nor does he tempt anyone; but each one is tempted when, by his own evil desire, he is dragged away and enticed" (James 1:13–14).

However, the prayer "Lead us not into temptation" is an acknowledgment of our own inability to deliver ourselves from our human tendency to sin. That is the clear message of one of Charles Wesley's hymns:

> Take away my bent to sinning,
> Alpha and Omega be;
> End of faith, as its beginning,
> Set our hearts at liberty.[2]

Temptation itself is not sin. Jesus was tempted by the devil (Matt. 4:1–11), but of course He did not sin. In fact, the writer of Hebrews declared, "For we do not have a high priest who is unable to sympathize with our weaknesses, but we have one who has been tempted in every way, just as we are—yet was without sin" (Heb. 4:15). He concluded, "Let us then approach the throne of grace with confidence, so we may receive mercy and find grace to help us in our time of need" (4:16). In other words, when tempted, *pray!* Ask the One who has overcome every conceivable temptation to help you.

To that helpful teaching, the apostle Paul added, "No temptation has seized you except what is common to man. And God is faithful; he will not let you be tempted beyond what you can bear. But when you are tempted, he will also provide a way out so that you can stand up under it" (1 Cor. 10:13).

When we pray, "Please don't lead me into temptation today," we can claim the promises of Scripture, knowing that the Lord never tempts us with evil. Only the devil does that. That is why Jesus also said we should pray, "But deliver us from the evil one" (Matt. 6:13).

Only the Lord can deliver us from evil and the evil one. We need to be led into paths of righteousness by our Lord Jesus, the One who has been tempted in every way we have been tempted or ever will be. But He never yielded to temptation; He never sinned. He is the source of our deliverance and of our righteousness.

We are to live by the Spirit (Gal. 5:16), to be led by the Spirit (5:18), and to keep in step with the Spirit (5:25). The New English Bible has a wonderful translation of verse 25: "If the Spirit is the source of our life, let the Spirit also direct our course." That is what our Lord desires to do for us. We are to allow the Holy Spirit to direct the course of our lives, to lead us in all we do.

Bill Hybels has written, "Hearing the Holy Spirit's leading is vitally important to a healthy Christian life. The Spirit nudges us to accept God's offer of salvation, assures us that we are members of God's eternal family, encourages us to grow and guides us along the path God has chosen for us. But often when the Spirit tries to get through to us, he gets a busy signal."[3]

Unfortunately, many Christians live as though the Holy Spirit does not even exist. Such an attitude reflects our culture, which is so focused on rationalism. Without realizing it, many believers are enslaved to a totally rationalistic philosophy of life. Hybels adds these helpful thoughts:

To these twentieth-century rationalists, the Holy Spirit's promptings seem to go against human nature and conventional thought patterns. Accustomed to walking by sight, steering their own ships and making unilateral decisions, they are squeamish about letting the Holy Spirit begin his supernatural ministry in their lives. They wish the package were a little neater. They would like his ministry to be quantified and described. The Holy Spirit seems elusive and mysterious, and that unnerves them.

So when they sense a leading that might be from the Holy Spirit, they resist it. They analyze it and conclude, "It isn't theological; therefore, I won't pay attention to it." They question the Spirit's guidance, rebukes and attempts to comfort.[4]

Of course, we certainly need to use the minds God has given us. But we should do so as we are guided by the Holy Spirit. Only when we are filled with and motivated by the Holy Spirit can we authentically follow Jesus as Lord and appropriate His protection.

ASKING OUR LORD TO DELIVER US FROM THE EVIL ONE

The Bible declares, "Your enemy the devil prowls around like a roaring lion looking for someone to devour. Resist him, standing firm in the faith" (1 Pet. 5:8–9). How do we resist the devil? How can we be delivered from the evil one?

The Scriptures offer at least three specific steps to follow. *First, we are to put on the whole armor of God so we can stand against the devil's schemes.* The Christian battle is a spiritual one. "Our struggle is not against flesh and blood, but against the rulers, against the authorities, against the powers of this dark world and against the spiritual forces of evil in the heavenly realms" (Eph. 6:12). One answer to this conflict is to "put on the full armor of God, so that when the day of evil comes, you may be able to stand your ground, and after you have done everything, to stand" (6:13).

Kent Hughes graphically describes this important spiritual exercise of regularly putting on God's armor.

> Ancient warfare was singularly horrifying. The experienced soldier knew that soon he would be facing a phalanx of razor-sharp spears thrusting and jabbing at his vitals, followed by foot-to-foot, hand-to-hand, breath-to-breath hacking and stabbing and bloody wrestling set to the terrible music of the howls and moans of battle. Trembling, the soldier begins to dress.
>
> First, he takes his thick leather war belt to which is attached his sword and cinches it tightly about him, drawing his sword close for battle and tucking in his tunic for mobility. Girt tight with God's Word, his whole person is bound in truth, so that his character and life exude truth. He has "truth in the inner parts" (Ps. 51:6). As a result he is "armed with . . . a good conscience" (1 Tim. 1:19, NEB). With truth holding his life together within and without, he can confidently face any spiritual enemy.

Second, he reaches, still trembling, for his metal breastplate, shaped to protect his chest and abdomen, his vital organs. . . . This is righteousness which first comes from God through faith in Christ—*imputed righteousness* (Phil. 3:9). As this righteousness is properly worn, it produces holy living. . . . God's righteousness protects his life. He cannot die in battle. And more, his righteous life allows him fearlessly to face the foe.

Third, he bends over and methodically laces the straps of his nail-studded legionnaire boots to his ankles and shins. His feet will be secure as he stands his ground in battle. He will not slip and will not retreat. The boots are peace *with* God (Rom. 5:1) and the peace *of* God (John 14:27)—*shalom*. . . . Thus grounded, the Christian warrior faces all onslaughts, never stepping back. Under the fiercest spiritual attacks, he simply regards his peace and, in the strength of his well-being in Christ, digs in.

Fourth, after tying the last boot thong, he picks up his great oblong shield, which he will use to catch the enemies' barrages of flaming arrows. The shield is faith in God and his Word.[5]

That is a vivid, helpful description of how the Lord wants us to put on His spiritual armor every day. I have found it helpful to "put on the full armor of God" early every morning as a strategic part of my quiet time. Actually, my early-morning time in the Word and prayer might be called a preparation time. It is the most important part of my day.

Like many people, I have been a "night person" virtually all my life. My parents were the same. In fact, I remember very few evenings in my formative years when my parents went to bed earlier than eleven o' clock. Most evenings, it was midnight or later. For years, my most creative hours were in the evenings. When I was in college, I seldom remember beginning a term paper before midnight. I loved and enjoyed the late hours.

But a few years ago that preference began to change. I do not believe it was merely a matter of my growing older. Instead, I found that as the demands of ministry grew greater and as the attacks of the enemy grew more fierce, I needed to spend more than five or ten minutes in prayer on the run or just before I fell asleep. Increasingly, I found that I needed more time in the Word and in prayer as I began each day. Preparation for the day's ministry became more and more important.

Contrary to my lifestyle for decades, I now enjoy the early mornings as the most significant hours of my day. In fact, I have asked God to wake me up whenever He desires. Increasingly I enjoy special times of prayer in the middle of the night. David wrote, "I think of you through the watches of the night" (Ps. 63:6). And Psalm 119:148 states, "My eyes stay open through the watches of the night, that I may meditate on your promises." I love to commune with God early in the morning before anyone else in our family is stirring. This begins the process of my communing with Him throughout the day.

At this stage of my life, I seldom accept breakfast appointments, after years of doing so virtually every day of the week except Sunday. In fact, I would frequently schedule two breakfast appointments back to back on the same morning. Now I try to reserve the best time of the day for my personal appointment with God.

May I encourage you to consider doing the same? I am convinced that such times can be transforming. If early morning does not work for you, then set aside another time of the day for prolonged, uninterrupted times with the Lord. And in your time with the Lord in the Word and prayer, consciously put on the full armor of God. It can make a significant difference!

Second, we are to use the sword of the Spirit as our offensive weapon. When the devil followed Jesus into the desert to tempt Him, Jesus immediately took the offensive. He understood that one of the major tactics of the enemy is to put us on the defensive. Each time the devil tempted our Lord, He responded with "the sword of the Spirit," the Word of God (Eph. 6:17). Jesus refuted and overcame the evil one by quoting Scripture (Luke 4:4–13).

This is not a new or radical insight to many Christian leaders. In fact, most pastors have probably preached on this subject a number of times. But a big difference exists between knowing a truth and doing it, between preaching an insight and practicing it.

I have found it extremely helpful to find a verse of Scripture that deals with each problem or temptation I experience in the ministry. As discussed in chapter 8, it is helpful to find a biblical promise we can claim for that given situation, and one we can quote to the enemy and *pray back* to our Father.

For example, when we are facing a particular temptation, we can claim the promise, "No temptation has seized you except what is common to man. And God is faithful; he will not let you be tempted beyond what you can bear. But when you are tempted, he will also provide a way out so that you can stand up under it" (1 Cor. 10:13). If our Lord Jesus, God incarnate, needed to use the Word to refute and defeat Satan, so do we. How can we do less?

Third, we are to use the shield of faith to extinguish all the fiery arrows of the evil one. The exercise of faith, both an offensive and a defensive weapon, is absolutely essential in the vital ministry of prayer. Praying without faith is not biblical praying. "And without faith it is impossible to please God, because anyone who comes to him must believe that he exists and that he rewards those who earnestly seek him" (Heb. 11:6).

Hughes describes the use of the shield of faith as follows: "Through faith, the warrior binds himself close to the heart and purpose of God. And when those burning shafts of doubt come flying toward him, up comes the shield of faith, into which they harmlessly thud. 'This is the victory that has overcome the world, even our faith'" (1 John 5:4).[6]

Every Christian leader needs the shield of faith in his or her praying. The statement, "The righteous shall live by faith," is repeated three times in the Scriptures (Rom. 1:17; Gal. 3:11; Heb. 10:38). O. H. Hallesby discussed this important subject of faith and prayer: "Without faith there can be no prayer, no matter how great our helplessness may be. Helplessness, united with faith, produces prayer. Without faith our helplessness would be only a vain cry of distress in the night.

"It is not intended that our faith should help Jesus to fulfill our supplications. He does not need any help; all he needs is access. . . . But He cannot gain admittance until we 'open the door,' that is, until we in prayer give Him an opportunity to intervene."[7]

After He caused the fig tree to wither, Jesus talked about the need for faith in our praying. "I tell you the truth, if you have faith and do not doubt, not only can you do what was done to the fig tree, but also you can say to this mountain, 'Go, throw yourself into the sea,' and it will be done. If you believe, you will receive whatever you ask for in prayer" (Matt. 21:21–22).

Faith in our Lord, and faith in His ability to supply what is needed, and faith to trust Him to do what is best in a given situation—these are at the heart of effective, powerful praying. By faith we can resist the devil in prayer, and he will flee from us. That is the clear promise in James 4:7–8, "Submit yourselves, then, to God. Resist the devil, and he will flee from you. Come near to God and he will come near to you." To have victory over the enemy, we need to be clothed in the Lord's full armor; we need to use the sword of the Spirit actively and regularly; we need to employ the shield of faith aggressively.

As our Lord calls us to frontline ministry, the devil's attacks increase in number and strength. Christians follow one of two ways of getting the devil "off their backs." The one most Christians employ is simply to shift into neutral, retreat into the "comfort zone" of Christianity, and become lukewarm in commitment to Jesus Christ as our Lord. It makes our Leader nauseous, but it thrills our enemy. Jesus simply does not tolerate lukewarmness. "I know your [the Laodecians'] deeds, that you are neither cold nor hot. I wish you were either one or the other! So, because you are lukewarm—neither hot nor cold—I am about to spit you out of my mouth" (Rev. 3:15–16). All of us need to guard against becoming lukewarm spiritually.

As considered in chapter 9, another way to quench the fiery arrows of the devil is to resist him. That can be done directly in prayer, at the beginning of the day and whenever we experience his attacks during the day. It is a simple and effective spiritual discipline all of us need to cultivate. As we *resist* him, the Word of God promises us that the devil will *flee* from us!

ASKING THE LORD TO BE OUR PLACE OF SHELTER

David told the Lord, "I long to dwell in your tent forever and take refuge in the shelter of your wings" (Ps. 61:4). That is the desire of everyone who is serious about following our Lord. As we encounter various trials and temptations of life, we can retreat into the safety and comfort of our Lord Himself.

But such an action is not a retreat into a comfort zone of neutrality or the nauseating place of the lukewarm life we have just discussed. Instead, we can be in God's shelter—in the hollow of His hand—when we face the battles of life. This is where our Lord wants us to dwell each moment. Jesus invited us, "Come to me, all you who are weary and burdened, and I will give you rest" (Matt. 11:28). When we face spiritual storms and battles, we can turn to the Lord and receive rest from Him. Dozens of times the psalmists wrote that God was their refuge. Comfort and assurance can be ours by meditating on these many references to the Lord as the One to whom we can turn for protection and security in hard times: Psalms 2:12; 5:11; 7:1; 9:9; 11:1; 14:6; 16:1; 17:7; 18:2, 30; 25:20; 31:1–2, 4, 19; 34:8, 22; 36:7; 37:40; 46:1; 57:1; 59:16; 61:3–4; 62:7–8; 64:10; 71:1, 3, 7; 73:28; 91:2, 4; 94:22; 104:18; 118:8–9; 119:114; 141:8; 142:4–5; 144:2.

Even Proverbs includes several assurances of God's availability as our refuge in difficult times: Proverbs 10:29; 14:26, 32; 22:3; 27:12; 30:5.

What Christian worker has not faced times of difficulty, distress, and even defeat? Yet we can find the Lord to be a "refuge for the needy in his distress" (Isa. 25:4). Jeremiah too affirmed that the Lord is our "refuge in time of distress" and "in the day of disaster" (Jer. 16:19; 17:17); and Nahum announced that the Lord is "a refuge in times of trouble" (Nahum 1:7). So in life's difficulties we can turn in prayer to the Lord for safety.

Prayer does not always deliver us from spiritual battles. But prayer can always prepare and equip and enable us for battle, and praying can keep us quiet and at rest as we trust in Christ Jesus (Phil. 4:7). As the psalmist wrote, "He who dwells in the shelter of the Most High will *rest* in the shadow of the Almighty" (Ps. 91:1, italics added).

Of course, our eternal rest lies ahead in heaven. But resting in the Lord now can refresh us and strengthen us for life's battle. As we seek to fulfill the Lord's command to "make disciples of all nations," we can rest in His promise that He will be with us "always, to the very end of the age" (Matt. 28:19–20). Praying "without ceasing" (1 Thess. 5:17, KJV) offers us a wonderful shelter.

ASKING OUR LORD TO PROVIDE ANGELS TO WATCH OVER US

Another wonderful means of protection is the ministry of the Lord's angels. The psalmist wrote that He commissions angels to watch over us. "If you make the Most High your dwelling—even the LORD, who is my refuge—then no harm will befall you, no disaster will come near your tent. For he will command his angels concerning you to guard you in all your ways; they will lift you up in their hands, so that you will not strike your foot against a stone" (Ps. 91: 9–12).

Prayer unleashes the ministry of guardian angels in ways we perhaps never fully comprehend. Frequently we are like Elisha's servant; he could see clearly the large Aramean army surrounding the city but could not see the Lord's horses and chariots of fire (2 Kings 6:17). Similarly perhaps we too fail to realize how often the Lord has commanded His angels to guard us. Sometimes, however, He gives us a glimpse of His protection.

That has happened to me several times. One of those dramatic experiences took place several years ago when my two sons, Dan and Mark, and I were returning home on New Year's Day from a Rose Bowl game. We left the game a few minutes early to beat the traffic. As we were driving on the freeway, I commented on how light the traffic was and how fortunate we were to get away before the rush began.

Suddenly, without warning, a car just ahead of us careened out of control. In a matter of seconds it crashed into the center divider and literally flew through the air, stopping abruptly in our lane and then exploding into flames. I instinctively cried out, "Lord, help us!" as I braced for the crash. I knew it was humanly impossible for me to stop the car in time to avoid the flaming wreckage, and it was impossible to change lanes because of other traffic. I was certain we were going to hit the other car.

Inexplicably, an opening appeared in the midst of the wreckage. We were guided through the fire and debris by an unseen guide. I sensed I was no longer in control of the car. We did not hit anything, nor were we injured in any way. It was absolutely amazing. In fact, it was humanly impossible.

I am convinced the Lord provided one or more angels to guide us. I will always be grateful for the Lord's protection that day. And I give God thanks for the many times His angels have protected us from harm, whether we were aware or unaware of their presence or involvement. Only eternity will reveal fully just how many times our Lord has protected us from harm and even death.

OUR LORD'S PROTECTION

He who dwells in the secret place of the Most High will abide under the protective shadows of the Almighty. This is not "pie-in-the-sky" theology. This is practical Christianity.

We need to ask our Lord to lead us each day as we commit ourselves to follow Him. He will guide us in the paths of righteousness if we but ask Him to do so. And we need to ask Him not to allow us to be led into temptation, and to deliver us from the evil one. Our Lord wants to protect us from harm.

We are wise to follow His instruction to "put on the whole armor" of God as we begin each day, and to use the sword of the Spirit as our offensive weapon. To triumph over the devil we must use the shield of faith to extinguish his fiery arrows, that is, his repeated temptations.

And let us not forget to take advantage of the protection our loving God gives us under the shelter of His wings, and to thank our Lord for the angels He lovingly and quietly provides to watch over us as silent sentinels.

<hr />

Dear Father,
Please don't lead us into temptation.
Instead, lead us into the paths of righteousness—
for Your name's sake.
And please deliver us from the evil one.
Grant us the protection, Lord,
that only You can provide.
Thank You for giving Your angels charge over us
to keep us safe in all of our ways!
We claim Your victory
through our Lord Jesus Christ!

11

Overcoming the Parochial through Prayer

⊙━━━⊙

JUST A FEW HOURS before His arrest, Jesus was praying.

Soon He would be taken before the Sanhedrin, then Herod, and finally Pilate. He would be humiliated in every possible way—mocked, scoffed, beaten, stripped naked, put on public display, taunted, spit on, disfigured—and finally hung on a cross to die. The only begotten Son of God would soon become the sacrificial Lamb of God, who would take away the sins of all who would believe in Him.

But now He was praying for something specific. He was praying for the spiritual unity of all who would follow Him.

That is not the usual way we pray. Spiritual unity is not a subject that captures the imagination of many people. In fact, the natural person seldom if ever thinks much about unity of any kind. Most people who pray seem to focus primarily on themselves and their own agendas. It is natural for us to focus on ourselves and "our kind" of people, and therefore to pray for "my needs," "my family," "our church."

However, in this prayer, often referred to as Jesus' "high priestly prayer," He prayed against that kind of parochialism. During the three years of His public ministry, He had often taught on that subject. Being concerned about others and focusing on God and His priorities were central subjects for Jesus.

125

At the same time, Jesus also addressed other subjects that run counter to the life of self-centeredness and parochialism. For example, He encouraged intercessory prayer, that is, praying for others and not merely for ourselves. And He asked His followers to gather in His name for corporate prayer. So praying for spiritual unity at this critical time in His life was consistent with who Jesus is and what He taught. Such praying focused on both the eternal and the temporal aspects of His kingdom.

Praying for spiritual unity, intercessory prayer, and corporate prayer will strengthen our prayer lives, and will help deliver us from the black hole of parochialism in our Christian living.

PRAYING FOR SPIRITUAL UNITY

As Jesus prayed for spiritual unity, He said to God the Father, "My prayer is not for them [His disciples] alone. I pray also for those who will believe in me through their message, that all of them may be one, Father, just as you are in me and I am in you. May they also be in us so that the world may believe that you have sent me. . . . I in them and you in me. May they be brought to complete unity to let the world know that you sent me" (John 17:20–21, 23).

No wonder this prayer is frequently called His "high priestly prayer," for in it He shared one of His highest priorities: the unity of His body, the church. William Barclay has given us some interesting thoughts about these verses.

> And what was His prayer for the Church which was to be? His prayer was that all its members would be one as He and His Father are one. What was that unity for which Jesus prayed?
>
> It was not a unity of administration or organization. It was not in any sense an ecclesiastical unity. *It was a unity of personal relationship.* We have already seen that the union between Jesus and God was a union of love and obedience. It was a unity of love for which Jesus prayed. It was a unity in which men loved each other because they loved Him. It was a unity based entirely on the relationship between heart and heart.
>
> It will never be that Christians will organize their churches all in the

same way. It will never be that they will worship God all in the same way. It will never even be that they will all believe precisely and exactly the same things. But the Christian unity is a unity which transcends all these differences, and joins men together in love. . . .

Still further, as Jesus saw it and prayed for it, it was to be precisely that unity which convinced the world of the truth of and of the place of Christ. It is more natural for men to be divided than to be united. It is more human for men to fly apart than to come together. Real unity between all Christians would be a "supernatural fact which would require a supernatural explanation."[1]

Has the church experienced this kind of unity for which Jesus prayed? Nearly a century ago E. M. Bounds wrote this commentary:

Notice how intently [Jesus'] heart was set on this unity. What shameful history, and what bloody annals has this lack of unity written for God's Church. These walls of separations, these alienations, these riven circles of God's family, these warring tribes of men, and these internecine, fratricidal wars! . . . The unity of God's people was to be the heritage of God's glory promised to them. Division and strife are the devil's bequest to the church, a heritage of failure, weakness, shame and woe.

The oneness of God's people was to be the one credential to the world of the divinity of Christ's mission on earth. Let us ask in all candor, are we praying for this unity as Christ prayed for it? Are we seeking the peace, the welfare, the glory, the might, and the divinity of God's cause as it is found in the unity of God's people?[2]

Now nearly ten decades after Bounds wrote that vivid description, there are some encouraging signs around us. The exaggerated and destructive focus on independence and individualism in Christianity is beginning to wane on some fronts, especially in the developing world.

"Turf wars" are beginning to be replaced with pastors of various communities gathering regularly to pray, to minister to each other, and to collaborate in mutual ministries. Many are going so far as to acknowledge that there is actually only one church in a given community, the true body of Christ, comprised of various congregations representing different denominations or traditions.

In the United States increasing numbers of pastors, local churches, denominations, and other Christian ministries are admitting, "We cannot do it alone." Many pastors and others from across the nation are posing the question, "What is God calling us to do together that we can do better than if we try to do it individually?" The Lord has also been calling pastors and other Christians to pray together for revival in the church, spiritual awakening in the nation, and the unity of the body of Christ so that the world may know that the Father has sent the Son (John 17:21, 23, 25).

That is the heart of the fast-growing ministry coalition known as Mission America, which focuses on mobilizing the church in America to join in praying for every man, woman, young person, and child in the nation and then in sharing the gospel lovingly and appropriately with every one of those persons by the end of the year 2000.

For this to take place, more than human organization or planning is required. The unity of the body of Christ for which He prayed so earnestly has become the major focus of corporate prayer and collaborative ministries for those involved in the Mission America coalition. William Hendriksen wrote about this kind of authentic spiritual unity.

> The unity for which Jesus is praying is not merely outward. He guards against this very common misinterpretation. He asks that the oneness of all believers resemble that which exists eternally between the Father and the Son. In both cases the unity is of a definitely *spiritual* nature. To be sure, Father, Son and Holy Spirit are one *in essence;* believers, on the other hand, are one in mind, effort, and purpose....
>
> There is more here than a mere *comparison* between the oneness of all God's children, on the one hand, and the oneness of the persons of the holy Trinity, on the other. The latter is not merely *the model;* it is *the foundation* of the former; it makes the former possible. Only such men as have been born from above, and are *in* the Father and *in* the Son, are also spiritually one, and offer united opposition to the world.[3]

Every Christian pastor and leader should be leading the way in praying for and being led by the Spirit in encouraging other Christians toward authentic spiritual unity. This has been the focus of a remarkable ministry called Prayer Summits, begun a decade or so ago by Joseph Aldrich, then president of Multnomah Bible College and Biblical Seminary in Portland, Oregon. The approach has been simple and very effective. Pastors from a given community are invited to a four-day prayer retreat. The format is to have no speakers or any set agenda. Instead, the pastors gather to pray and wait on the Lord.

A striking result of many of the prayer summits is a new sense of spiritual unity among the pastors and churches in a community. In this context Aldrich wrote about spiritual unity as one of God's key battle plans for local and world evangelism.

> What's the battle plan for the church? John 17 lays out Christ's strategy for members of his army.
>
> Commander Christ places unity at the heart of his military operation. His troops are to stand undivided. Four times he asks his Father to enable believers to achieve this difficult objective. Why?
>
> Unity releases power.
>
> Unity attracts the blessing of God.
>
> Unity captures the attention of an unbelieving world.
>
> Psalm 133 reads: "How good and pleasant it is when brothers live together in unity. . . for there the Lord bestows [commands] his blessing" (vv. 1, 3).
>
> Where does the Lord command his blessing? Where does he direct his enablement? In what kind of an environment does he release his power?
>
> Where there is unity.
>
> Christ's prayer for his rag-tag army is one of the hinge-points of human history. It's a revolutionary prayer, uttered by one who intends to unleash exactly that—a revolution.
>
> It's a neglected prayer whose time has come. It's a prayer about how God wants to use His children to impact their world with the glorious gospel.
>
> Please note that the goal for all believers is unity; evangelism is the by-product.[4]

This says it well. Our enemy seeks to divide and destroy us. In response, our Leader, Jesus Christ, has prayed and is still praying, I believe, for the unity of His body. Can we do less than join Him earnestly in that prayer, and then make ourselves available to be used by Him to do all we can to encourage and promote the unity of the body of Christ?

In his outstanding book on revival Brian Edwards writes insightfully on this important subject.

> One of the greatest benefits of revival lies in its effects upon human relationships. In society, those converted to Christ are reconciled not only to God, but to neighbours, workmates and others. Family feuds are healed, gossiping and slanderous tongues are silenced and class and social barriers are pulled down. The gospel that makes us "all one in Christ Jesus" and the Savior, in whom there is "neither Jew nor Greek, slave nor free, male nor female" (Gal. 3:28), unites those who are unnecessarily divided.
>
> It was reported from Wales in 1904 [after the Welsh Revival] that women who "sued one another in the courts, [now] prayed side by side in the same meeting." An old miner, speaking of the feuds between union and non-union members prior to the 1859 revival in Wales, claimed: "I have seen neighbors refuse to speak to each other, although they had been great friends. I have seen some refuse to descend the mine in the same cage with men who did not belong to the Federation, or to speak to them below ground, except with an oath. The revival has stopped all that, and colliers [coal miners] look upon each other, in spite of all the differences, as friends and companions. Some of the Non-unionists were among the best of men, and, at the meeting I have just left, one of them was leading the prayers, and Unionists joining in!"
>
> Nowhere is this seen more obviously than in the life of the churches. One of the sad marks of the church in its normal life is that it is often found uniting with those from whom it should separate, and separating from those with whom it should unite. Too often denominational ties and traditions are far more important than the loyalty to the truth. Revival, as we have already said, is an evangelical experience; it is the glory and gift of the evangelical churches, whatever their denomination. Revival highlights the big issues that unite, rather than the secondary issues that divide. . . .
>
> It must be re-emphasized that unity like this is always an evangelical unity, and never an ecumenical unity where the true gospel is lost among the baggage of error and pretense.[5]

Reading this kind of description of past revival reminds us of the great need for revival we are facing today in the church. During my three decades in the ministry, I have learned that no kind of church polity, church constitution, organization, or legislation can bring spiritual unity to a church or any gathering of Christians. Only when people's hearts are right with God can they be right with others. Authentic unity in the church can only be wrought as the Holy Spirit unites the hearts of Christian believers who are living under the lordship of Jesus Christ.

Christian leaders do well to join their Leader, Jesus Christ, in praying for true unity in the body of Christ. May we be brought to the "complete unity" of the Father, Son, and Holy Spirit so that the world may believe.

PRAYING FOR OTHERS

Our Lord has also instructed us to be involved in the prayer ministry of intercession. Kyu Nam Jung, of Korea, has defined this ministry as "prayer in which the petitioner asks God for something on behalf of someone or something else."[6]

Jesus is our example and model for intercessory praying. During the three years of His earthly ministry, He often interceded for others. In fact, His high priestly prayer is primarily a prayer of intercession. He first interceded for His disciples (John 17:6–19), and then for all believers (17:20–26).

Of course, Jesus interceded for His disciples on other occasions. In the Last Supper, He shared the fact that He had been praying for Peter as He said, "Simon, Simon, Satan has asked to sift you as wheat. But *I have prayed for you*, Simon, that your faith may not fail. And when you have turned back, strengthen your brothers" (Luke 22:31–32, italics added).

Since He ascended to be with the Father, Jesus has continued His ministry of intercessory praying (Heb. 7:25). It is remarkable to understand that He has been interceding for His people for twenty centuries.

One of the dangers Christian leaders face is to think that intercessory prayer is something others provide for them, without realizing the responsibility and potential of being involved themselves in intercessory praying for others.

My wife, Jeannie, and I have a team of wonderful intercessors who pray regularly for us in our ministry. In recent years we have enjoyed praying for them as they pray for us. When we send our prayer requests to those committed to pray for us, we enclose a prayer request card for them to send back to us, so that we can be involved in praying for them even as they pray for us.

I have come to love the ministry of interceding for these dear brothers and sisters. It is a source of great joy to pray for them. And the joy increases greatly when we see them being blessed as a result of God's answers to prayer. In the best sense of the term intercessory praying is a win-win situation. Both the intercessor and the recipient are blessed.

Admittedly, however, intercessory praying is not a "natural" activity. It requires discipline, initiative, and time. As Sammy Tippit put it, "Intercessory prayer is hard work. It involves communion with the King and compassion for the multitudes. It is understanding the passion of Christ for souls. It is waiting on God to endue us with power from on high in order that we might lead those souls into the kingdom."[7]

Jesus' intercessory ministry has practical implications for His followers. "Since Jesus ever lives to intercede, any time you pray—day or night—Jesus is already interceding. Every time you go to prayer you can be Jesus' prayer partner."[8]

Intercession is a ministry of partnership with both God and others. "When I learn what intercession is," Jack Hayford observed, "and how to respond to the Holy Spirit's prodding to do it, I am moving into partnership with the Father in the highest sense."[9] And that partnership of intercession has an awesome potential to affect the lives of those we love and for whom we pray. In fact, Jesus has encouraged us to pray not only for those we love but also for our enemies.

Charles Spurgeon's following words on this subject are encouraging:

> Remember that intercessory prayer is the sweetest prayer God ever hears ... and is exceedingly prevalent. What wonders it has wrought!
>
> Intercessory prayer has stopped plagues. It removed the darkness that rested over Egypt, drove away the frogs that leaped upon the land, scattered the lice and locusts that plagued the inhabitants of Zoan, removed the thunder and lightning, stayed all the ravages that God's avenging hand

did upon Pharaoh and his people. We know that intercessory prayer healed diseases in the early church. We have evidence of it in old Mosaic times. When Miriam was smitten with leprosy, Moses prayed and the leprosy was removed. Intercessory prayer has raised the dead. . . .

As to how many souls intercessory prayer has instrumentally saved, only eternity shall reveal it! There is nothing that intercessory prayer cannot do. Believer, you have a mighty engine in your hand—use it well, use it constantly, use it now with faith, and you shall surely prevail.[10]

Wesley Duewel has shared his vision for the wonderful potential of intercessory praying.

God has a wonderful plan by which you can have world-wide influence. This plan is not just for a chosen few. It is for you. . . .

Through prayer you can accompany any missionary to remote reaches of the earth. . . . Through prayer you can contribute to the ministry of any pastor or evangelist in a church or gospel hall anywhere in the world. . . . Through prayer you can take a suffering infant in your arms. Through prayer you can touch a fevered brow in any hospital, mediating the healing love of Jesus.

God has given you a way to make your presence count, a way to be a true partner in His kingdom's work, if you really want to be. . . . There is no reason in the world why you cannot become so steadfast in your personal prayer life that Christ will count on you to help build His church . . . in many parts of the world.

You yourself can influence more people for God and have a greater role in advancing Christ's cause by prayer than in any other way. It is not the *only* thing you must do, but it is the *greatest* thing you can do.[11]

Intercessory praying is one of the most significant ministries in which any of us can be involved! In most of my years of ministry I have been an activist. God has enabled me to minister long hours and with great intensity. I have tried to be a faithful steward of the gifts and resources He has entrusted to me. There have been months in which I have traveled thousands of miles and have preached literally dozens of times, along with countless meetings, appointments, and counseling sessions. Without realizing it, I have sometimes been impressed by how much I have been able to do for Christ and His church.

But in recent years the Lord has led me into a new dimension of ministry. I accept fewer speaking engagements. I no longer get on an airplane unless I have the strong conviction that the Lord is calling me to do so. I spend less time in meetings. And by God's grace I spend more time alone with Him in prayer and intercession.

I am not suggesting that preaching, counseling, meetings, and ministry activity are no longer important. It is just that God has been gracious enough to teach me more about balance in the ministry, more about both "inhaling" and "exhaling"—inhaling the presence and the power of the Holy Spirit so I can be more effective in my outward, exhaling ministry. For example, I have come to understand that most spiritual battles are won in the prayer closet or in corporate prayer meetings with my Christian brothers and sisters rather than on the battlefield itself.

Like David, I have come to believe that we need to face the giants of life with the conviction that "the battle is the Lord's" (1 Sam. 17:47), and He will give the victory. That kind of conviction does not come merely by positive thinking or spiritual hype. It comes only when we have wrestled in prayer with our heavenly Father. As we engage in this kind of intercessory praying, our ministries will be strengthened and will bring glory to the Lord.

PRAYING WITH OTHERS

There is a kind of praying that is even more effective and powerful than a single person praying alone. That is when a group of God's people pray together. On the Day of Pentecost the church was born in such a group prayer meeting, when a little band of 120 followers of Jesus gathered for prayer. "They all joined *together* constantly in prayer. . . . When the day of Pentecost came, they were all *together* in one place" (Acts 1:14; 2:1, italics added).

In response to their corporate prayers, the power of the Holy Spirit came on them, and the church was born supernaturally by the Spirit. Peter and the others were filled with the Holy Spirit, and as they stood together on the streets of Jerusalem, Peter preached of the life, death, and resurrection of Jesus Christ. Some three thousand listeners believed in Jesus and became a part of the church in just one day.

After Pentecost, the members of the early church continued to gather together and to pray together on a regular basis. "All the believers were *together....* Every day they continued to meet *together* in the temple courts" (2:44, 46, italics added). Every afternoon at three o'clock they gathered in the temple courts to pray (3:1). And when the leaders of the early church faced their first crisis, the believers "raised their voices *together* in prayer to God" (4:24, italics added).

Praying together became a way of life for the early Christians. I believe it was in response to the teaching of Jesus, who said, "Again [apparently He had spoken to them about this matter on other occasions] I tell you that if two of you on earth agree about anything you ask for, it will be done for you by my Father in heaven. For where two or three come together in my name, there am I with them" (Matt. 18:19–20).

Concerning this significant passage, Andrew Murray wrote the following:

What an unspeakable privilege [is] united prayer . . . and what a power it might be. If the believing husband and wife knew that they were joined together in the Name of Jesus to experience His presence and power in united prayer . . . ; if friends believed what mighty help two or three praying in concert could give each other; if in every prayer meeting the coming together in the Name, the faith in the Presence, and the expectation of the answer, stood in the foreground; if in every Church united effectual prayer were regarded as one of the chief purposes for which they are banded together, the highest exercise of their power as a Church . . . O who can say what blessing might come to, and through, those who thus agreed to prove God in the fulfillment of His promise.[12]

God honors corporate praying—in which Christian leaders pray with their spouses (if they are married) and with their families, and then with their elders or staff or other leaders of a given local church or Christian ministry. Broken marriages, dying churches, and ineffective ministries can be transformed by the strategic ministry of united prayer.

The benefits of corporate praying are many. The pages of church history are filled with the wonderful results of corporate prayer. Charles Spurgeon recounted a few of those benefits.

As many mercies are transported from heaven in the ship of prayer, so *there are many special mercies that can only be brought to us by the fleets of united prayer.* Many are the good things that God will give to his lonely Elijahs and Daniels, but if two of you agree as touching anything that you ask, there is no limit to God's bountiful answers (Matt. 18:19).

Peter may have never been brought out of prison had it not been that prayer was made without ceasing by all the church for him (Acts 12:5). Pentecost might never have come had not *all* the disciples been with one accord in one place (Acts 2:1), waiting for the descent of the tongues of fire. God is pleased to answer individual prayers, but at times He seems to say, You may entreat My favor, but I will not see your face unless your brethren are with you. Why is this? I take it that our gracious Lord is setting forth His own esteem for the communion of saints. "I believe in the communion of saints" is one article of the great Christian creed, but how few saints understand it. And yet there is such a thing as real union among God's people.

We cannot afford to lose the help and love of our brethren. Augustine says, "The poor are made for the rich, and the rich are made for the poor." I do not doubt but the strong saints are made for the weak saints and the weak saints bring special benedictions upon mature believers. There is a completeness in the whole body of Christ—each joint owes something to every other joint, and "the whole body is bound together by that which every joint supplies. . . . "

The value placed upon union and communion among the people of God is seen by the fact that there are certain mercies that are bestowed only when the saints pray unitedly. How we ought to feel this bond of union! How we ought to pray for one another! [13]

Our dear heavenly Father,
teach us how to pray for spiritual unity
and with spiritual unity.
Help us experience
the kind and depth of unity for which our Lord Jesus prayed.
Deliver us from being Lone Rangers
who focus on ourselves—
and help us to enjoy the great privilege of intercessory praying.
Help us to experience Your power
and the results
that are especially unleashed
through corporate prayer—
praying together
in the name and presence
of our Lord Jesus.

12

AVOIDING THE PHARISEES'
APPROACH TO PRAYER

LUKE 18:10–13 RECORDS one of the most remarkable parables Jesus ever told "Two men went up to the temple to pray, one a Pharisee and the other a tax collector. The Pharisee stood up and prayed about himself: 'God, I thank you that I am not like other men—robbers, evildoers, adulterers— or even like this tax collector. I fast twice a week and give a tenth of all I get.' But the tax collector stood at a distance. He would not even look up to heaven, but beat his breast and said, 'God, have mercy on me, a sinner.'"

Two kinds of men prayed two kinds of prayers. The first man, a Pharisee, was religious. In fact, he was a leader of the religious. The Pharisee prayed *about* himself rather than praying *to* God. His was the personification of the kind of self-centered praying we have considered in a couple of earlier chapters. He violated several of the principles of praying already discussed. His was certainly far from being a model prayer!

Proud of himself, the Pharisee compared his behavior to others. He was delighted that he was not like them. He boasted that he did not rob others or commit adultery. And he certainly was not like the tax collector who was in the temple that very moment. The Pharisee was devout. He fasted not just once a week, but twice. He gave a tithe of everything he received. In short, he was extremely impressed with himself, and he wanted God and others to notice how righteous he was.

By contrast, the tax collector did not know how to pray according to religious traditions or guidelines. He was a sinner and he knew it. He would not even lift up his eyes toward God as he cried out to Him. He beat on his chest in contrition and humility. Admitting he was a sinner, he pleaded to God for mercy. He prayed, "God have mercy on me, a sinner," but a more accurate translation of his request is, "God have mercy on me, *the* sinner." He evidently looked on himself as the worst of sinners.

This is one of the few parables Jesus explained. "I tell you that this man [the tax collector], rather than the other [the Pharisee], went home justified before God. For everyone who exalts himself will be humbled, and he who humbles himself will be exalted" (18:14).

The lesson is clear. If we want to be justified before God, and if we want our prayers to be heard and answered, we must pray like the tax collector, not like the Pharisee.

WE NEED TO HUMBLE OURSELVES

The Pharisees and other hypocritical religious leaders believed in prayer. In fact, they seemed to enjoy praying in public. But their approach was wrong. It was not acceptable to God. In fact, Jesus said the religious leaders were actually providing a model of how *not* to pray.

The implications for contemporary Christian leaders are both obvious and ominous. We must be careful how we pray. Those who follow our leadership should be able to learn how to pray from us. Our Lord has made it clear that He wants us to humble ourselves before Him as we come into His presence to pray. He "opposes the proud, but gives grace to the humble" (James 4:6; 1 Pet. 5:5).

This is the same message the Lord shared with Solomon after he had led in the dedication of the temple. The Lord appeared to him at night and told him his people were to "humble themselves and pray" (2 Chron. 7:14). Pride and prayer don't mix.

For some reason, when people think they have "arrived" in the realm of the religious or have won God's favor because they have followed certain steps, they tend to approach God in pride and tell Him what to do and how to do it.

Although I do not suggest we critique the prayers of others, it is interesting to note the vocal tone and attitude of people when they pray in public. Some pray-ers sound angry. Others attempt to dictate orders to God and often present their demands with great volume and velocity. On occasion I have not been able to avoid noticing that such prayers sound a lot like the resounding gongs and clanging cymbals Paul warned about in 1 Corinthians 13:1. God is not impressed with that kind of praying.

God is God, and we are mere sinners saved by His grace. He is the Source of all we need, and we are those who are in need. He is all-powerful, and we are weak and fragile. We do not impress him by pretending to be otherwise.

That was one of the major challenges the Pharisees faced. They attempted to earn the favor of God and people. They seemed to be most concerned about being heard by others and making a favorable impression on them. The major focus of their prayers was on themselves rather than on the God to whom they supposedly prayed. As a result of their pride, God would humble them, not accept them (Luke 18.14).

WE ARE NOT TO PRAY LIKE THE HYPOCRITES

This was not the only time Jesus encouraged us not to pray like religious people. In the Sermon on the Mount He declared, "And when you pray, do not be like the hypocrites, for they love to pray standing in the synagogues and on the street corners to be seen by men. I tell you the truth, they have received their reward in full" (Matt. 6:5).

Jesus then continued, "But when you pray, go into your room, close the door and pray to your Father, who is unseen. Then your Father, who sees what is done in secret, will reward you. And when you pray, do not keep on babbling like pagans, for they think they will be heard because of their many words. Do not be like them, for your Father knows what you need before you ask him" (6:6–8).

Jesus used the negative model of "how not to pray" in order to teach some important positive principles. Unfortunately the Pharisees and other religious leaders were modeling the wrong kind of praying, and others were following their lead. And so Jesus taught them how they should pray.

It can be helpful for us to summarize the basic principles of prayer practiced by the Pharisees and other hypocritical religious leaders, not to pass judgment on them but to be duly warned to avoid their kind of praying.

First, we should not pray with a spirit of pride. The Pharisee in Jesus' parable prayed, "God, I thank you that I am not like other men" (Luke 18:11). He then listed the sins he thought others were committing, and then he compiled an impressive list of what he considered his outstanding religious achievements. Viewing himself as righteous, he rejoiced in the fact that he was significantly better, he thought, than other people. But he failed to realize that prayer is not an occasion for focusing on ourselves or comparing ourselves with others. Instead, as we have seen, prayer is the means whereby we come humbly into the presence of the One who alone is holy and righteous.

Authentic Christian humility begins with seeing God as He really is and seeing ourselves as God sees us. This was Isaiah's experience. "In the year that King Uzziah died, I saw the Lord seated on a throne, high and exalted, and the train of his robe filled the temple. Above him were seraphs, each with six wings. . . . And they were calling to one another. 'Holy, holy, holy is the LORD Almighty; the whole earth is full of his glory.' At the sound of their voices the doorposts and thresholds shook and the temple was filled with smoke" (Isa. 6:1–4).

Isaiah's immediate response was what many of us have experienced when we have sensed we are in the presence of God: " 'Woe to me!' I cried. 'I am ruined! For I am a man of unclean lips, and I live among a people of unclean lips, and my eyes have seen the King, the LORD Almighty' " (6:5).

Ushering us into the very presence of God, prayer reminds us of who God is and who we are, of the Creator and the created. Prayer puts into graphic perspective why we so desperately need God. It fulfills our innate desire to worship and fellowship with the One who made us.

Genuine prayer can dissolve and even eradicate our temptation to bask in our self-righteousness. When we realize that in prayer we are in God's holy presence, we can be delivered from the pharisaical error of attempting to impress God and others with any self-centered or self-reliant religious activities.

Prayer humbles us. By contrast, pride is subtle. Pride is far easier to detect in the lives of others than it is to recognize in our own. In fact, if we are not careful, we can become proud about what we perceive to be our own humility!

I find it is helpful for me to fall prostrate, literally, before God in prayer early every morning, envisioning Him as He really is, high and lifted up, asking Him (a) to show Himself to me and to reveal myself to me as He sees me, (b) to search my heart and cleanse me, (c) to overwhelm me with a sense of His holiness and purity, and (d) to give me an authentic hunger for His holiness in my life.

At times I feel His presence much more than others. In those moments I can see Him more clearly in all His beauty and holiness. But the act of falling before Him, looking up at Him, and praying to Him from a prone posture of worship is always meaningful, regardless of the presence or absence of any special feelings. That kind of praying then flows into a time of worship and praise. You may have a better or more meaningful way of doing it. But whatever the approach, I believe we need to begin every day humbling ourselves before God as faithfully and volitionally as we can.

Second, we should not pray to impress others. Jesus said the hypocrites loved to pray as they stood in the synagogues or on the street corners so they would be seen by others. Within their culture, such a display of religious piety evidently received the approval and even accolades of others.

Such a display would hardly be well received in our culture today. It reminds me of an experience I had on a commercial airplane recently. Some young Muslim clerics were on the plane. When their traditional time of prayer arrived, without warning they walked down the aisle to the first-class section of the airplane. They unrolled their prayer mats and began to pray. They seemed to be praying with much the same spirit as the Pharisee whom Jesus described in His parable. Their actions were not well received by the flight attendants, the passengers in the first-class section, or those of us in the coach class.

One of the major problems of the Pharisees is that they failed to realize their approach to praying led them to focus more on themselves than on God. They were affecting the temporary and not the eternal. As a result, as Jesus said, the only reward they would receive would be the approval of some of the persons who observed them. Seeking to be honored by God, they would be rejected by Him.

On the other hand, authentic prayer has incredible implications for the eternal. In fact, only eternity will reveal all the results of the prayers of God's saints. Some one hundred years ago, Andrew Murray addressed this great potential in his classic book *With Christ in the School of Prayer.* "Who can say what power a Church could develop and exercise, if it gave itself to the work of prayer day and night for the coming of the Kingdom, for God's power on His servants and His word, for the glorifying of God in the salvation of souls? Most Churches think their members are gathered into one simply to take care of and build up each other. They know not that God rules the world by the prayers of His saints; that prayer is the power by which Satan is conquered; that by prayer the Church on earth has disposal of the powers of the heavenly world."[1]

As I have shared this quotation in my preaching over the past few years, I have found some Christian leaders have objected to what Murray was saying. Murray's statement was completely foreign to their experience in prayer. As a result, some of them have rejected his insights on prayer as radical or invalid.

Without realizing it, some pastors and other Christian leaders have neglected the awesome work of prayer for so long that it is difficult for them to comprehend its potential. They are so busy in honorable ministry activity that they believe only more people and more labor will help them accomplish what are often worthy ministry goals. Methods, programs, church-growth theories, management principles, business practices, and other good and profitable ventures frequently consume all their time and energy in the ministry, not to mention the constant needs of people both within and outside the church.

Somehow, there is simply not time for prayer. Many church calendars are so full of activities that the good has squeezed out the best. The important has usurped the place of the most important. Pastors and parents and other Christian leaders are often fatigued, discouraged, and even disheartened. They desperately need the power of God, but they have forgotten how to receive it. To that kind of ministry approach, E. M. Bounds has responded this way: "What the Church needs today is not more machinery or better, nor new organizations or more and novel methods, but men [and women] whom the Holy Ghost can use—men of prayer, men mighty in prayer. The Holy Ghost does not flow through methods, but through men. He does not come on machinery, but on men. He does not anoint plans, but men—men of prayer."[2]

The greatest need of the church in America is to rediscover the ministry of prayer, beginning with prayer in the lives and families of Christian leaders. I believe such actions could contribute greatly to the possibility of revival in the church and spiritual awakening in our nation.

The church is virtually exploding in many nations of the world today. The church is growing rapidly in one Third-World nation after another. Yet many churches in the United States are either declining or maintaining their congregations. And a number of the growing churches are increasing in number by attracting members from other churches in the community.

Pastors and leaders are buying one book or audiocassette after another, attending seminars almost constantly, and implementing one new program after another. But many ideas do not seem to be working well. We are finding it is difficult to franchise programs or to transfer ideas effectively from one church to another.

Not that these approaches are wrong or worthless. In fact, many may be very worthy. But they are insufficient to meet our deepest needs in ministry. We need to return to our Lord's basic principles. Many of us have neglected prayer long enough. It is time to humble ourselves before God and each other—and to pray.

Our sin is often in sharp contrast to that of the Pharisees, who loved to pray in public to impress people. Many of us have done just the opposite. We have neglected prayer both in public and in private, in our homes and our churches.

But in the words of Jesus, the results are essentially the same. We have already received whatever rewards we are to get. And for great numbers of Christian leaders in America, those rewards are inadequate, inconsequential, and insignificant. Only when we learn to pray as Jesus taught us to pray will we be different. That kind of praying will radically affect our lives, our ministries, our families, our churches, our nations—and the world.

Third, we should not think God will hear our prayers based merely on how many words we utter. Jesus called that kind of praying "babbling"

(Matt. 6:7). The Greek word for "babble," used only here in the New Testament, means to speak without thinking. He said the pagans did that, assuming that the more words they prayed (without thinking!) the more they would get God's attention. He warned us not to fall into that temptation: "Do not be like them," He said. We have a loving Father who already knows what we need long before we ask Him (6:8). We simply need to ask.

We receive God's answers only when we humbly come into His presence asking Him for what we need, that is, what we genuinely need. Authentic praying transforms us from focusing on our personal agendas to being concerned about accomplishing His will. We no longer ask merely for what we think we need. We now ask for what our Lord knows we need. We surrender to Him and the fulfillment of His will. We pray as He taught us to pray, "Your will be done on earth as it is in heaven" (6:10).

The apostle John stated this truth about prayer in a most practical and applicable way: "This is the confidence we have in approaching God: that if we ask anything according to *his will,* he hears us. And if we know that he hears us—whatever we ask—we know that we have what we asked of him" (1 John 5:14–15, italics added).

That is the key to answered prayers. God is not impressed with our worldliness or our lengthy but thoughtless prayers. Nor does He respond to our tactics, quarrels, or fights. Instead, our Lord answers the prayers of His children who come into His presence humbly, seeking to fulfill His will.

The Westminster Shorter Catechism summarizes this profound theological truth in simple terms: "Prayer is offering up of our desires unto God, for things agreeable to His will, in the name of Christ, with confession of our sins, and thankful acknowledgment of His mercies."[3] Catherine Marshall stated that same truth in a slightly different manner: "The purpose of prayer is to find God's will and to make that will our prayer."[4]

WE ARE TO PRAY AS JESUS PRAYED

The Lord Jesus practiced what He preached. He did not pray in the synagogues and on the street corners so He could impress people. Instead, He prayed privately (Mark 1:35; Luke 5:16). One time He prayed all night in a solitary place in the hills (Luke 6:12).

The Pharisees viewed prayer as a religious obligation; to Jesus, prayer was a wonderful opportunity to commune with His Father. The Pharisees viewed prayer as an avenue to impress others with their religious accomplishments; to Jesus, it was an opportunity to focus on God.

The hypocrites viewed prayer as a way to demonstrate their self-righteousness; Jesus viewed prayer as an opportunity to advance God's work. The hypocrites' view was shortsighted, quickly bringing all the rewards they would ever receive. In contrast, Jesus promised that His Father would reward all those who truly prayed. The hypocrites thought God would be impressed with how many words they prayed. But Jesus said our Father knows what we need before we even ask Him.

The Pharisees and other religious hypocrites abused prayer and missed out on one of the greatest blessings life can offer: enjoying intimate communion with the God of the universe. Unfortunately many Christian leaders today face the same tragic consequences. Ignoring prayer robs us of one of the greatest sources of joy and spiritual power available.

In communing with the Lord, we need to avoid misusing prayer as the Pharisees did. Being involved in corporate prayer with other Christians must be preceded by personal, private, intimate times of communion with God. Like a husband sharing intimately with his wife, or a wife with her husband, so God delights in sharing intimately with us. John Dawson, a young prayer leader of this generation, has written, "God knows the weakness of the human heart towards pride. If we speak of what God has revealed and done in intercession, it may lead to committing sin. God shares his secrets with those who are able to keep them."[5]

RESPONDING TO OUR FATHER'S INVITATION

Jesus' model prayer (Matt. 6:9–17) shows us we are to pray not with a proud spirit, but with authentic humility; not to try to impress others, but to commune with Him intimately from our hearts; not to try to impress God with the length of our prayers or the amount of time we spend in prayer each day, but to talk to Him because we love Him.

To pray is to invite Jesus into our hearts. To pray is to communicate with the God of all creation. To pray is to surrender to the will of God, to receive His provision and protection. To pray is to entrust all to our Father, and to trust Him utterly. To pray is to ask that His kingdom come and that His will be done on earth as it is in heaven.

Father, forgive us when we pray like the Pharisees.
We do not want to pray with a spirit of pride
or merely to impress others
or to offer babblings to You.
Instead, we want to pray as our Lord Jesus taught us to pray.
With love—
With awe and adoration—
With worship and praise—
With confession and humility—
To fulfill Your will
and to advance Your work!

13

PERSISTING IN THE SCHOOL OF PRAYER

c—✶—o

CHARLIE RIGGS understands the basics of prayer. He has learned them from experience, first as an oil-field worker who came to know Christ through the Navigators ministry and then during his many years as director of counseling and follow-up for the Billy Graham Evangelistic Association.

He has grasped the fact that prayer is practical—that it works—and that it needs to be a part of our lives each day, just as much as eating, sleeping, and working are parts of our daily schedules. Riggs describes how practical prayer has become in his life.

Most of my adult life I have been out of my league socially, educationally and spiritually. My work has put demands on me that have stretched me to the limit and beyond. In other words, I have been over my head. I've been doing things that are not natural for me to do, and it has been good for me. I have had to spend a lot of time on my knees, looking up to a sovereign God who has been a constant helper.

I have learned that prayer is more of an attitude than a posture or a form of expression. An attitude of dependence on God. A realization that I am not sufficient and need help. I can't do it but God can help me do it. As the song says, "I need thee every hour," or "Learning to lean." Our whole life, when it is lived to the glory of God, can be a form of prayer. We learn to lean on Jesus throughout every day for help to live a supernatural life in a tough, worldly environment. It is like "praying without ceasing."[1]

Like Charlie Riggs, Rosalind Rinker has been one of my "instructors" in the school of prayer. As a young missionary she began to learn some of the practical precepts of prayer that she in turn has shared with hundreds of thousands of us who have read her books. "Prayer is the expression of the human heart in conversation with God. The more natural the prayer, the more real He becomes. It has all been simplified for me to this extent: *prayer is a dialog between two persons who love each other.*"[2]

These two seasoned servants of the Lord have come to realize over the years that prayer is to be much more than a religious activity. It begins with our attitude toward God. It flows in and out of our lives as we commune with Him.

Prayer can also make a great difference in our public ministries. Another great prayer warrior and prayer leader, Evelyn Christenson, addressed this matter in a most practical way in an article in *Pray* magazine.

The pastor of the large Texas church and his wife walked me slowly to the car after an all-day prayer seminar for 2,000 people. When I had given the invitation to pray aloud in their groups, over one-fourth of these people, many weeping, had repented and boldly invited Jesus into their hearts.

The pastor stopped, looked me in the eye, and asked, "To what do you owe that kind of power?" Taken aback, I responded, "Well, prayer, of course."

"What kind of prayer?" he quizzed.

"First of all, the prayer of the committee who invited me to come here. They signed a contract promising to get a representative from the churches in the community and pray together for at least six months before I came—I said I wouldn't come unless they did. Then last night, I dropped in to their group and kicked off the seminar with an evening of prayer, once again pleading for those who didn't know Jesus.

"My own board members pray every day. I have a prayer calendar that includes a special intercessor of the day. My telephone prayer chains pray three times a week. Thousands of my newsletter subscribers pray. We have a group that prays around the clock for special events and overseas trips. Plus the prayer of friends, family, and my own prayers several hours each day."

The pastor looked at me in silence. Finally, he said, "What would happen if I, as pastor of this church, had that kind of prayer?"

"Sir," I replied, "you wouldn't be able to get all the new believers into your overcrowded sanctuary."[3]

She is right. Most of our ministries would be affected greatly if prayer were a major focus of our ministries.

Over the years evangelist Billy Graham has been asked repeatedly about the reasons for the remarkable success of his ministry. Again and again he has responded with all sincerity by saying, "There are three basic ingredients that have been key in our crusades. The first is prayer. The second is prayer. And the third and final ingredient is prayer!" Prayer has been Billy Graham's foundation and key spiritual dynamic, resulting in great spiritual harvests in crusade services over the years.

The benefits of cultivating a life of prayer are numerous. In one sense, it is virtually impossible to assess fully the profitability of a life of prayer. Just the privilege of communicating with God in prayer is beyond human description.

As we have explored the subject of prayer together, we have considered many of its benefits, such as enjoying intimate communion with God in His presence, receiving His provision and protection, being able to make significant contributions to the lives of others, and gaining increased spiritual power and purpose in our lives. Two additional aspects are exceedingly important.

PERSISTING IN PRAYER

Prayer is a joy, a delight, a privilege. But at times prayer can be hard work. It requires commitment, discipline, and perseverance—things that seem to pose a special challenge in our culture. Wesley Duewel writes cogently about our need for prevailing prayer as follows:

The great need of our world, our nation and our churches is people who know how to prevail in prayer. Moments of pious wishes blandly expressed

151

to God once or twice a day will bring little change on earth or among the people. Kind thoughts expressed to Him in five or six sentences, after reading a paragraph or two of mildly religious sentiments once a day from some devotional writing, will not bring the kingdom of God to earth or shake the gates of hell and repel the attacks of evil on our culture and our civilization.

Results, not beautiful words, are the test of prevailing prayer. Results, not mere sanctimonious devotional moments, are the hallmark of the true intercessor.

We need great answers to prayer, changed lives and situations—answers that bear upon them the stamp of the divine. . . . We need mighty answers to prayer that will bring new life to the church and new strength, faith, and courage to faint believers; that will silence, dumbfound, and convict evil men; and that will thwart, defeat, and drive back the assaults of Satan. . . .

The great and godly people of the church have always been those who know how to prevail in prayer. There is nothing higher or holier in Christian living and service. In prevailing prayer you rise to your full potential as created in the image of God and as exalted to the heavenlies to share with Christ His intercessory throne. . . .

You have no greater ministry or no leadership more influential than intercession. There is no higher role, honor, or authority than this. You have been saved to reign through prayer. You have been Spirit-filled to qualify you to reign by prayer. You reign as you prevail in prayer.[4]

Those insights shared by one of the great prayer leaders of our generation are both sobering and encouraging. Persisting or prevailing in prayer can make a great difference. Dutch Sheets agrees. In his book *Intercessory Prayer* he has shown from Elijah's experience why persisting in prayer is so important.

In 1 Kings 18:1 the Lord said to Elijah, "Go, show yourself to Ahab, and I will send rain on the face of the earth." God didn't say, "I might." He didn't say, "If you pray hard enough." He didn't say, "I'm thinking about it." He just said, "I'm going to do it." It was God's timing, God's idea, God's will.

Yet, we are told at the end of this chapter that Elijah labored in prayer diligently seven times in the posture of a woman in travail before clouds appeared and the rain came. He didn't casually walk to the top of the mountain and say, "Lord, send the rain," and immediately it was done. That's not the "effectual, fervent prayer" James 5:16–18 tells us Elijah did to first stop and then bring the rain.[5]

You do not have to agree fully with Dutch's interpretation of this passage in order to benefit from his basic insight. Elijah is a great example to us in the arena of persisting in prayer. Even though God had assured him of His forthcoming answer, Elijah fervently continued to pray until the answer came. Persevering in prayer does not mean we "twist God's arm," trying to force Him to act. Instead it means continuing to let God know of our needs. We do not insist; we persist.

WAITING ON GOD

That introduces us to one of the most difficult aspects of prayer—namely, waiting for God's answers. Waiting on God is an experience that every Christian has encountered at one time or another.

This is not merely a twentieth-century phenomenon. The psalmist addressed this challenge. "I wait for the LORD, my soul waits, and in his word I put my hope. My soul waits for the Lord more than watchmen wait for the morning, more than watchmen wait for the morning" (Ps. 130:5–6). Several times David encouraged us to wait for the Lord. "Wait for the LORD; be strong and take heart and wait for the LORD" (27:14). "Be still before the LORD and wait patiently for him (37:7). "Wait for the LORD" (37:34). And he testified, "In the morning I lay my requests before you and wait in expectation" (5:3). And "I wait for you, O LORD; you will answer, O Lord my God" (38:15). And an anonymous psalmist affirmed, "We wait in hope for the LORD" (33:20).

Waiting, of course, is difficult.

But sometimes the Lord answers even before we ask. The Lord shared an amazing promise through His prophet Isaiah. "Before they call I will answer; while they are still speaking I will hear" (Isa. 65:24).

Perhaps you have had that kind of experience in your praying. In fact, most of us would like to enjoy more of that kind of immediate answer when we pray. But the decision is not ours. It is up to God. He is our sovereign Lord. And a part of the mystery of prayer is that sometimes the answers come even while we are asking, and other times we have to wait, sometimes for a long time.

My wife and I have had that kind of experience in our praying on a number of occasions. One of the most dramatic took place a number of years ago when our daughter, Debbie, was stricken by a virus when she was eighteen months old. She lay in a coma for several days and was not expected to live. Then on Christmas morning, when I was praying by her hospital bed, the Lord graciously touched her. She opened her eyes and smiled at me. That was the beginning of her recovery.

In our praying, both Jeannie and I had sensed assurance from the Lord that Debbie would recover. We knew the Lord was capable of touching her and healing her instantaneously. That is what we expected. But the Lord had other plans. He invited us to wait on Him—to trust Him with all our hearts. Little did we know how long we would wait before our prayers were totally answered.

As Debbie began her recovery, complications began to take place. Debbie underwent some 150 surgeries over a period of thirteen years. Only then was her healing completed.

Today she is a healthy wife and mother. We rejoice at God's grace and provision as we waited on God day after day, month after month, year after year. We learned so much from our gracious Lord over that period of time. He was so patient and faithful with us.

One of the lessons God taught us during those years of praying and waiting was not to become preoccupied with the "why" of the situation. Why was a question God did not answer for Job, nor has He answered it for us. Instead, He gave us an unusual opportunity to trust Him implicitly.

Also it became clear to us that the "how" of prayer is also in God's sovereign hands. He is in charge of when He responds to our prayers as well as how He answers them. Our Lord has declared, "For my thoughts are not your thoughts, neither are your ways my ways" (Isa. 55:8). Waiting on God helps us learn to trust Him more fully.

In his classic book *He Leadeth Me* V. Raymond Edman wrote, "For God's trusting child in need of guidance there are times when he must wait and other times when he must walk onward in calm confidence despite no outward indication of divine direction. There are no occasions, however, when he should worry. If we are troubled we are not trusting; conversely, if we are believing we are not bewildered."[6]

Communing with God in prayer and in His Word will bring us into an ever deeper and trusting relationship with our Lord Jesus Christ.

KEEP ON PRAYING

Waiting on God teaches us never to give up in our praying. Jesus' wonderful parable on this subject should be a source of great encouragement to us in our praying. "Suppose one of you has a friend, and he goes to him at midnight and says, 'Friend, lend me three loaves of bread, because a friend of mine on a journey has come to me, and I have nothing to set before him.' Then the one inside answers, 'Don't bother me. The door is already locked, and my children are with me in bed. I can't get up and give you anything.' I tell you, though he will not get up and give him the bread because he is his friend, yet because of the man's boldness he will get up and give him as much as he needs. So I say to you: Ask and it will be given to you; seek and you will find; knock and the door will be opened to you" (Luke 11:5–9). This man in the parable did not want to be bothered. By contrast our Lord eagerly wants us to come to Him with our requests.

Nor is God like the unjust judge in Luke 18:1–8 who had to be persuaded to provide justice for a needy widow. God does not keep putting us off (18:7) the way the judge did with the woman.

It is always appropriate to ask of the Lord, to seek, and to knock. It is right for us to persist in prayer until God answers us or until we sense the leading of His Spirit to do otherwise. And it is always right for us to trust in the Lord with all our hearts and to leave the results of our praying to Him.

David had that experience when his son was dying. Nathan, the prophet, had rebuked the king for his sin with Bathsheba. Then the Lord struck their baby boy, and he became ill. David pleaded with the Lord in prayer for the child. He fasted and spent nights lying on the ground in prayer. Yet after seven days, the baby died. His servants were afraid to tell David for fear he would do something desperate (2 Sam. 12:15–19).

But when David received the news of the death of his son, he did a curious thing. He got up from the ground, washed, changed his clothes, and then went to the house of the Lord to worship (12:20). David trusted God. While his son was alive, he cried out to the Lord in prayer. But when God took his son, David released his child and himself to the will of God. That is an important lesson for us to learn. In the midst of his pain and grief David experienced the peace of God. He acknowledged that although his son would never return to him, he would someday join his son. The hope of eternal life was his.

Like the man in the parable in Luke 11:5–9 who asked help from his neighbor at midnight, and like the widow in the parable of Luke 18:1–8, we should persist in our praying. As stated earlier, this does not mean we are to cajole God to do something against His will. Nor does it suggest that God is reluctant to respond and that He needs to be influenced by us. Persevering in prayer means continuing to seek His face, not to nag, pressure, pester, or seek to coerce Him.

Remembering God wants us to commune with Him continually, we must recognize He has His own timing for answering. For example, Jesus' delay in answering the Syro-Phoenician's request suggests He was testing her faith (Mark 7:24–30).

Roy B. Zuck says this about persistent praying: "The Bible affirms that we should continue to pray for whatever we know in God's Word is His will. We know that God longs for people to be saved (1 Tim. 2:3–4; 2 Pet. 3:9), so we should continue to pray for the salvation of others. Also we should pray for daily provision of food (Matt. 6:11). Other matters for which we should continue to pray, without giving up, are these: strength to resist temptation (Matt. 6:13), sanctification (1Thess. 4:3), needs of other Christians (Eph. 6:18), leaders (1 Tim. 2:2), our enemies (Luke 6:28), and missionaries (Luke 10:2)."[7]

Sometimes God may seem unreponsive to our prayers. Troubled by God's silence, Job exclaimed, "Though I cry, 'I've been wronged!' I get no response; though I call for help, there is no justice" (Job 19:7). "Oh, that I had someone to hear me! . . . Let the Almighty answer me" (31:35). David, too, felt God was unresponsive. He wrote, "O my God, I cry out by day, but you do not answer" (Ps. 22:2), and "My prayers returned to me unanswered" (35:13). "O God, whom I praise, do not remain silent" (109:1).

The prophet Habakkuk was disturbed by God's silence. "How long, O LORD, must I call for help, but you do not listen?" (Hab. 1:2).

God's silence, however, does not mean He is unconcerned. Job, David, and Habakkuk all discovered God was indeed aware of their needs and did something about them. His seeming lack of response to our prayers simply means His timing differs from ours. In our impatience we want immediate answers. Delays disturb us. But the Lord is seldom in a hurry.

Sometimes when we sense the answer to our requests is not forthcoming, we need not persist in prayer. For example, as Zuck observes, Paul "prayed three times that his 'thorn in the flesh' would be removed; but when he sensed God would not remove it, he stopped praying (2 Cor. 12:7–9)."[8] As William Klein wrote, "It's doubtful that three is the divine, appointed number of times we ought to request something, but there does come a time when we must accept a 'no' and go on from there."[9]

When David asked the Lord to spare the life of his and Bathsheba's child, the child died on the seventh day (2 Sam. 12:14–18). And God denied Elijah's foolish request that He take the prophet's life (1 Kings 19:4). Why did the Lord deny the requests of Paul, David, and Elijah? He wanted them to see His greater purposes for their lives. Through his "thorn in the flesh" Paul learned more of God's strength in his weakness. David learned that serious sin bears serious consequences. And God showed Elijah He still had work for him to do. In each of these no answers God was more glorified than if He had answered yes.

DOES PRAYER CHANGE THINGS?

We often hear the motto, "Prayer changes things." But does it? In one sense no, and in another sense yes. As already stated, our persistence in prayer is not for the purpose of manipulating God or getting Him to do something He is reluctant to do or that is contrary to His will. So in one sense prayer does not change God or what He has sovereignly decreed will take place. However, the Bible does occasionally refer to God's changing what He had in mind to do in certain situations. When God threatened to destroy Israel because of their idolatry (Exod. 32:9–10), Moses prayed on their behalf and God answered his prayer by not carrying through on

His threat (32:11–14). Later Moses prayed that God would not bring His threatened plague on Israel because of their unbelief, and God answered that prayer too (Num. 14:12, 20).

True, God is immutable; He does not change His essential character (Ps. 102:24–27; Isa. 46:9–10; Mal. 3:6; James 1:17). But sometimes in answer to prayer He does alter His attitude or intention toward specific situations or individuals. Thomas Constable explains it this way:

> There are many instances in Scripture where God altered His attitude or intended action in response to certain conditions (Gen. 6:6–7; Ex. 32:14; Num. 14:20; Deut. 32:36; Judg. 2:18; 1 Sam. 15:11; 2 Sam. 24:16; 1 Chron. 21:15; Pss. 90:13; 135:14; Jer. 18:8, 26:3, 13, 19; 42:10; Hos. 11:8; Joel 2:13–14; Amos 7:3, 6; Jonah 3:9–10; 4:2; Rev. 2:15–22).
>
> But what about the verses that say God does not change His mind? There are several of these in the Bible (cf. Num. 23:19; 1 Sam. 15:29; Ps. 110:4 [also quoted in Heb. 9:21]; Rom. 11:29). The point of these statements is that God does not change His mind as man changes his. God is not fickle or capricious, nor will His ultimate purposes change. God will not change His mind with respect to the major aspects of His decree. He has, however, changed His mind with regard to minor negotiable matters.
>
> The parent-child analogy is . . . helpful. There are some things about which a good father who is in control of his family will not change his mind no matter how hard his child may try to convince him. "No, you may not play on the highway. You may as well stop asking me because there is nothing you can say that will convince me to let you do that." But there are other things about which he is open to influence. "Yes, you may have a chocolate ice cream cone rather than strawberry, if you prefer." Or, "Since you have done what I asked you to do, I am going to take you to the baseball game this weekend."[10]

In other words, some of God's actions are dependent on other conditions. "If the Israelites would obey Him, He would bless them; but if they disobeyed, He would discipline them (Deut. 27–28; Josh. 8:30–35). If Christians walk in loving obedience to the Lord, He will cause them to increase and abound in their spiritual benefits (Eph. 3:14–19; Col. 2:6–7)."[11]

On the other hand, no amount of praying will alter certain purposes of the Lord. This is seen, for example, in His promise to bless Abraham and His descendants (Gen. 12:1–3; 15:7–21) and in His promise never again to destroy the world with a flood (8:21–22). And if a person dies without receiving Christ as his or her Savior, that individual will not have eternal life (Matt. 25:46; John 3:18, 36). Joshua's praying did not alter God's intention to punish Achan for his sin (Josh. 7:6–13). Nor did prayer keep the Lord from sending the people of Judah into captivity as a result of their continued rebellion (Jer. 14:11–12).

Prayer, however, is one of the means by which God accomplishes certain plans. He has designed that we pray for the salvation of the lost (e.g., Rom. 10:1), for the sending of more missionaries (Matt. 9:38), and for the spiritual growth of believers (Col. 1:9–12). He has chosen to do certain things in response to prayer. He delivered Lot and his family in response to Abraham's prayers (Gen. 18), and the Lord spared the Israelites when they were under attack by the Philistines in response to Samuel's intercessory praying (1 Sam. 7:5–9).

Sometimes, then, prayer does change certain things—God's actions, people's responses, circumstances. In another sense some things will never be changed. But another aspect of change that *can* come about through prayer is our own attitudes. Prayer can change *us*. We benefit ourselves by praying. We mature spiritually as we depend on God in prayer; we experience spiritual blessings as we fellowship with the Lord in prayer; we are encouraged as we pray.

EXPERIENCING THE PEACE OF GOD THROUGH PRAYER

God has promised us His peace. Not "just" peace, but an extraordinary, unexplainable, inexpressible peace. Jesus described it as an uncommon kind of peace. "Peace I leave with you; my peace I give you. I do not give to you as the world gives. Do not let your hearts be troubled and do not be afraid" (John 14:27).

What does that kind of peace have to do with prayer? Everything!

We can experience His divine peace as we commit our needs and concerns to Him in prayer. In Paul's epistle to the Philippians, he wrote, "Do not be anxious about anything, but in everything, by prayer and petition, with thanksgiving, present your requests to God. And the peace of God, which transcends all understanding, will guard your hearts and your minds in Christ Jesus" (Phil. 4:6–7).

Years ago I memorized this passage from *The Living Bible*. I have turned to it again and again. I have found it to be a wonderful prescription for escaping from anxiety and worry and for basking in the sunshine of God's peace. I have turned to it frequently in my own life and have often quoted it from the pulpit when I have been preaching. It is a wonderful paraphrase of Paul's message on prayer: "Don't worry about anything; instead, pray about everything; tell God your needs, and don't forget to thank him for his answers. If you do this, you will experience God's peace, which is far more wonderful than the human mind can understand. His peace will keep your thoughts and your hearts quiet and at rest as you trust in Christ Jesus."

We need not worry. We need not walk through life burdened with anxiety. Instead, we can enjoy peace, God's peace.

Still, worrying is so natural for us. In fact, most areas of worry have little to do with reality. The concerns of worry are often the "what if" questions: "What if this or that happened?" "What if he doesn't show up?" "What if I get sick?" "What if I don't have enough money?"

Most people, even Christians, spend a lot of time worrying. The "Don't worry about anything" statement of Paul is rather radical. If we did not worry, what would we do with all our spare time? What would we substitute for worry? Paul's concise and practical answer is, "Instead, *pray* about everything." *Prayer helps replace worry.*

The practical results of this insight are impressive. No longer do we need to be uptight and irritable. No longer do we need to toss and turn with sleepless nights. No longer do we need to complain or fear. Instead, we can experience God's peace, which is "far more wonderful than the human mind can understand."

Worry can be dangerous to our health. It can bring ulcers, insomnia, or even heart attacks. In contrast, prayer can bring peace, the very peace of God.

Charles Swindoll has written about this great passage in his wonderful book, *Laugh Again.*

Paul writes of God's peace which "shall guard your hearts and your minds." When he mentions peace as a "guard," he uses a military term for "marching sentry duty" around something valuable and/or strategic. As we rest our case, we transfer our troubles to God. "Corporal Peace" is appointed the duty of marching as a silent sentry around our minds and our emotions, calming us within. How obvious will it be to others? Go back and check—it will "surpass all comprehension." People simply will not be able to comprehend the restful peace we will model. In place of anxiety— that thief of joy—we pray. We push the worrisome, clawing monster of pressure off our shoulders and hand it over to God in prayer. I am not exaggerating; I must do that hundreds of times every year. And I cannot recall a time when it didn't provide relief. In its place, always, comes a quietness of spirit, a calming of the mind. With a relieved mind, rest returns.[12]

Prayer opens the doors of our hearts to this remarkable peace. As Paul wrote, "Let the peace of Christ rule in your hearts, since as members of one body you were called to peace. And be thankful" (Col. 3:15). God's peace can be so authentic and present in our lives in times of turmoil and trouble that others are amazed and can't understand it. At the same time, such situations give us a wonderful opportunity for Christian witness. When people inquire about our peace, we can share with them sensitively and lovingly that the source of that incredible peace is our Lord Jesus Christ.

Jeannie and I experienced that several times when our daughter was critically ill. Although the outward circumstances were very bad and the situation bleak, the inner peace of God ruled our hearts. It was a powerful witness of the presence and power of Christ.

Our Lord's peace is available to each of His children all of the time. We simply need to avail ourselves of this priceless treasure by offering to our Lord prayers of faith.

GIVING GOD THANKS

Thanksgiving is probably the most neglected area of prayer. It is so human for us to ask and seek and knock. In our praying, we are often like little children who need to be taught how to say "Please" and "Thank you."

Again the Word of God has much to teach us about prayers of thanksgiving. The Book of Psalms frequently encourages us to thank the Lord. "Glorify him with thanksgiving" (Ps. 69:30). "Let us come before him with thanksgiving" (95:2). "Enter his gates with thanksgiving and his courts with praise; give thanks to him and praise his name. For the Lord is good and his love endures forever; his faithfulness continues through all generations" (100:4–5). "Give thanks to the Lord, for he is good; his love endures forever" (Ps. 106:1). For a refreshing devotional study look up these many references in the Book of Psalms that mention giving thanks to God: 7:17; 28:7; 30:12; 35:18; 75:1; 105:1; 106:1, 47; 107:8, 15, 21, 31; 118:1, 19, 21, 28–29; 119:62; 136:1–3, 26; 147:7.

Paul often thanked the Lord for blessings in his life (e.g., Rom. 1:8; 6:17; 7:25; 1 Cor. 1:4; 14:18; 15:57; 2 Cor. 2:14; 8:16; 9:15; Eph. 1:16; Phil. 1:3; Col. 1:3; 1 Thess. 1:2; 2:13; 1 Tim. 1:12; 2 Tim. 1:3; Philem. 1:4). And he often encouraged believers to be thankful to the Lord, as seen in these verses: "In everything, by prayer and petition, with thanksgiving, present your requests to God" (Phil. 4:6); be "overflowing with thankfulness" (Col. 2:7); "be thankful" (3:15); "giving thanks to God the Father" (3:17); "being watchful and thankful" (4:2); "give thanks in all circumstances, for this is God's will for you in Christ Jesus" (1 Thess. 5:18).

Leslie Flynn told of a friend of his who, when a student at New York's Juilliard School of Music, was invited to an outdoor picnic at the home of the president of a prestigious Eastern divinity school. "Everyone sat down on the benches and started right in to eat. Commented my friend who had been raised in a strong Christian background, 'I sat with open mouth in surprise, so accustomed was I to saying grace before meals. Yet here in my first contact with this prominent seminary, no one asked the blessing—despite the presence of dozens of ministerial students and their president. I almost stood up and prayed out loud, but wisely gave a silent thanks.'"[13]

Although we must be careful not to point our fingers at others as the Pharisees would do, we do need to draw nearer to the One from whom all blessings flow. We need to ask Him for more grateful hearts, to cultivate the attitude of thanksgiving, and to express our gratitude to Him. Closing the day with specific prayers of thanksgiving is a wonderful way to calm our hearts for the night and to prepare us for the next day.

Dear Father,
Thank You for inviting us—
even encouraging us—
to keep persisting in prayer.
Lord, we would wait on You
as we pray,
even when things look hopeless
or impossible.
We would trust You with all of our hearts
and would joyfully receive Your peace,
which is more wonderful than we can comprehend.
Thank You, Thank You!

PART 3

Continuing a Life of Prayer

14

DEVELOPING YOUR
PERSONAL PRAYER LIFE

———

When I was in fifth grade, our family moved to a beautiful little town in northern Minnesota. On my first day in the new school, the band director came to my class to invite us to take music lessons so we could eventually play in the high school band.

I volunteered immediately and enthusiastically. I could envision myself becoming a great trumpet player someday. But when I discussed it that evening with my parents, they had other plans. Since John, my older brother, already played the trombone, and since I could learn on his instrument, they felt that would be the more economical plan. Also it would allow me to decide whether I would enjoy playing an instrument at all.

So I proceeded on the pathway to become another Glen Miller. In fact, after taking lessons for just a few weeks, I was making such good progress that the band director asked me to play in the high school band right away. I was elated.

Little did I know the challenge before me. On the first day of practice, I was overwhelmed. I looked at the music and tried to read the notes, but the band was playing much too fast for me. By the time I played one measure of notes, they had progressed to the next page.

It was impossible for me to keep up, until in desperation I discovered another way to play in the band. I began watching the trombone slide of the girl sitting next to me. I thought all I had to do was to keep up with her. It seemed much easier than trying to read the notes.

The good news was that I was no longer a page behind everyone else. The bad news was that I was still at least one or two notes behind the rest of the band, since by the time I duplicated the position of the girl's slide, she had already moved on to the next note. In short, I was destined always to be behind.

The band director soon found out that I was not as ready for the "big time" as he had first thought. He promptly demoted me back to the grade school band, where I needed to be.

As you smile at my story, you might also relate it to our common experience in the school of prayer. Most of us would like to be great prayer warriors like Praying Hyde, Andrew Murray, or E. M. Bounds. But we must begin our prayer lives at an elementary level. Prayer requires practice, just like playing a trombone. It is not helpful to us nor to anyone else to try to take shortcuts or to skip over the foundational elements of prayer.

We need to grow and mature in our lives of prayer. Our Lord has provided the best teacher for us—namely, Himself. With the guidance of His Word and the Holy Spirit, every believer can become effective and powerful in prayer.

The first two sections of this book addressed some of the biblical and spiritual principles of prayer. Now the chapters in this third section explore how to put those principles into practice.

One of the great things about being a Christian is that we do not need to be seasoned prayer warriors in order for our prayers to be effective. In fact, even a new Christian can bear fruit in his or her praying. Prayer always makes a difference, whether it flows from the mouth of a baby Christian or from a seasoned disciple of Christ.

How do we develop and build a meaningful prayer life? What do we do? Where do we begin? What are some first steps we can take?

First, we can begin by mastering the principles of prayer in the first thirteen chapters of this book. Pray over that material. Ask the Lord to help you understand it and apply it.

Second, establish a strong personal devotional time each day, which includes, of course, a strategic prayer time. We will begin to explore that important subject in this chapter. Then chapter 15 discusses the devotional life in much more detail, as do appendices A and B.

Third, consider developing a more extensive prayer life. The next four chapters in this section share some practical steps and point to some excellent resources useful in building an effective prayer life.

In this chapter I offer six options by which to develop your prayer life. I am not suggesting that you do all six at once. Instead, prayerfully consider which of them seems to have the potential of helping you most in your praying. Then, guided by the Holy Spirit, proceed in taking those steps that will enhance your great adventure of following Jesus deeper into the life of prayer.

In other words, begin with one or two of the following six options. The first suggestion, however, is really not an option at all. Include it absolutely in your overall plan.

OPTION 1: BEGIN AND/OR STRENGTHEN
YOUR DAILY DEVOTIONAL TIME

Because our devotional life is so foundational to our Christian walk, we need to give major attention to it. It is my opinion that this is the most important of all the recommendations in the last four chapters of this book. In fact, this is the heart of this book.

All of us who are truly concerned about strengthening our prayer lives need to *spend significant time alone with God every day*. Most committed Christian leaders at least attempt to have a personal devotional time of one kind or another. Some call it a "quiet time," while others refer to it as "personal devotions." I have one friend who used to call his devotional time "three minutes with God."

For many Christian leaders, however, trying to establish a healthy daily devotional time is akin to making a New Year's resolution every year and never seeming to achieve it. The desire is sincere, but somehow the goal is never accomplished.

For many, it will be helpful to begin just by clarifying what a daily devotional time might include and how much time it would take. Though this information is basic to many Christians, it is still worth reviewing and using as a checklist.

First, your devotional time can occupy as long or as short an amount of time as you would like. Second, there is much latitude as far as content is concerned. There are many options and a lot of variety available for our daily devotional times.

The dynamics of our devotional time should be kept as simple as possible. Actually there are only three essential requirements for a meaningful devotional life. *The first element is a regular time.* Probably most Christians schedule their daily time with God at the start of their day. But whatever the time, be sure you actually establish an appointment with God. Write it on your calendar or in your datebook. Then keep the appointment just as you would with anyone else on your ministry schedule.

For couples with small children, it is important to establish a schedule accommodating uninterrupted devotional time for each parent.

The second element is a regular place. Most of us find it immensely helpful to have a regular place where we go every day to spend an uninterrupted time with God. Those of us who have spouses or children need to work out the details with them. You may use a family room, a corner in your basement, or even a bathroom, but you need to be all alone with God.

As a pastor or leader of a Christian ministry I have found that it is difficult to use my church or ministry office for my devotional time. As soon as I enter my place of employment, my attention focuses on my work. I find it much better—even imperative—to have my devotional time before I go to my office.

The third element is a practical format. The old saying, "Different strokes for different folks," certainly applies to the question of format in our devotional times. The Bible does not teach a single approach; instead the Lord has given us great latitude on how we may approach Him in our devotional times or sessions of prayer. However, we find some similarities and common elements in many of the prayer times recorded in Scripture.

Of course, it is always appropriate to offer different kinds of prayers for different occasions in our Christian lives, such as praying for God's intervention at a time of specific crisis, praying as you prepare a sermon or lesson, offering a prayer of thanksgiving just before a meal, or praying for the Lord's protection before departing on a trip.

It seems obvious that the reason for which we are praying will often help us determine how we should pray. For example, in times of crisis, we do not ask ourselves, What format or outline should I use? Instead, we just pray fervently for whatever the need may be. And frequently in times of crisis we do not know exactly how we should pray, so we invite the Holy Spirit to help us in our praying (Rom. 8:26–27).

Over the years I have been introduced to a number of formats or outlines of how to make devotional time meaningful.

For example, a common format for prayer is based on the acronym *ACTS*, a simple approach that includes four prayer elements.

A—Adoration. This aspect of prayer consists of adoring God by offering Him praise and worship.

C—Confession. The next step is to offer the Lord prayers of confession and repentance from sin.

T—Thanksgiving. The third focus is to offer to the Lord prayers of specific gratitude for blessings received.

S—Supplication. Here specific prayer requests are offered for oneself as well as intercessory prayers for others.

Others prefer to begin with a time of confession and humbling themselves before the Lord before they offer worship and thanksgiving. If you prefer that, then you can use the outline one of my sons has referred to by the acronym *CATS*—Confession, Adoration, Thanksgiving, and Supplication.

I have found it helpful to vary the format from time to time so that this important time does not become stale. I do not want to get in a rut that is harmful in any way to communicating with the Lord.

However, the approach I have found most helpful is one I have used for many years and continue to use. I recommend it to you not merely because it has been meaningful to me, but because it was shared with us by our Lord Jesus Christ.

"One day Jesus was praying in a certain place. When he finished, one of his disciples said to him, 'Lord, teach us to pray, just as John [the Baptist] taught his disciples.' He said to them, 'When you pray, say: "Father, hallowed be your name, your kingdom come. Give us each day our daily bread. Forgive us our sins, for we also forgive everyone who sins against us. And lead us not into temptation"'" (Luke 11: 1–4).

Jesus shared this same prayer as a significant ingredient in the Sermon on the Mount. "This, then, is how you should pray: 'Our Father in heaven, hallowed be your name, your kingdom come, your will be done on earth as it is in heaven. Give us today our daily bread. Forgive us our debts, as we also have forgiven our debtors. And lead us not into temptation, but deliver us from the evil one'" (Matt. 6:9–13).

Some ancient New Testament manuscripts include the phrase, "For yours is the kingdom and the power and the glory forever. Amen." Many have learned that portion of the prayer in their formative years.

This prayer, often called the "Lord's Prayer," is recited in the weekly worship services of many churches around the world. Some criticize this use of the Lord's Prayer as mere tradition or vain repetition, or even "babbling" in the sense Jesus warned us about (6:7). Although I agree that this beautiful prayer can be reduced to any one of those, I would contend that it offers us a practical and powerful format for our praying.

How does the Lord's Prayer serve as a pattern for our praying? How can we incorporate that pattern into our prayer notebooks? That is the focus of the next chapter. However, before proceeding to that important topic, several other practical steps for strengthening our spiritual lives are suggested.

OPTION 2: STUDY THE WORD AND SOME KEY BOOKS ON PRAYER

Reading is an excellent means by which to grow spiritually. The Lord has given us incredible resources on the subject of prayer. If you have never done so, I would suggest you begin by reading the many passages in the Bible on prayer.

Make an in-depth word study on the subject of prayer, or if you have done so, review it thoroughly. In other words, this is the time to focus on and study the subject of prayer in your personal devotions, and to consider studying all the great prayers of the Bible as deeply, thoroughly, and prayerfully as you can.

Also, do not rush through the study to complete the task so you can move on to other things. Make this a thorough, once-in-a-lifetime biblical study on prayer. Pray about the passages you study. Meditate on them. Then, just as you would counsel others to do, ask the Lord to help you prayerfully integrate into your life the principles of prayer found demonstrated in the Bible's prayers.

Where can you find all the prayers in the Bible? Herbert Lockyer's *All the Prayers of the Bible*[1] discusses more than three hundred prayers recorded in the Scriptures. Walter A. Elwell lists hundreds of verses on prayer in his *Topical Analysis of the Bible*.[2] Another helpful source is *Drawing Near* by Kenneth Boa and Max Anders. This prayer guide lists almost five hundred Bible passages, giving the verses in full as guides for prayer under eight headings: prayers of adoration, for forgiveness, for reward, for personal needs, for others, of affirmation, of thanksgiving, and closing prayers.[3] A helpful article that refers to many of the Bible prayers is J.G.S.S. Thomson, "Prayer," in *The Illustrated Bible Dictionary*.[4]

Moses' intercessory prayers are especially worthy of study and meditation. These are recorded in Exodus 32:11–13, 31–32; 33:12–16; 34:9; Numbers 11:11–15; 14:13–19; 2:7 and Deuteronomy 9:18; 10:10.

The Book of Psalms is a book of prayer. As you read the Psalms, note every statement that includes some aspect of prayer and observe the things the psalmists prayed for. Kyu Nam Jung discusses five kinds of prayer in the Psalms: petitionary (e.g., Ps. 13), penitential (e.g., Ps. 51), intercessory (e.g., Ps. 72), thanksgiving (e.g., Ps. 40), and hymnic or adoration (e.g., Ps. 113).[5]

After completing a study of the biblical passages on prayer, begin to explore other books on prayer. Start with some of the excellent resources listed in the bibliography at the end of this book. Do not hesitate to approach others for their recommendations, asking, "What is the best book you have ever read on prayer?" or "What book on prayer has helped you more than any other?"

In addition to reading good books on prayer, you may want to listen to audio tapes or videotapes on prayer. Give prayer a high priority in your reading and studying, and, if you are a pastor, in your preaching and teaching. Allow the Lord to be your Teacher as you participate in His school of prayer.

OPTION 3: FIND A PRAYER PARTNER TO
PRAY WITH REGULARLY

You will find your spiritual life greatly strengthened by praying more frequently with others. It is my conviction that every one of us in ministry leadership needs to have at least one special prayer partner.

If you do not have such a person, ask the Lord to lead you in that direction. If you are married, begin by inviting your spouse or another family member to join you. Of course, if you select a prayer partner beyond your family, be sure you share with a person of the same sex. I have found it especially helpful to have a prayer partner who is involved in ministry leadership. But, of course, it is not imperative to do so.

Pray specifically for the Lord to provide the right person—even someone who may live or work some distance from you. In this culture, effective praying can take place over the telephone when necessary. And requests can be shared regularly and immediately by e-mail or fax.

Pray with your prayer partners at least once a week. You may meet just before or after a church service or during your lunch hour. You may even want to fast and pray together during one lunch hour a week.

Do not allow this prayer relationship to remain formal. We are talking about a deep friendship relationship—with the Lord and each other. You need to be available to each other when you need special prayer, counsel, or encouragement. This is an "iron-sharpening-iron" kind of relationship (Prov. 27:17). Two or more persons praying together in agreement can have a significant and powerful prayer ministry. Partnership praying can make a significant contribution to your life and ministry.

OPTION 4: JOIN AN EXISTING PRAYER GROUP
OR HELP START ONE

There is perhaps one thing you can do that is even more strategic than having a prayer partner. That is belonging to a small prayer group of peers. Perhaps pastors in your community meet in prayer groups, and you could join one of them. This would give you opportunity to be on the front lines of the needs and advances of churches in your community and beyond.

I cannot imagine being in the ministry and not being a part of a group of fellow ministers of the gospel in a prayer-and-accountability relationship. I began that practice early in my ministry. In fact, I have usually belonged to more than one group at the same time.

The benefits are many. You do not have to be the Lone Ranger in ministry; you can team with others by loving them, praying for them, and supporting them in their ministries as they do the same for you. This kind of ministry helps manifest the unity of the body of Christ.

If you cannot find such a group, consider initiating one. I am in the process of doing that right now. Jeannie and I have recently moved to a community where we know very few people. I have begun to pray and ask the Lord to lead me to a group of brothers with whom I can meet, pray, and share regularly.

In the meantime I still commute periodically several hundred miles to meet with my previous group. Those brothers have become a very important part of my life. I love them deeply and continue to pray for them regularly.

Remember, it only takes two or three people to form a small, effective, and potentially powerful prayer group. Again, I assure you that such a group can make an incredible difference in your life and ministry.

Once the group is functioning, plan to meet at least every couple of weeks at a specified time. When you are together, spend most of your time praying. Do not just talk about prayer; do it! And, of course, spend some time studying the Word and sharing prayer requests. In short, talk, learn, strategize, grow, and most importantly, pray together.

OPTION 5: ATTEND A PRAYER SUMMIT OR SEMINAR

Many Christian leaders are barraged with invitations to conduct and/or attend seminars and workshops. I would encourage you to take time in the next few weeks or months to attend a special *prayer* seminar, workshop, or conference.

If you are unaware of any such seminars, I would recommend you begin by participating in a Prayer Summit for pastors and/or church leaders. I know of no other prayer experience for Christian leaders that can be more significant. (You may discover more about Prayer Summits by contacting Multnomah Bible College and Biblical Seminary, 8435 N.E. Glisan St., Portland, Oregon 97220.)

Of course, there are other fine prayer seminars and workshops. As you are helped by a given seminar or workshop, contact some of your friends who are Christian leaders and explore hosting such a prayer seminar in your own community.

OPTION 6: GIVE RENEWED LEADERSHIP TO YOUR CHURCH'S PRAYER MINISTRIES

If you are a pastor or a member of a pastoral team, and if your prayer life is becoming more meaningful to you, God may be preparing you to begin to give strategic leadership to the prayer ministry of your church.

If you want to be encouraged and helped in this area, I recommend the book *Fresh Wind, Fresh Fire*, by Jim Cymbala, pastor of the Brooklyn Tabernacle, and Dean Merrill. Pastor Cymbala has been used of God to mobilize that church for praying in a truly remarkable way. This approach may not be the exact blueprint for your local church, but you will be encouraged and helped as you prayerfully explore how to make your church "a house of prayer."

There are so many significant prayer ministries that can be launched in a local church. If you are not the pastor of the church you attend, and if you find that your church does not offer a regular prayer meeting or any specific prayer ministries, do not scold the pastor or leave for another church that has more to offer. Instead, commit yourself to pray for your pastor and church consistently and fervently. Make yourself available to the Lord and to your pastor to help develop a meaningful prayer ministry in your church under your pastor's supervision.

PRAYERFULLY CONSIDER THE SIX OPTIONS

These are six options for you to consider prayerfully as you cultivate and strengthen your prayer life. Pray specifically about what your priorities should be. All six options should not be attempted at the same time. But you can begin with the most foundational option—establishing and strengthening your daily devotional time. Hopefully, it will not be the only option you will eventually pursue, but it should be the first. Because it is so important and foundational, I discuss a daily devotional and prayer time in more detail in the next chapter.

⊙━━◆━━⊙

Dear Lord,
There are so many opportunities for us to pray.
Help us to be good stewards
of those opportunities—
especially the time we spend in our
daily devotional times.
And please lead us to other brothers and sisters
with whom we can pray together.
And, Lord,
Use us to help mobilize Your church to pray.
Above all, help us not only to understand
the basic principles of prayer.
Help us to do them—
to put them into practice.
We pray in the precious name of Jesus.
Amen.

15

PRACTICING YOUR
DAILY PRAYER TIME

FOR MANY YEARS I have used a prayer notebook for my daily devotional time. I have found it to be exceedingly helpful. Although it is very personal to me and I have not shared the more intimate details of my daily praying with many, I would like to open my prayer notebook with you. I hope it will help and encourage you in your intimate times of prayer with our Lord.

In Appendix A you will find the basic outline of my prayer notebook to help you create your own notebook, if you choose to do so. Appendix B contains some of the contents from my prayer notebook in more detail. Again, I hope this will encourage you in your own prayer life. Creating a prayer notebook is not an end in itself. It is merely a vehicle to guide you in your time of daily devotions.

As you consider the best approach or format for your daily devotional time, I would suggest the following steps for your prayerful consideration. Please understand that I am not using myself as a perfect model. Some of you reading these pages are much more advanced in your understanding and practice of prayer than I am.

However, in writing on this important subject, I believe it is my responsibility to open my heart and even put myself at some risk by sharing a deeply intimate area of my life. I do so with the sincere prayer that what I share will be helpful.

PREPARING FOR PERSONAL DEVOTIONS

I find it difficult to rush into my morning time of prayer. I need some time and space for preparation after I get up in the morning. Since I am not a coffee drinker, I usually drink a glass of water or juice and then go into the bathroom to freshen up a bit. Sometimes I will take a shower before my devotional time, but usually I simply wash my face with cool water to help wake up.

Some people prefer to go for a jog, take a shower, read the morning paper, or watch the news on television before having their devotional time. Those kinds of things, however, can become distractions. I personally need the discipline of *beginning* the day with God. I want to give Him my very first attention before I become distracted or involved with anything else.

Then I go to my place of appointment with God. As stated earlier, it is important for me to have a private place where I can pray aloud and sing, laugh, cry, or do whatever else is appropriate in prayer without fear of interrupting others. I enjoy being in an environment that sets me free to commune with God without becoming self-conscious.

For me, that place is my study, which is located in a far corner of our house. When I have traveled with my wife, I have often had my devotions in a hotel bathroom with a fan running to obscure the sound of my praying. At other times, it is better for me to retreat to a corner of the hotel room and commune quietly with the Lord.

The important thing is to be in an environment that allows you to pray freely and without interruption. That is why it is also important to schedule a specific amount of time for your devotions. You may need to take the phone off the hook, put a sign on your door, or ask your family not to disturb you for a given number of minutes; or you may need to ask your secretary to do the same if you are in your office. Whatever it takes, do all you can to protect your daily time alone with God.

I have found it to be most freeing not to be aware of time during prayer. I usually do not wear my watch or look at a clock during my devotional time. But I do believe it is important to reserve a specific time for your prayer appointment when you are first planning and developing your devotional time. It may be well to begin by reserving a fifteen-minute block if you are not accustomed to longer periods of praying. You can always extend the time. But you do not want to be looking at your watch to see if your time is up so you can move on to other things. We want our times of prayer to be meaningful and productive. Our devotional times should bring glory to God and joy to us as His servants.

Another part of preparation is spiritual. I have found it helpful and even necessary to quiet my heart before I begin praying. Often this includes a time of confession and asking the Lord to search my heart, cleanse me, and prepare me to commune with Him.

This is the matter of coming to the Lord with clean hearts and clean hands, as discussed in chapter 6. Our hearts (our thoughts) are made clean by our confession, and our hands (i.e., our conduct) are made clean by our repentance.

PARTICIPATING IN PRAYER

I begin my appointment with God by spending time in His Word. This is not the same as my study time for a message. It is a communication time with the Lord in which I invite Him to speak to me through His Word. For that reason, I believe it is important to get away from my desk or the place where I would normally study.

I usually sit in a chair, offer a brief prayer of invitation for the Lord to come and speak to me through His Word, and then I prayerfully begin to read the passage for the day. Over the years I have used different approaches to my daily Bible reading. For example, for years I have used the *Daily Light* devotional book of Scripture verses for my evening Bible reading just before retiring.

For my morning reading, however, I usually am involved in reading though a given book of the Bible. I alternate my reading between the Old and New Testaments. As I read, I mark my Bible profusely. Instead of reading through a biblical book, you may wish to read topically or to use another arrangement of Scripture. It is not enough to read a book with someone else's devotional thoughts, although they may certainly be used in our devotional time. It is important to spend most of your time reading the Bible itself and meditating on it.

In fact, it would be tragic to go through any day of the year without giving the Lord the opportunity of speaking to us and communing with us. We need to spend uninterrupted, quality, focused time with God and His Word every day.

When it is time to pray, I divide my prayer time into the various segments or sections of the prayer Jesus taught us. I have found this to be extremely helpful in my own praying. However, as I have said, you may prefer to use another approach or format. One such variation to what I am suggesting below is the 125-page "Scripture Prayer Guide," included as part three of the book *Drawing Near*, by Kenneth Boa and Max Anders, mentioned in the previous chapter. This prayer guide gives suggestions for prayer topics and related Scriptures for each of thirty-one days.[1]

Adoration/worship/praise: "Our Father in heaven, hallowed be your name." As stated in chapter 7, the first and most appropriate thing for us to do when we come into the presence of God—after our prayers of confession—is to offer Him our praise.

We need to enter His presence reverently and humbly, not casually and hurriedly. We need to see Him as He is—high and lifted up, holy and pure, loving and powerful. And we should bring Him the kind of sacrifice He is always ready to accept. "The sacrifices of God are a broken spirit; a broken and contrite heart, O God, you will not despise" (Ps. 51:17).

My words of praise and worship often flow from my times of Bible reading and meditation. Then I express to Him some words of praise and worship from one of the psalms or another passage of Scripture. (Examples are given in Appendix A.) I pray those expressions from the Scriptures as my own prayer, as my own expressions of praise and adoration to God. I follow them with a song of praise. As I mentioned in chapter 7, I use both hymns and contemporary praise songs. I have purchased several hymnals and praise songbooks, cutting out pages to insert in my prayer notebook.

Sometimes a certain song or hymn of praise will come to mind when I am meditating on my Bible reading or when I am reading one of the psalms as an expression of praise and worship to God. Otherwise, I proceed sequentially through my hymns and praise songs. I usually sing just one song each morning, although sometimes I find I need extended times of singing to the Lord.

Usually I conclude my time of praise and worship by praying several verses of Scripture to the Lord. The first such verse I "pray" is Hebrews 13:15. "Through Jesus, therefore, let us continually offer to God a sacrifice of praise—the fruit of lips that confess his name." Then I pray that my mouth would continually offer Him praise throughout that day, that praise would pour forth from my heart and my lips all day long.

The second verse I pray in praise to God is Psalm 71:8. "Let my mouth be filled with Your praise and with Your glory all the day" (NKJV).

The third verse is Colossians 3:17. "And whatever you do, whether in word or deed, do it all in the name of the Lord Jesus, giving thanks to God the Father through him." I pray that I may do everything that day in the name of the Lord Jesus and to His glory (1 Cor. 10:31).

Then I give Him thanks. I try to recount everything that has happened in the previous twenty-four hours and to give specific thanks for everything the Lord has provided and for every way in which He has protected. It is a wonderful time. Thanksgiving is a strategic part of true worship. It helps us focus on the Lord and His many expressions of love and grace to us. My time of thanksgiving often concludes with another song or chorus of praise and thanksgiving.

Recommitment/release/surrender: "Your kingdom come, your will be done on earth as it is in heaven." The next step in my worship time is to surrender anew to Jesus Christ as my Savior and Lord. I find that as I begin each new day, it is important to recommit myself to Christ and to doing His will. It is a constant challenge to avoid getting in a rut or merely sharing formal or trite words that do not come from my heart.

These are examples of the commitment prayers I pray: "Lord, I commit myself anew to seek first You, Your kingdom, and Your righteousness. May Your kingdom come and Your will be done in and through my life—to Your glory!" "Lord, I surrender anew to You and to doing Your will. I submit to You in all things—to Your lordship and sovereignty. I will seek to follow You today, obeying Your Word and being guided by the Holy Spirit." (Appendix B includes additional expressions of surrender and recommitment.)

Sometimes our prayers of surrender and commitment need to be specific. We need to get rid of spiritual baggage, to throw off anything that hinders us or any sin that may be weighing us down (Heb. 12:1). Peter put it this way: "Cast all your anxiety on him because he cares for you" (1 Pet. 5:7).

Provision: "Give us today our daily bread." This next area of prayer pertains to God's gracious provision for us. It is the segment that usually requires the greatest amount of time, since it includes the sharing of our personal petitions as well as praying prayers of intercession for others.

I begin by claiming the wonderful promise of God, "And my God will meet [supply] all your needs according to his glorious riches in Christ Jesus" (Phil. 4:19). I thank God that He will supply everything I need that day—and I acknowledge that only He understands fully what I need. Then I release all my requests to Him for Him to determine what and how He will supply.

I pray something like this: "Lord, I ask You for the needs that I now recognize and for anything and everything I do not see or understand. I trust You with all my heart and rely on Your provision." Next I pray for specific people and particular needs by various categories. In a prayer list I include the names of the persons and ministries for which I pray regularly.

I use the word *regularly.* I cannot pray for every person on my list daily. Of course, there are some people and ministries for which I do pray every day, including members of my family and my ministry colleagues.

Others I pray for every three or four days, and some I pray for once a week. However, one of the wonderful ministries of the Holy Spirit is to bring people to mind who need our prayers at a given time for a specific reason. Our prayer lists need not control or limit our praying; they are simply tools to help us be consistent and faithful. At the same time, I marvel at the wonderful way our Lord leads us in our praying if we are open to His guidance.

My prayer list includes the following categories of persons and ministries. (For a more complete explanation of the preparation and use of prayer lists, see Appendix B.)

a. My family. I pray daily for each family member, along with specific requests for them, including God's provision and protection, His presence and His peace, His perspective and His power, His patience and perseverance.

b. Our pastor and church family. I pray by name for our pastor and for other members of the pastoral team, our church leaders, our church family, and the ministry of our local church.

c. My ministry colleagues. For years I have prayed daily for my ministry colleagues by name. I believe it is one of the most important investments I can make on their behalf.

d. Pastors and missionaries. I pray regularly for a significant list of friends who are serving the Lord as pastors or missionaries, including national and international denominational leaders.

e. My support-group members. For years I have belonged to a small group of Christian brothers with whom I meet at least monthly and pray for regularly.

f. Ministry leaders. I pray for a long list of friends who are serving as national or international leaders in the ministry of our Lord. In addition, I pray regularly for a number of Christian leaders whom I have never had the privilege of meeting, but whom I believe God has called to strategic ministry roles.

g. Other ministry colleagues and friends. Once again, it is a privilege to pray for many brothers and sisters in Christ on a regular basis. For example, Jeannie and I have several scores of friends who are a part of our Ministry Prayer Team. As they pray for us, we enjoy praying for them.

h. Non-Christian neighbors and friends. One of the great privileges of praying for others is to pray for neighbors and friends who have never come to faith in Christ.

i. Our nation and the world. I have a systematic approach for praying regularly for the leaders of our nation, state, and community. In addition, I pray regularly for various nations of the world and for specific unreached people groups. Each day I pray for at least three key "gateway cities" to the unreached people groups.

j. Personal requests. After praying for others, I usually pray for myself. Daily I ask for the Lord's provision of wisdom, love, generosity, purity, holiness, self-control, the fear of the Lord, freedom, faith, absence of anger, a forgiving spirit, and a good name and reputation. And I pray that I may glorify my Lord both in life and in death.

k. Special and urgent requests. I usually close this segment of prayer by falling prostrate before the Lord and bringing to Him urgent requests that have been shared by others. I keep these special requests on a loose-leaf page in my prayer notebook with the date the requests have been shared with me printed to the left of the actual request. Then in the right column I reserve space to record the date when the prayer is answered in an observable way. Most requests are answered graciously by the Lord in a matter of days. Others are in my notebook for a few weeks or even months. Some requests have been there for several years.

I keep praying until I discern that the Lord has answered according to His will. For example, within the past year I have had the names of two friends who live in different parts of the country who were both dying from cancer. One of those dear friends died a few months ago. He was a very godly man with a deep commitment to Jesus Christ. I visited him a few weeks before he died. He was totally surrendered to the Lord and to His will. Although he expected to be healed, he was resting fully in Christ. In God's loving providence, He took him home to Himself. My friend finished his race well.

Our other friend, who was expected to live for only days, was miraculously healed by our gracious Lord. Today she is living a perfectly normal life with no signs of cancer.

God answered both of those prayers according to His love and grace and according to His will. And so we ought "not [to] become weary in doing good" (Gal. 6:9, KJV) but should continue to persist in prayer until the Lord answers in ways we can recognize and we have the joy of seeing His will accomplished.

Forgiveness: "Forgive us our sins, for we also forgive everyone who sins against us" (Luke 11:4). I confess that this is one of the most difficult areas of my praying. I usually am not able to wait this late in the sequence of prayer to pray for forgiveness. As I mentioned earlier, I find it better to ask God to search my heart and to cleanse me from all unrighteousness during the time of preparation for prayer, before I ever begin following the model provided by the Lord's Prayer.

However, at the same time, I reserve this time in my praying for drawing even closer to the Lord and for asking specifically if there is anyone in my life whom I have not forgiven, or if there is any hidden sin or undetected offense against another that remains in my life and needs to be resolved.

Here too, I pray specific and appropriate passages of Scripture back to the Lord. Frequently I use the following passages: "Search me, O God, and know my heart; test me and know my anxious thoughts. See if there is any offensive way in me, and lead me in the way everlasting" (Ps. 139:23–24). "But if we walk in the light, as he is in the light, we have fellowship with one another, and the blood of Jesus, his Son, purifies us from all sin. If we claim to be without sin, we deceive ourselves and the truth is not in us. If we confess our sins, he is faithful and just and will forgive us our sins and purify us from all unrighteousness" (1 John 1:7–9).

Guidance: "And lead us not into temptation." My praying at this point is both simple and direct. I ask our Lord, "Please, dear Lord, keep me from being led into temptation today; instead, lead me in your paths of righteousness for Your name's sake." Then I ask Him to lead me that day by the Holy Spirit (Gal. 5:18, 25).

In recent months I have prayed in response to our Lord's command in Ephesians to "put on the whole armor of God" (Eph. 6:11–18). I pray through the various articles: the belt of truth, the breastplate of righteousness, the gospel of peace, the shield of faith, the helmet of salvation, and the sword of the Spirit, the Word of God. Putting on the full armor of God daily helps me take my stand against the devil's schemes. Our enemy will do all he can to oppose our commitment to follow the Lord's leading (Eph. 6:12). So, understandably, that kind of praying is often intensive.

I close this segment of praying by asking the Lord, "Help me to be sensitive to Your leading and to be open to every person You want me to encounter and every experience You want me to have."

Protection: "But deliver us from the evil one." As I ask the Lord to lead me and help me put on His full armor, I then ask Him to deliver me from Satan, our enemy.

For this area of praying, I refer very clearly to the Scriptures. Specifically, I claim God's promise in James 4:6–10. I respond to that wonderful passage by humbling myself before God and submitting myself to Him. Then, as He has instructed us to do, I seek to resist the devil in the name of Jesus and by the power of the Holy Spirit. By faith I claim God's promise that the devil will "flee" from me (4:7). I thank God for victory through our Lord Jesus Christ.

In addition, I often pray a paraphrase of the statement David made when he went out to meet Goliath. My statement goes something like this: "Lord, as you know, Satan comes to me with his power and deception, but, Lord, I thank You that I can respond to him in the name of my Lord Jesus Christ, who has defeated him once and for all at Calvary. It is You, O Lord, who saves. And the battle is the Lord's. You have won the victory over the enemy, and You will win the victory for me today. I trust in You!"

Then I close this segment of praying with giving God thanks for His protection. I pray daily that wonderful passage of David as my own, "Thank You, dear Lord, for commanding Your angels to guard us in all our ways and to protect us in all that we do. I do not presume on You, dear Lord. I just thank You for Your wonderful protection in days past and for Your protection today as I follow You" (based on Ps. 92:9–14).

Claiming the victory: "For yours is the kingdom and the power and the glory forever. Amen." This prayer that Jesus taught ends on a joyous, victorious note. Of course, much of the Bible emphasizes this truth of God's future victory when Christ returns to reign.

The day is coming when it will be declared, "The kingdom of the world has become the kingdom of our Lord and of his Christ, and he will reign for ever and ever" (Rev. 11:15). It is not a matter of if; it is merely a matter of when. The kingdom of God is coming in its fullness. Jesus will return to reign as King of kings and Lord of lords (Rev. 17:14; 19:16).

Each morning I close my devotional time by claiming a wonderful promise of God not only for the future but also for the present. The world and even the church can look dark and desperate. It is easy for us to lose perspective, to be discouraged and defeated by Satan. Yet the promise to us is clear: "But thanks be to God, who *always* leads us in triumphal procession in Christ and through us spreads everywhere the fragrance of the knowledge of him" (2 Cor. 2:14, italics added). Our times of intimate communion with God at the beginning of every day will help put things in proper perspective. Jesus Christ is our Victor! That's what the "Amen" is all about in our praying. It means simply, *So be it!*

What a way to close a prayer—acknowledging who He is and committing ourselves and our prayers to Him with the assurance that He hears us, loves us, and will answer us. The victory is His, not just sometimes, not just one out of ten times or even nine out of ten times, but *ten* out of ten times. He is *always* victorious. Praise be to God!

CONTINUING THE DAY IN PRAYER

But that is not the end of our praying. As exciting as it may be and as spiritually "pumped" as we may feel after our daily devotional time, it is only the beginning.

Early morning praying (or whatever time is best for you) launches us into the day with God. It prepares us to continue in the "spirit of prayer" throughout the day. It prepares us to *commune* with Jesus morning, noon, and night. It helps us understand what Paul was writing about when he told us to "pray continually" (1 Thess. 5:17). That does not mean we must live in a cave so we can pray all day without interruption, or that we should retreat to our rooms to pray all the time. It means to live in a spirit of prayer throughout each day.

You will not regret being involved in a time of personal devotions daily. Anything you sacrifice in order to do it will pale in comparison to the lasting value and sheer joy you will derive from communing daily with the Lord.

Dear Lord,
Thank You for Your invitation to us
to spend personal and intimate time with You every day.
Forgive us when we have failed to do so.
Teach us how to maximize
our times with You.
Come, Lord Jesus.

16

PREPARING TO BE
MORE EFFECTUAL IN PRAYER

◦━━━◦

FRANKLIN GRAHAM tells a wonderful story of the late Bob Pierce, founder of World Vision International. When Franklin was a young man just beginning in the ministry, he was traveling with Dr. Pierce from India to Iran. On that trip Bob introduced him to the concept of having "God room."

"What do you mean?" I asked him once when he started talking about "God room."

He gave me a glance that was close to disgust, almost as if to say, "Don't you know?" He took a deep breath and sighed before he said, "'God Room' is when you see a need and it's bigger than your human abilities to meet it. But you accept the challenge. You trust God to bring in the finances and the materials to meet that need.

"You get together with your staff, your prayer partners, and supporters, and you pray. But after all is said and done, you can only raise a portion of the resources required.

"Then you begin to watch God work. Before you know it, the need is met. At the same time, you understand you didn't do it. God did it. You allowed Him room to work."[1]

This is one of the principles of the life of prayer. We increasingly walk by faith (2 Cor. 5:7) as we are led by the Holy Spirit (Gal. 5:18). The life of prayer leads us to new thresholds of faith and obedience. We escape from the comfort zone of the rational and comfortable to the exciting place of "God room." What a wonderful place to be! Henry Blackaby wrote about God's initiative in believers' lives. "All the way through Scripture, God takes the initiative. When He comes to a person, He always reveals Himself and His activity. That revelation is always an invitation for the individual to adjust his life to God. None of the people God ever encountered could remain the same after the encounter. They had to make major adjustments in their lives in order to walk obediently with God."[2]

When we talk about "proceeding" in our prayer lives, we are talking about much more than mere mechanics or methods. We are talking about *experiencing God*—about consistently walking with Him in obedience.

And there are some specific things we can do to nurture our prayer lives and our relationship with God. As discussed previously, prayer does not move God to our agenda; it moves us to His agenda.

Blackaby put it this way: "God is the Sovereign Lord. I try to keep my life God-centered because He is the One who is the pace setter. He is always the One to take the initiative to accomplish what He wants to do. When you are God-centered, even the desires to do the things that please God come from God's initiative in your life."[3]

As we follow Jesus and obey Him, He leads us in the ways we should go. Increasingly His agenda becomes more important to us than our own. His will, rather than our will, becomes the focus of our lives. The Olympic-champion-turned-missionary Eric Liddell said it well: "Obedience to God's will is the secret of spiritual knowledge and insight. It is not willingness to know, but willingness to [obey] God's will that brings certainty."[4]

This chapter explores seven significant steps (in addition to the options suggested in chapter 14) we can take to draw nearer to God, to advance His will, and to give leadership to prayer by enlisting and mobilizing others to join us in the ministry of prayer.

PERSONAL PRAYER RETREATS

A wonderful way to enhance your prayer life is to set aside periodically a day or a portion of a day for prayer. That suggestion may not sound appealing at first, but a personal prayer retreat can become a most enjoyable and profitable experience.

The schedules of most Christian leaders are so full that the thought of setting aside a full day, or even a few hours, for a personal prayer retreat may seem unrealistic. Most of us need less to do, not more. Yet spending such a period of time alone with the Lord can be an incredibly meaningful experience. In fact, once you have done it, you will probably want to continue it on a regular basis.

For a number of years, I have tried to set aside such a day at least four times a year. I cannot begin to express fully just how meaningful and significant those times have become to me.

There are a number of ways you can approach the adventure of arranging your schedule and the details. You can simply take your Bible and prayer notebook to a place of seclusion and spend the entire day reading the Word, meditating on it, and praying in response to what the Lord is saying to you. This has been a very meaningful experience for many.

However, others sense the need for more structure. A second approach is to use your prayer notebook as your guide by following the same basic outline you use each day in your personal devotions. One great benefit will be that you will not be limited by the same time constraints you experience in your daily devotional time. For example, instead of having just a few moments for praise and worship, you can now enjoy a longer, uninterrupted period of time worshiping the Lord by using the Word, hymns and spiritual songs, and your own words of expression of praise and adoration. Then you can spend time worshiping in quietness, in stillness and unspoken praise to God. I found it to be freeing and wonderfully fulfilling to take off my watch and spend an uninterrupted time of worship and praise without any concern for how long it is taking.

Other times you may prefer a more active approach, such as a prayer walk along the beach or a prayer hike into the countryside, or even an overnight prayer retreat in the mountains or some other secluded setting. I especially enjoy times of praying and communing with the Lord as I walk along the beach. And within that context I stop periodically to spend some more focused time in the Word and in prayer.

The important thing is to enjoy the privilege of spending time alone with the Lord, communing with Him, listening to Him, talking to Him, opening your heart to Him, committing your needs and concerns to Him, and basking in His presence.

One good way to begin your personal prayer retreats is with a prayer walk of an hour or two. Or if you prefer, you can spend an hour alone with your Bible and prayer notebook in a quiet setting. Then you can extend your personal prayer retreats to longer periods. And, of course, you can vary the approach and format according to the Spirit's leading.

As a Christian leader, a personal prayer retreat can be exceedingly productive for you and your ministry. As you develop that prayer ministry in your own life, you may enjoy introducing this idea to others, especially members of your family and your ministry leadership team.

Over the years I have had the privilege of introducing the personal prayer retreat to other members of the ministry teams on which I have served. These retreats have been used of God to transform the lives of some of these colleagues.

LEADERSHIP PRAYER MEETINGS

Board and committee meetings are usually consumed with business items, which seem to be extremely important and often urgent. As a result, many Christian leaders do not have much time to pray together. In fact, the thought of taking time in a board or committee to pray is viewed by some as an interruption.

I found this to be true when I was pastoring a wonderful church several years ago. During my first months I attempted to introduce a prayer session at the beginning of each board and committee meeting. Although I tried to do so with love and sensitivity, it was not well received by a number of the leaders. Although they believed in prayer, they did not think we had time to pray when there was so much important business to transact.

As I prayed and sought the Lord's guidance in the matter, I sensed Him leading me to suggest a practical solution. Since some of the leaders were reluctant to mix "business and prayer" in the same meeting, I suggested we move all our board and committee meetings to the same night of the week in which we held our all-church prayer meeting (which was poorly attended).

The plan was to begin the prayer meeting at 7:30 P.M., dismissing the board and committee members at 8:00 to go to their business meetings. Those who did not have such a meeting could remain to pray until 8:30. This worked quite well. As a result, many of the church leaders became faithful participants in our church prayer meeting, growing in their spiritual lives and their effectiveness in prayer.

Of course, it is not productive to attempt to "force" or manipulate people to pray; instead, we can only invite them. We need to offer friendly and appealing opportunities for them to learn to pray. I have sometimes made the mistake of *telling* leaders they should join with us to pray rather than being a loving vehicle of the Holy Spirit *inviting* them to gather with others to pray. Many people have an inherent fear when they are invited to participate in prayer meetings. For example, some are shy about praying aloud. Others have had negative experiences in the past in which they have felt violated in some way. For many, it is simply a new idea that does not have much appeal.

I was reminded of this recently when I was visiting with a Christian lay leader who has become a great man of prayer. He told me of some wonderful answers to prayer, then mentioned that he and another lay leader were launching a new prayer ministry for men in their church. He was excited about how the Lord was answering their prayers in many ways.

Sensing his great enthusiasm for prayer, I was reminded of a conversation with him more than a decade ago. At that time I was his pastor and he was a key lay leader of the church. I had called the leaders of the church together for an evening of prayer. Although many responded and we enjoyed a significant prayer gathering, this particular brother was not present. A few days later I casually said to him, "We missed you at the prayer meeting the other night."

He was a man of great integrity, and he answered with transparency. He said something like this, "Pastor, I could have been there that evening, but I decided not to come. The reason is that I have tried prayer at different times in my Christian life and have found that it just doesn't work for me."

I remember answering him with deep appreciation for his honesty. With loving sensitivity I told him I sympathized with him and I was sorry for his negative experiences with prayer. But, at the same time, I assured him that I had good news for him—that prayer could become very meaningful to him.

I told him about a small group of men who were meeting in my study one morning a week for a time of sharing in the Word and praying together. Most of them were leaders of the church whom he knew well. I invited him to join us the next week to "try it." He could come without any sense of obligation, observing the group and participating in any way he would like.

I was delighted when he accepted my invitation. He not only came to that initial meeting but he continued to attend. God used that experience powerfully in his life. He has become a great man of prayer. He now not only "believes" in prayer; he is leading and training others in the school of prayer.

LEADERSHIP PRAYER RETREATS

Prayer retreats as a group can be another effective approach for providing meaningful experiences in prayer for Christian leaders. However, as mentioned previously, we need to proceed with the understanding that many leaders may not initially show much eagerness for such a retreat if they are not already men and women of prayer.

As shared in earlier chapters, corporate or united prayer has so many benefits for us personally and for the Lord's work. According to Armin Gesswein, one of the great prayer leaders of the twentieth century, "There are plenty of differences among us, and if we dwelt on these we could have trouble in a hurry. But we have learned that these do not divide, because our unity does not lie there—it is *centered in Christ.* Christ unites."[5] This important matter of unity has strategic implications as well. Dick Eastman has written, "Stated simply, *without unity, world evangelization is impossible.*"[6]

Perhaps that is why Jesus prayed so passionately that His disciples would be united. In fact, in His high priestly prayer He mentioned unity at least five times (John 17:17–23). Twice He explained why He prayed for unity: "that the world may believe" and "to let the world know" (17:21, 23). "Essential to the ultimate fulfilling of the Great Commission will be the networking of perhaps hundreds of ministries and strategies committed to the task."[7]

Quite early in my ministry I learned this principle of united prayer from Lloyd Ogilvie, now chaplain of the United States Senate. During my first year on the pastoral staff of Hollywood Presbyterian Church, where he was serving as senior pastor, he led the elders of the church on a weekend prayer retreat. This included both the pastoral team members and the lay elders who comprised what Presbyterians call the "Session."

It was a memorable time. He introduced me to a new concept of prayer that weekend. He stated categorically that the elders needed to spend more time in prayer together and especially more prayer time in their monthly business sessions. He contended that he believed such concerted prayer times actually saved time in business sessions rather than requiring additional time.

His reasoning was simple and logical. If church leaders would only spend more time together in prayer, there would be more of a sense of Christ's presence and of authentic spiritual unity. Therefore the business sessions would go more smoothly and efficiently.

It did not take long for me to discover that what he said was true. Over the years of my ministry since then I have emphasized the importance of our leadership teams spending quality times of prayer together. For example, in my present ministry leadership role, we bring our national leaders together for a two- to three-day retreat every month. We usually spend up to a third of our time praying together. God has honored that time of united prayer in significant ways.

In short, if God has called you to a leadership role, seek to provide significant times of prayer for those entrusted to your care.

PRAYER JOURNALING

As you encourage others in the ministry of prayer and especially as you invite leaders to participate with you in corporate prayer settings, you will need to continue to strengthen your own prayer life. In addition to the various options and recommendations made in earlier chapters, let me suggest another.

You may find that keeping a diary or journal of your personal prayer retreat times or your daily devotional prayer time can make a significant contribution to your spiritual growth. Putting things in writing can help solidify spiritual truths and lessons. I have found prayer journaling to be that kind of experience. Many others have affirmed that experience in their prayer lives as well.

Journaling can take a number of different forms. For example, I keep a simple prayer diary in which I write just a few sentences each day, reflecting some of my prayer experiences of the previous day along with some specific answers to prayer.

Interestingly, nothing seems to motivate our praying more powerfully than clear answers to prayer. I find it immensely helpful to recount those answers from the previous day every morning during my devotional time, and then to record them in my prayer diary. None of us should be like the nine lepers who were healed by Jesus but never returned to express their thanks (Luke 17:11–19).

Recognizing what God has done for us and giving Him thanks for His goodness is not merely an obligation. It is one of the great joys of our lives. It is wonderful to write those things down and to review them from time to time. How great is our Lord, and how gracious and generous He is to us. Thanksgiving can be a very important part of our prayer journaling experience.

Sometimes much of my prayer diary page for a given day is filled simply with expressions of praise to God. One of the most significant contributions of communing with God in prayer is to focus on Him and to offer Him praise. I have found it helpful at times to put some of those expressions of praise into writing.

Other times, even in the midst of our thanksgiving and praise, we may be experiencing difficult times or great challenges. Within that context, I like to write down some of my deepest concerns and most urgent prayer requests I am facing at a given time. In addition, sometimes it is exceedingly helpful to express our deep concerns or pain in writing in the form of a prayer to God. Usually I write in my prayer diary a mixture of praise and thanksgiving, a review of some of the highlights of the previous day, and then some specific requests, which I write as a prayer to God.

As I have said, my prayer journaling is very simple. Others find it more meaningful to be more creative and comprehensive in their journaling.

For example, some Christians enjoy writing a prayer to the Lord every day. In it they share their hearts very personally and intimately. That approach to prayer journaling is somewhat akin to a personal diary in which people record intimate details of their lives.

I would suggest you keep a place in your prayer notebook to do some type of journaling. Try some different approaches. Find out what is most helpful to you. Do not be afraid to vary your approach from day to day as you sense the Spirit of God leading and guiding you.

INTERCESSORY PRAYER TEAMS

One of the most significant and blessed ministries in which my wife and I have been involved in recent years has been that of building a personal team of intercessors. These are family members and Christian friends who love us and who believe in the ministry God is entrusting to us. I cannot imagine attempting to carry on without the support and involvement of a personal prayer team. It is impossible to express adequately our love and appreciation for those who support us and encourage us daily in prayer.

The guidelines for building a ministry prayer team are quite simple. In fact, for many of you they will be almost obvious. For example, my wife and I ask that each person who agrees to serve on our prayer team make a personal commitment to pray for us and for our ministry daily. Although that may not seem like a difficult requirement, we have found that kind of commitment provides an effective screening device to identify those who are truly committed to pray for us. It is interesting to realize that we live in a culture—even within the church—in which many people are reluctant to make commitments of any kind.

Therefore when brothers and sisters commit to pray for us daily, we take that commitment seriously. We recognize it as a gracious and generous gift. When people share that kind of sacrificial gift with us, we send them a personal letter expressing our deep appreciation and assuring them that we have placed their names on our prayer team list. That begins our ongoing communication process.

At the end of each month we mail a prayer memo to all the members of our prayer team. The memo is designed to fit into a Bible or prayer notebook so that the prayer team members can use it with ease. It contains four specific kinds of prayer information.

The first is a list of specific *praises and answers to prayer* from the previous month's prayer memo. Second is a list of specific and often urgent *prayer requests* for the coming month. Third, we enclose our *ministry calendar and itinerary* for the month just ahead so that our prayer team members know where we are and what we are doing. We want them to pray for us as specifically as possible. Then in addition to sharing our personal and ministry prayer requests with our prayer partners, we invite them to share their prayer requests with us. Fourth, each month we send them *a prayer request card* with the invitation for them to send us their requests.

When they return their cards with their specific prayer requests, my wife compiles them on a monthly "prayer request sheet" that both of us insert in our prayer notebooks. In turn, we pray for those requests regularly. Since the list is usually so long, we often cannot pray for each request every day, but we pray for each of them at least weekly until we receive the new requests the next month. As our prayer team members pray for us, and we pray for them, we experience the privilege of mourning with those who mourn and rejoicing with those who rejoice (Rom. 12:15).

Paul carried on such a ministry. For example, he prayed for the Colossian Christians, "We always thank God, the Father of our Lord Jesus Christ, when we pray for you, because we have heard of your faith in Christ Jesus and of the love you have for all the saints" (Col. 1:3–4). Then later on in that same letter, Paul wrote, "Devote yourselves to prayer, being watchful and thankful. And pray for us, too, that God may open a door for our message, so that we may proclaim the mystery of Christ, for which I am in chains. Pray that I may proclaim it clearly, as I should" (4:2–4).

I know of no more generous gift that one Christian can share with another than that of regular and consistent prayer.

MOBILIZING/MENTORING/HELPING OTHERS TO PRAY

I have never established a "prayer mentoring" relationship with another person. However, I have been involved in a number of mentoring relationships over the years that have included mentoring in the ministry of prayer. I have found that it is virtually impossible to mentor a younger person in the ministry without giving a high priority to prayer.

The term *mentoring* may seem a bit challenging or even formal to some. Many contemporaries prefer the term *discipling* or *disciple-making*. Whatever you call it, this is an important ministry. I believe every one of us who has been called of God to Christian ministry has a responsibility to invest in the lives of younger leaders, whether formally or informally.

While it is important to teach younger leaders ministry skills, it is even more important to teach them spiritual disciplines such as prayer. I would recommend we teach them the kind of basic principles of prayer that are shared in this book. But even more than that, we should mentor others in the life of prayer by praying with them—teaching them to pray by "doing" and not just "telling." In other words, we would do well in mentoring on every level—including prayer—to follow the model of our Lord Jesus Christ. He spent significant time with His disciples. Besides telling them what to do, He showed them how.

The most effective kind of mentoring is the informal approach of merely taking younger people with us as we are involved in daily responsibilities of ministry. Allow them to observe you and to ask questions of you (at appropriate times) and to dialogue with you. Let them hear you pray in your hospital visits, in your business sessions, before you begin an important appointment, before you depart on a trip, or as you visit with a grieving family. In this real-life process of sharing with you in ministry, they will be mentored in praying!

PRAYER-WALKING

Another significant way for you to grow in your prayer life and to mentor others is prayer-walking. In recent years prayer-walking has become an increasingly significant ministry for many Christians. I well remember the first time I was introduced to this concept. It came from a very unexpected source.

While I was pastoring in Southern California a number of years ago, one of the couples in our church family lived just two blocks from our house. Sometimes early in the morning, I would see them walk by our house.

One day I happened to mention to them that it was good to see them out walking together. They responded by saying they enjoyed it greatly and that one of the things they had begun to do was to pray for Jeannie and me and our family every morning when they passed our house. Soon they were praying not only for us but for other neighbors as well. Without fully realizing it, they were involved in a prayer-walking ministry.

Steve Hawthorne and Graham Kendrick have written a very helpful book entitled *Prayer-Walking: Praying on Site with Insight.*

Across the globe God is stirring ordinary believers to pray persistently while walking their cities street by street. Some use rather well-arranged plans. Others flow with Spirit-given prompts. Their prayers run the gamut from lofty appeals to pinpoint petitions, ranging beyond their own homes to their neighbors. It's hard to stop there, so most of them eventually burst into prayers for the entire campus or city or nation. No quick fix is envisioned. But expectancy seems to expand with every mile. Most of these pray-ers don't imagine themselves to be just bravely holding flickering candles toward an overwhelming darkness. Rather, long fuses are being lit for anticipated explosions of God's love. Every day believers are praying, house by house, in their neighborhoods.[8]

Peter Wagner has shared an example of a rather sophisticated and systematic approach to prayer-walking that focuses on evangelistic outreach.

Most prayerwalking to date has been spontaneous. Ministry and results have been good. But suppose we went beyond doing it here and there. Suppose that once a week every single block of every single street in our city were covered by a prayerwalk. Would you believe that within a year this would be a different city? I believe it would, but it would take more effort, more leadership and more coordination.

My friend John Huffman has pioneered that kind of citywide neighborhood prayerwalking that might give us the clues about how to do it in our own city. His initial field experiments, called "Christ for the City," were done in Medellin, Colombia.

Although all synchronized neighborhood prayerwalking does not have to be done this way, John Huffman's plan is explicitly evangelistic. . . . The general idea is to mobilize as massive an amount of intercessory prayer for the neighborhood as possible for 14 days preceding an evangelistic event. The more targeted the prayer the better, so each neighborhood is mapped block by block. . . .

A suggested prayer program for the 2 weeks has been outlined by Huffman, but any variations the Lord indicates are welcome. The schedule includes, among other things, preparation of the intercessors, prayers of blessing, warfare praying, fasting and prayer for special groups.[9]

Prayer-walking can vary, from simply praying in general for our neighbor's needs to praying for the salvation of entire city blocks.

PRAYING ON ALL OCCASIONS

As we have seen in this chapter as well as in previous chapters, there are many ways to become involved in the strategic ministry of prayer. I am not advocating or even suggesting that all of us will be called of God to become involved in every one of these expressions of prayer. But seek the Lord's guidance regarding which of these prayer opportunities you should select.

The Lord Jesus Christ is our "Headmaster" in the school of prayer. He is the One who must guide us in our praying. He is the One with whom we commune in prayer, the One to whom we go with the petition, "Lord, teach us to pray!"

Thank You, dear Lord,
for the many ways You invite us to pray,
and for the many opportunities You extend to us.
Help us to enjoy times of
personal prayer retreats with You,
and help us to invite You
to our business meetings
and to every area of our lives.
And, Lord, even when we feel inadequate,
help us to help others to pray
in retreats or meetings or small groups
or prayer-walks.
Lord, teach us to pray,
and help us to teach
others to pray!

17

Promoting the Lord's Agenda through Prayer

A LITTLE OVER A DECADE AGO I taught a seminary course on spiritual disciplines. My students ranged from seasoned pastors and Christian leaders to relatively young seminarians who were just beginning their preparation for the ministry.

One of the spiritual disciplines I introduced to the class about midway through the course was fasting. I began by asking how many of the students had ever heard about fasting as a spiritual discipline in the Christian life. Only one or two students raised their hands—with some uncertainty. And when I asked how many of them had ever fasted, virtually no one responded. Most of them knew literally nothing about spiritual fasting.

In past decades relatively few Christians in America ever fasted. But that has changed radically in the past few years. Many Christians are talking about fasting today, and increased numbers of them are actually doing it.

FASTING AND PRAYER

Bill Bright has been used of God in a remarkable way in mobilizing Christians to fast and pray. He and his wife, Vonette, have hosted some wonderful national fasting and prayer conferences. In his excellent book,

The Coming Revival, he shares some helpful insights on fasting and prayer, including the following list of some biblical and practical reasons for fasting.

> The writings of Scripture, the Church Fathers, and many Christian leaders of today offer several biblical insights into the spiritual need for fasting:
> - It is a biblical way to truly humble oneself in the sight of God (Psalm 35:13; Ezra 8:21).
> - It brings revelation by the Holy Spirit of a person's true spiritual condition, resulting in brokenness, repentance, and change.
> - It is a crucial means for personal revival because it brings the inner workings of the Holy Spirit into play in a most unusual, powerful way.
> - It helps us better understand the word of God by making it more meaningful, vital, and practical.
> - It transforms prayer into a richer and more personal experience.
> - It can result in dynamic personal revival—being controlled and led by the Spirit and regaining a strong sense of spiritual determination.
> - It can restore the loss of one's first love for our Lord.[1]

Wesley Duewel has written an excellent sketch of the importance of fasting and its significant place in the history of the Christian church.

> Fasting was a powerful God-blessed strategy of the early church, and in the lives of many of the leaders God raised up. Paul prayed with fasting in every church (Acts 14:23).
> Epiphanius, Bishop of Salamis (born A.D. 315), wrote: "Who does not know that the fasts of the fourth and sixth days of the week are observed by the Christians throughout the world?" In the thirteenth century, Francis of Assisi went through the streets of Italy singing, preaching, testifying, praying, and fasting until thousands of the youth were saved. Martin Luther was criticized for too much fasting. John Calvin fasted and prayed till most all of Geneva was converted, and there was not a house without at least one praying person. John Knox fasted and prayed until Queen Mary said she feared his prayers more than all the armies of Scotland. Latimer, Ridley, Cranmer, in fact, most of the reformers, were known for their fasting added to their prayer.[2]

Duewel then concluded, "Fasting is sti
and strengthen prayer. You will be the poc
life will never be what God wants it to be i
of fasting. . . . Biblical fasting is a form of s
and His kingdom. It is a deliberate abstine
spiritual purpose. It demands a deep level (

Increasing numbers of pastors and Ch
tion and around the world would agree wi
deep and growing conviction among many
calling His people to their knees to humb
seek His face. Fasting is one of the means G
focus more on Him and less on ourselves a

I would encourage you to do some seric
becoming involved in the ministry of fastii
explore the purpose and benefits of spiritu
spective, I would recommend the books by
from which I have just quoted.

In addition, the Word of God spoken th
to be exceedingly appropriate for Christiar
cloth, O priests, and mourn; wail, you who n
spend the night in sackcloth, you who mir
grain offerings and drink offerings are witl
God. Declare a holy fast; call a sacred assen
all who live in the land to the house of the L
the LORD" (Joel 1:13–14).

In the second chapter of Joel, the Lord a
the people of Judah back to Him, and to re
" 'Even now,' declares the LORD, 'return to
fasting and weeping and mourning. Rend y
ments. Return to the LORD your God, for he is
slow to anger and abounding in love, and he
ity' " (Joel 2:12–13).

Judah's spiritual condition was so bad that
national repentance by fasting and prayer. Noi
be voluntary. It was never required in the Mosa

on the D
phrase "d
The (
neous fas
of stone
fasted wh
Abner's (
faced tin
109:24–2
from Bat
when he
ites, whe
was read
4:16); Da
9:3); Ann
ing and
Barnaba
Barnaba
fasted wl
of fastin;
Othe
Jonathai
Jews in I
the Nine
Fasti
pressed :
spiritual
is a legit
times of
in humi
Dona
(not one
Neh. 1:4
press gri
Esth. 4:1

y of Atonement (Lev. 16:29, 31; 23:27, 29, 32: Num. 29:7). The
ny yourselves" in these verses probably included fasting.
'd and New Testaments record a number of occasions of sponta-
ing. Moses fasted on Mount Sinai before he received the tablets
·ith the Ten Commandments (Exod. 34:28; Deut. 10:10). David
·en he mourned Saul's and Jonathan's deaths (2 Sam. 1:12) and
·ath (3:35); he fasted when his son was ill (12:16) and when he
·es of spiritual agony (Ps. 35:13–14) or opposition (69:10–11;
·). Ezra fasted when he and others set out on a dangerous journey
·lon to Jerusalem (Ezra 8:21–23). Other examples are Nehemiah,
·eard the bad news about Jerusalem's walls (Neh. 1:4); the Israel-
·they confessed their sins (9:1); Esther and Mordecai, when Esther
·to go before the king with her request on behalf of the Jews (Esth.
·niel, when he prayed about the Jews' return to their land (Dan
·a, whose worship in the temple was often accompanied with fast-
·rayer (Luke 2:37); the church leaders at Antioch, when they set
·and Saul apart for missionary work (Acts 13:2–3); and Paul and
·, when they appointed church elders (14:23). And of course Jesus
·en He faced the devil's severe temptations (Matt. 4:2). Jesus spoke
·as a time of mourning (9:15).
Old Testament examples of fasting included Israel (1 Sam. 7:6),
(20:34), Ahab (1 Kings 21:27), Jehoshaphat (2 Chron. 20:3), the
·ersia (Esth. 4:3), Baruch (Jer. 36:6–8, Daniel (Dan. 10:1–3), and
·vites (Jon. 3:5).
·g was often carried out in times of crisis or sorrow. Fasting ex-
·orrow for one's sins or the sins of others, or acknowledged one's
·need for guidance, protection, healing, or victory. "Fasting then
·mate response to dangers, trials, heartaches, or sorrows. . . . In
·hysical or spiritual need Christians realize their inadequacy and
·ty and repentance look to the Lord."[4]
· S. Whitney points up ten purposes for fasting given in the Scriptures
·of which is to earn God's favor!): to strengthen prayer (Ezra 8:23;
·Acts 13:3), to seek God's guidance (Judg. 20:26; Acts 14:23), to ex-
·' (2 Sam. 1:11–12), to seek deliverance or protection (2 Chron. 20:3–4;
·), to express repentance and the return to God (1 Sam. 7:6; Joel

2:12; Jon. 3:5–8), to humble oneself before God (Ps. 35:13), to express concern for the work of God (Dan 9:3), to minister to the needs of others (Isa. 58:6–7), to overcome temptation and dedicate yourself to God (Matt. 4:1–11), and to express love and worship to God (Luke 2:37).[5]

Fasting should never be "for show," as Jesus said, for that was hypocritical (Matt. 6:16–18). It should be done in private. And it was always to be carried out with humility (Isa. 58:3–5).

Praying can be greatly enhanced as we occasionally—in times of deep spiritual need—spend times of fasting.

EVANGELISM PRAYING

Several years ago I was invited by Ed Silvoso to speak at a conference in Argentina. One of the assigned subjects was "Praying for the Unconverted." As I was preparing for that plenary session, I drafted an outline of my presentation that was to be distributed to the participants gathering from all over the world.

The title I recommended for the session was simply "Prayer *As* Evangelism." However, when I arrived in Argentina and received my copy of the reproduced outline, the middle word had been misprinted. It read "Prayer *Is* Evangelism."

As I reflected on that typographical error, I concluded that the revised title was better than the one I had proposed. The truth is that prayer is an effective and powerful approach to the ministry of evangelism. Prayer and evangelism are not synonymous, but prayer is an essential ingredient in any vital ministry of evangelistic outreach.

The apostle Paul prayed that all of Israel would be saved (Rom. 10:1). And he encouraged Timothy to be involved in praying for others, even kings and others in authority (1 Tim. 2:1–2). The apostle concluded, "This is good, and pleases God our Savior, who wants all men to be saved and to come to a knowledge of the truth" (2:1–4).

Prayer is not the only thing we do in evangelism, but it is the most important. As I mentioned earlier, Billy Graham's evangelistic ministry has depended primarily on God's people, who are mobilized first to pray for loved ones and friends, and then to invite them to a crusade service where the gospel is preached clearly and powerfully and an invitation is extended to receive Christ.

Some Christians debate whether praying for the lost violates the sovereignty of God or the free will of non-Christians. I do not believe either is true. Instead, I have found that praying for lost people by name somehow unleashes the special ministry of the Holy Spirit to woo, draw, and convict them of sin and of their need of the Savior (John 16:5–11). Years ago Lewis Sperry Chafer emphasized this truth in his book *True Evangelism*.[6]

For years I have kept in my prayer notebook a list of names of friends and family members who, so far as I know, have never come to personal faith in Jesus Christ. As I have prayed and others have prayed for those individuals, we have seen literally scores of them come to Christ.

When I was a pastor I was often asked to pray for a church member's non-Christian husband, child, or friend. Jeannie and I took those requests seriously. Frequently we would covenant with that Christian to pray daily for the person who needed to come to Christ.

I remember one young wife who came to see me for a counseling session. Her husband was a non-Christian and militantly so. He was reluctant even to allow her to go to church. Jeannie and I began to pray daily for that man, whom we had never met.

Several months later, I greeted the young lady one day with the words "I'm still praying for your husband every day." Her response was one of astonishment and appreciation. She replied, "Oh, I have some wonderful news for you. My husband came to Christ a few weeks ago. There has been a radical change in his life. In fact, he is involved in a small-group Bible study and has been attending church with me every Sunday. It's wonderful!"

Over the years, I have had similar experiences frequently. As the apostle Paul wrote, "I planted the seed, Apollos watered it, but God made it grow" (1 Cor. 3:6).

That is what evangelism praying is about. Prayer is an important part of the planting and watering process. God uses it to prepare the hearts of the lost to receive the good news of the gospel—and it prepares our hearts to share the love and grace of Jesus Christ with them. Jesus spoke of this dynamic when He said, "No one can come to me unless the Father who sent me draws him" (John 6:44). I believe that praying for the salvation of lost people is a ministry in which every one of us should be strategically involved.

Ed Silvoso has shared another important dimension of praying for the lost:

> In order to pray effectively for the unsaved, we must become aware of the difference between the most important need a person has and what that person feels is his most important need—what is known as the "felt need." Usually these two are not one and the same in the mind of the unsaved. Man's most important need has already been determined by God: the salvation of his soul. However, the felt needs of the lost are defined by the lost themselves; it is what *they feel* is most important to them.
>
> The lost are unable to clearly see their most important need because "the god of this world has blinded the minds of the unbelieving" to the gospel (2 Cor. 4:4). When we pray for their felt needs and God answers, their eyes are opened to the reality and the power of God, and this in turn leads them to recognize their need for salvation. This is what Paul may have had in mind when he said that the Lord sent him "to open their eyes so that they may turn from darkness to light and from the dominion of Satan to God" (Acts 26:18).[7]

Very likely someone or a number of people were praying for you before you became a follower of Jesus Christ. And by God's grace He can use your prayers in bringing others to Christ.

RELATIONAL PRAYER WITNESSING

Recently I heard of an exciting approach to evangelism being used by Howard Tryon, a minister in Phoenix, Arizona. For years he had used a confrontational style of witnessing, but found that many people were turned off by that approach. They were not interested in hearing the plan of salvation. Howard began to wonder if there was some other, more effective way of winning people to Christ.

While studying 1 Timothy 2:1–8, Tryon was struck with the thought that prayer should be the major focus, not a side issue, in evangelism.

He recalled that when he was in seminary he had witnessed to a man who had little response until Tryon asked him if he had some problem he could pray about. The man gladly shared a personal problem he was facing.

Excited about this simple approach to getting an entrée to a person's interest in spiritual things, Howard decided to go door to door, telling people he was a pastor and asking them if he could pray for some need in their lives. To his surprise and delight, he found that eight of the nine people he approached in the cul-de-sac where he visited were pleased that someone would care enough to write down their need and promise to pray for them. This led to continued contacts with these and other neighbors, and as a result within one year twenty people accepted Christ as their Savior!

Tryon then began to encourage other Christians to do the same with their family members, friends, and work associates. Many believers who are hesitant to confront the unsaved with the gospel have been greatly encouraged to use this "tool" of evangelism, and many individuals who have been approached in this way—with a friendly, prayerful concern—have become believers.

Seeing the effectiveness of this approach, Tryon now teaches seminars in churches across the country on how to use this method of prayer evangelism. He calls his ministry "Praying for You." As Joseph C. Aldrich, president emeritus of Multnomah Bible College and Bible Seminary, states, " 'Praying for You' can take the fear out of reaching others for Christ."

For more information on this simple but remarkable ministry, see Howard Tryon's book *Praying for You* (Grand Rapids: Kregel, 1996), two audiocassettes on how pastors and laypeople can lead others in this approach, and four videocassettes produced by Praying for You, P. O. Box 35834, Phoenix, Arizona 85069 (telephone: 602-375-9914).

GREAT COMMISSION PRAYING

Until just a few years ago the term *Great Commission Praying* was probably seldom used. Now it has become well known to millions of Christians around the world.

The term describes the praying that we do for individual persons and people groups who are a part of what missiologists call "unreached people groups." These are the various nations, tribes, and other people groupings who do not yet have an indigenous Christian church. Ralph Winter, Patrick Johnstone, and many other missiologists note that more than seventeen hundred unreached people groups are in the world today.

The "AD 2000 and Beyond" movement has focused particularly on mobilizing the church around the world to reach these special people with the love and grace of our Lord Jesus Christ. One of the goals of this enterprise is to help establish a viable church in every one of those groups by the end of the year 2000.

A special outreach called "Joshua Project 2000" has been formed with the goal of recruiting local churches and denominations to adopt various groups of unreached peoples. The response to that initiative has been very positive.

As a part of the strategy to reach the nations of the world with the gospel of Jesus Christ, the United Prayer Track of the AD 2000 and Beyond movement is mobilizing millions of Christians worldwide each October in a special united prayer effort called "Praying through the Window." Last year approximately 36 million Christians from 105 nations participated in praying for the unreached peoples of the world.

The particular prayer focus is on the nucleus of people in the world who have not had the chance to hear the gospel even once and who live in what is called the "10/40 Window." This area, from 10 degrees latitude south to 40 degrees latitude north, stretches across North Africa, the Middle East, India, and Asia.

You can participate in praying for unreached peoples who live in the nations located in the "10/40 Window," in other nations of the world, in the United States, and even in your own community. Thankfully the Lord is marshaling a great army of prayer warriors in these critical days to pray for the world's many unreached peoples.

REVIVAL PRAYING

Possibly more books and articles have been written on the subject of revival within the past few years than at any other time in the history of the church. There is no doubt that our Lord is moving in the hearts of an increasing number of Christians to pray for revival in the church and spiritual awakening in our nation and the world. The Lord is moving in the hearts of many of His people, nudging and even urging many of them to be involved in praying for revival.

This is an encouraging development. Two great spiritual awakenings in our nation's history are called the First and Second Great Awakenings. A third revival movement, which occurred shortly before the Civil War, is known as the Great Prayer Revival or sometimes the Third Great Awakening. Thus well over a century has passed since there was a great movement of God in this nation that touched not only His church but also had deep and lasting impact on our culture and society.

A number of Christian leaders are observing some encouraging signs in America and other nations that are reminiscent of the kinds of things that took place in past revivals, both as recorded in the Old Testament and in the pages of church history.

Tom Phillips, in *Revival Signs*, describes the insights of one of these Christian leaders.

If anyone has his finger on the pulse of the current revival stirrings in North America, it may be Dr. Lewis Drummond. This respected, godly scholar has written several noted books on revival and has held the Billy Graham Chair of Evangelism at Beeson Divinity School (Samford University) in Birmingham, Alabama, since 1991.

I met Dr. Drummond in 1976 at the Southern Baptist Theological Seminary in Louisville, Kentucky, where he was then teaching. At the time, talk of spiritual awakening in this country was almost nil. "There was not near as much interest in revival or prayer back then as there is today," he recalls.

Today, more than eighteen years later, Dr. Drummond is seeing the kind of revival stirrings that preceded our nation's Great Awakenings.

"I'm seeing at least two things I've never seen in my lifetime, two things that make me think America may be ripe for a new spiritual awakening," he says. "First, there's never been so much concern and interest in revival. I'm seeing this renewed interest in pastors, and to some extent, in laypersons as well.

"The second thing that's remarkable about the potential for revival in America is the increasing interest in prayer and the formation of prayer groups we've been seeing throughout our nation. Though it's still in the developmental stage, there's so much prayer for revival today. Again, I've never seen anything quite like it in my lifetime."[8]

David Bryant, chairman of the U.S. Prayer Committee, agrees: "I believe—with unshakable conviction—that we are on the threshold of the greatest revival in the history of the church. This is what I hope. I have no doubts that it is coming. In fact I can 'see' it as if it were already completed. I can't explain this sense of things. I realize it sounds quite subjective—and to a degree it is. Some might call my hope a "prophetic insight," while others would simply call it a hunch. I only know that I believe God is not only able and willing to once again give revival to his church worldwide, but I believe he is ready to do so at this very moment."[9]

With all the encouraging signs emerging today for the possibility of a great revival movement in the United States and elsewhere, there are also some challenges. Neil Anderson and Elmer Towns share some insights from the late A. W. Tozer. At first glance, the words of Tozer seem extremely strong. And, if we are not careful, they can be misunderstood. "Sometimes praying is not only useless, it is wrong. . . . We must have a reformation within the church. To beg for a flood of blessing to come upon a backslidden and disobedient church is to waste time and effort. A new wave of religious interest will do no more than add numbers to churches that have no intention to own the lordship of Jesus and come under obedience to His commandments. God is not interested in increased church attendance unless those who attend amend their ways and begin to live holy lives. . . . Prayer for revival will prevail when it is accompanied by radical amendment of life; not before."[10]

In other words, if authentic revival is to take place in the church, and if a spiritual awakening is to sweep across this nation, it must begin with the people of God praying. But that prayer must be authentic. And revival requires true repentance, turning from sin to God. Prayers must flow from the hearts of those who have been cleansed. One of the marvelous things about revival praying is that each one of us can be involved. You can be on the front lines of this great prayer effort.

Tom Phillips has addressed this issue with the following words of encouragement and exhortation.

> As a slumbering Church, as individuals indifferent to our own spiritual fatigue, we're missing the sunlight of the day with Christ. We're missing the wonderful meals we could be having with Him. We're missing the fellowship with other believers that could be so unbelievably fulfilling and joyous. We're missing a little bit of heaven on earth. In short, we could be our own worst obstacles to the awakening we so desperately need and want. And we don't even know it.
>
> True spiritual awakening that once turned our nation back to God (and may turn us to Him again) will take place once more because God chooses to love human beings who choose to receive Him. The only thing that can possibly stand in the way of the next Great Awakening (and it's a big "only"), the only obstacle to experiencing revival in all its fullness, will be if you and I are unwilling or unable to receive the blessing God is ready to give.
>
> You and I won't hinder revival because we stand in the way of an all powerful, all-caring God, but because we simply aren't willing to receive the great love He wants to pour out. If you're concerned about possible obstacles to revival, don't expect to find a satisfying "answer" in the eternal, theological tug-of-war of God's sovereignty vs. man's free will. The relevant questions we need to be asking are these:
>
> Do I want to be part of an extraordinary movement of the Holy Spirit in this nation?
>
> Do I long for God's forgiveness and healing in this country, a movement that can come only from Him?
>
> If your answer to both is yes, if deeper spiritual life is what you seek, then be ready to experience two very distinct and opposing forces. The first is God's infinite desire to bring our nation to Himself. The second is our own imperfect nature that causes you to look out for self. It's in this flawed, human interior where the potential obstacles to revival dwell.[11]

The questions then become, How can God use us in revival praying? How should we pray and for what should we pray?

For the answer to these two important questions, we do well to listen to Jonathan Edwards, who was born in 1703 and who was God's anointed leader of the First Great Awakening:

> I have often said it would be a thing very desirable, and very likely to be followed with a great blessing, if there could be some contrivance, that there would be an agreement of all God's people in America, that are well affected to this work, to keep a Day of Fasting and Prayer to God; wherein we should all unite on the same day. . . . Some perhaps may think its being all on the same day is a circumstance of no great consequence; but I can't be of that mind. . . . It seems to me, it would mightily encourage and animate God's saints, in humbly and earnestly seeking God, for such blessings which concerns them all, and that it would be much for the rejoicing of all, to think, that at the same time, such multitudes of God's dear children, far and near, were sending up their cries to the same common Father for the same motives.[12]

This is something we can all do as we seek to be involved in effective revival praying. Tens of thousands of Christians across the nation are setting aside the first Friday of each month as a special day of prayer and fasting for revival in the church and spiritual awakening in our nation and the world. In addition, many of us have made the commitment to observe a day of prayer and fasting for revival every Friday.

I invite you to join us.

Also we can all be involved in participating in the National Prayer Accord. Robert Bakke, director of the National Prayer Advance, discovered this wonderful prayer tradition when he was doing research for his doctoral dissertation on the Concert of Prayer movement. Bakke discovered that Jonathan Edwards and other revival leaders instituted a wonderful ministry of concerted prayer that led up to the First Great Awakening and continued through the Second Great Awakening and the Great Prayer Revival.

The plan was both simple and unusually effective. Christians were asked to focus on praying for two things: the revival of the church and evangelism. These pray-ers followed three steps in their concerted (united and cooperative) praying. First, each participant prayed weekly, focusing on the Prayer Accord either privately or in a small group for at least one half-hour. Second, they gathered monthly in their local churches to pray for the Prayer Accord, focusing on revival and evangelism. Third, every three months, they gathered with Christians from other churches in the community for a Community Prayer Concert with the same prayer focus of the Prayer Accord.

Thousands of Christians and hundreds of churches participated in the Prayer Accord, particularly in New England. Their commitment to such concerted and focused praying for revival and evangelism lasted well over a hundred years. And it is interesting to note that all three major spiritual awakenings took place during the time those Christians were actively involved in concerted praying.

By God's grace that Prayer Accord is being revived in our day. Again thousands of Christians and hundreds of churches across the nation have become involved. And, because of the technology now available, an additional element has been added. A nationally televised Concert of Prayer is broadcast each year. Now virtually every Christian and every local church in the nation has the opportunity to be involved in the National Prayer Accord in a meaningful way.

I would encourage you to get involved in such praying and to invite other Christians and churches in your community to participate. For a more complete description of the Prayer Accord, see Appendix C.

In studying the influence and effectiveness of the National Prayer Accord in the eighteenth and nineteenth centuries, Bakke shares the following counsel.

Pastors and ministry leaders should recognize the enormous value of establishing a rhythm of prayer for the revival of the church and the advancement of Christ's Kingdom. Such a rhythm—whether weekly, monthly, quarterly, etc.—weaves prayer for the promotion of Christ's reign into the fabric of people's lives. Furthermore, that the rhythm of prayer alternated between individual or small group praying, and large group multi-denominational praying, meant that each Christian was regularly reminded of the breadth of the evangelical world and the common interest among all Christians for God to pour out his Spirit upon the earth. Today's need for a equivalent instrument to teach us similar lessons couldn't be more acute.[13]

What can you do to become more effectual in your praying? Let me summarize the several recommendations that have been made in this chapter. First, you can prayerfully explore the ministry of fasting and praying by reading one of the excellent books on the subject listed in the bibliography of this book. And you can become involved with a growing number of other Christians in observing a special day of prayer and fasting for revival on the first Friday of every month or even every Friday.

Second, you can become involved in the exciting and fruitful ministry of prayer evangelism. Third, you can be used of God to "touch the world" through focused Great Commission praying. Fourth, you can join with hundreds of thousands of other Christians across America and around the world in revival praying. Even more specifically, you can become involved in the National Prayer Accord and encourage others to join you.

In the late summer of 1989 I stood at "Checkpoint Charlie" at the infamous Berlin Wall. For years I had wanted to visit that site. Although I had ministered in eastern Europe and Russia, I had never had the privilege of visiting Berlin.

Our flight into Berlin took us right over the wall. It was one of those rare times that I was sitting next to the window. I was grateful. As I looked down at the wall and the no-man's-land that separated East Berlin from West Berlin, I was overcome with the contrast in the appearance of the two cities. It was startling.

The next day, as I stood at the wall and looked across the barren divide, I was moved to tears at what the wall represented: the enslavement of people, the division of families and loved ones, and aggressive rebellion against God. Suddenly I felt prompted by the Holy Spirit to pray. I bowed my head and began to ask God to "break down the wall." Soon I found myself weeping and pleading to God for His divine intervention.

Some nine weeks later, on November 9, 1989, the impossible happened. With very little warning, the wall came down! As one of my sons expressed it, in a real sense a kingdom of darkness fell, and the walls followed.

I remember watching it happen on television along with so many other millions of Americans and others around the world. It was astounding, unbelievable, indescribable.

World leaders, journalists, government officials, political scientists, and others have tried to interpret and give rationale for why the walls came down, but to no avail. To this very day, there is no plausible cause, except one.

God intervened. God answered the prayers of millions of His people who had prayed fervently for years for the Berlin Wall to fall. I was only one of a great host whose prayers were answered that momentous day. Our Lord heard the prayers of His people offered up to Him for decades, and He graciously answered.

A few months after the Berlin Wall fell, Jeannie and I made another visit. Again I stood at Checkpoint Charlie. It was remarkable. Most of the wall was completely gone. Much of it had been literally ground into cement dust. Only a few remnants of the actual wall remained as a memorial—to help us all remember what had been and what is now.

I have a piece of the wall on my desk in my study. I look at it almost daily. It reminds me of who God is—and of the power of prayer.

That is the focus of this book. The message is simple and powerful. Our God is the Creator and Ruler of heaven and earth. He is the Lord of human history. And He has invited us to pray, to commune with Him daily in personal, intimate conversation. He wants to use us to advance His agenda, to fulfill His will, to further His work in every way.

Brothers and sisters, it is time to pray!

Thank you, dear Lord,
for your wonderful invitation to us
to pray.
Help us to be on the "cutting edge"
of what You are doing around the world.
Lord, teach us more about fasting and praying
and lead us into evangelism praying,
and Great Commission praying,
and revival praying.
And use us as Your instruments
to help break down the walls
our enemy has constructed
to divide Your people.
Lord, teach us to pray!

Appendi₃

❦

My Personal Prayer Nc

C.

1. *My Preparation Time*
   (Make notes about what you have don
   for your appointment with God.)

2. *My Time in the Word of God*
   A. *Bible Passage for Today*

   B. *What God said to Me Today through I*
      (List the specific insights the Lord sh
      and meditated on the passage of the

D

3.

1. _____

2. _____

3. _____

4. _____

5. _____

6. _____

7. _____

What I Am Going to Do about It—My "Action Steps" for Obeying God
(Write down the specific steps you plan to take as you respond to
  God's Word in obedience to what the Lord has said to you today.)

1. _____

2. _____

3. _____

4. _____

5. _____

6. _____

7. _____

A Key Verse (or Verses) I Want to Remember

My Time of Prayer: Communing with God

Adoration/Worship/Praise/Thanksgiving
("Our Father in heaven, hallowed be your name.")

1. *Adoration*
   Share words (and an attitude) of adoration with God, such
   as "Father, I bow before You and adore You. I express my love
   to You from the depths of my heart. I see You high and holy
   and lifted up."

2. *Worship/Praise*
   Read verses of Scripture expressing worship and praise to God, such as Psalms 92, 93, 95, 100, 103, 104, 113, 150.

Sing a hymn or song of praise to God.

Share with the Lord your desire to be involved in offering Him the sacrifice of ongoing praise throughout the day as you read these passages:

Hebrews 13:15

Psalm 71:8

Colossians 3:17

1 Corinthians 10:31

Express joyous praise to the Lord in your own words.

3. *Thanksgiving*
   "It is good to praise the LORD, and make music to your name, O Most High; to proclaim your love in the morning and your faithfulness at night" (Ps. 92:1–2).

Pause to give God thanks for everything you can think of that He has done for you and your loved ones in the past twenty-four hours.

B. *Recommitment/Release/Surrender*
   ("Your Kingdom come, your will be done on earth as it is in heaven.")

1. Offer to the Lord a prayer of recommitment and surrender, such as the following. (See examples in Appendix B.)

"Lord, I surrender anew to You and to doing Your will. I submit in all things to Your lordship and sovereignty. I will seek to follow You today in all I do in obedience to Your Word and the guidance of the Holy Spirit."

"Lord, I would die anew today. I seek to be dead to self and alive to You" (based on 1 Cor. 15:31).

"Lord, I would abide in You today. Thank you for your promise that as I do, You will abide in me and I will bear much fruit for You. Lord, I acknowledge that without You I can do nothing, but I rejoice that with You I can do anything You call me to do—by the strength that comes from You" (based on John 15:5 and Phil. 4:13).

"Lord, I would open the door of my heart wide to You today in every area of my life. Please come in and commune with me throughout the day just as You promised. Thank You for the great joy of communing with You today" (based on Rev. 3:20).

"Lord, I ask to be filled anew by the Holy Spirit. I long to put to death the works of the flesh and to walk in the Spirit. Help me, dear Lord" (based on Gal. 5:19–23 and Eph. 5:18).

2. Surrender to the Lord any and all burdens you are carrying. Name them and release them to God specifically one by one. "Cast all your anxiety on him because he cares for you" (1 Pet. 5:7).

C. *Asking for God's Provision*
   ("Give us today our daily bread.")

1. Begin by claiming the wonderful promise of God, "And my God will meet [supply] all your needs according to his glorious riches in Christ Jesus" (Phil. 4:19).

2. Ask the Lord to provide for specific needs of yourself, your family, and others. Use a prayer list of persons and ministries for which you will pray regularly. The following categories may be helpful:

    My family:

    My pastor and church family:

    My ministry colleagues:

    Pastors and missionaries:

    My support-group members:

    Other ministry colleagues and friends:

    Our nation and the world:

    Personal requests:

    Special and urgent requests:

    (See Appendix B for additional information on praying for urgent needs.)

D. *Asking God for His Forgiveness as I Forgive Others*
    ("Forgive us our sins, for we also forgive everyone who sins against us," Luke 11:4.)
    1. Ask God to search and cleanse your heart. The following passages will be helpful as you pray.

        "Search me, O God, and know my heart; test me and know my anxious thoughts. See if there is any offensive way in me, and lead me in the way everlasting" (Ps. 139:23–24).

"If we claim to be without sin, we deceive ourselves and the truth is not in us. If we confess our sins, he is faithful and just and will forgive us our sins and purify us from all unrighteousness" (1 John 1:8–9).

2. Ask the Lord to bring to mind any persons whom you need to forgive. Then take the necessary steps to forgive them, whoever they may be.

E. *Asking God for Guidance*
("And lead us not into temptation.")

1. Ask the Lord, "Please do not lead me into temptation today, but lead me in Your 'paths of righteousness.'"

2. Then ask Him to lead you today by the Holy Spirit (Gal. 5:18, 25).

3. Then in prayer "put on" the whole armor of God (Eph. 6:10 18). Pray through the various articles that comprise the armor He has instructed us to don the belt of truth, the breastplate of righteousness, the gospel of peace, the shield of faith, the helmet of salvation, and the sword of the Spirit, the Word of God.

4. Close this section of prayer by asking the Lord, "Help me to be sensitive to Your leading and to be open to every person You want me to encounter and every experience You desire for me to have."

F. *Asking God to Protect Me and Others*
("But deliver us from the evil one.")

1. Begin by asking God to deliver you from our enemy, the devil.

2. Claim God's promise in James 4:7. Pray through each part of the verse. Submit yourself to God, resist the devil in the name of Jesus and by the power of the Holy Spirit, and claim God's promise that the devil will "flee from you."

3. Close this segment of praying with giving God thanks for His protection. Thank Him specifically for commanding His angels to guard us in all our ways and to protect us in all we do (Ps. 92:9–15).

G. *Claiming Victory through Our Lord Jesus Christ*
("For yours is the kingdom and the power and the glory forever. Amen.")

1. Thank God for victory through Christ.

2. Give thanks that our Lord has won the battle. He is victorious. He will reign as King of kings and Lord of lords (Rev. 17:14; 19:16).

3. Claim the wonderful promise that God "always leads us in triumphal procession in Christ and through us spreads everywhere the fragrance of the knowledge of him" (2 Cor. 2:14).

4. *Continuing the Day in Prayer*
("Pray continually," 1 Thess. 5:17.)
As you close your prayer notebook and conclude your devotional time, commit yourself to continue in the spirit of prayer for the rest of the day. Your prayer time is not ended. You have just begun your communion with the Lord throughout your day's activities.

Appendix B

My Personal Prayer Notebook, Part II

(Note: The following material offers additional details of how I personally use my prayer notebook. Although some of the material is somewhat personal, I share it with the prayer that it will be of benefit to you.)

Sample Prayers of Recommitment/Release/Surrender
("Your kingdom come, Your will be done on earth as it is in heaven.")

"Lord, I would commit myself anew to seek first You, Your kingdom, and Your righteousness. May Your kingdom come and Your will be done in and through my life—to Your glory! In the name of Jesus I pray. Amen."

"Lord, I surrender anew to You and to doing Your will. I submit to You in all things—to Your lordship and sovereignty. I will seek to follow You today in all that I do in obedience to Your Word and the guidance of the Holy Spirit."

"Lord Jesus, reign in my life today as my Lord. I will seek to do Your will today and not my own—by the grace that You supply and by the power of the Holy Spirit."

"Lord, I would die anew today. I would seek to be dead to self and alive to You."

"Lord, I would deny myself again as I begin this day. And, by your grace and the power of the Holy Spirit, I will take up my cross and follow You."

"Lord, I would abide in You today. Thank you for your promise that as I do, You will abide in me—and I will bear much fruit for You. I acknowledge that without You I can do nothing, but I rejoice that with You I can do anything You call me to do—by the strength that comes from You."

"Lord, I ask to be filled anew by the Holy Spirit. I long to put to death the works of the flesh and to walk in the Spirit. Help me, dear Lord!"

"Lord, I would open the door of my heart wide to You today in every area of my life. Please come in and commune with me throughout the day just as You promised. Thank You for the great joy of communing with You today."

"Lord, I would inhale Your presence and would exhale anything that is displeasing to You. Please fill me anew with Yourself now and throughout this day. Thank You."

Of course, there are many other expressions of surrender and recommitment we can express to God. And sometimes our prayers of surrender and commitment need to be more specific. Too often we carry things we should not be carrying. This is the time in our praying for releasing and committing everything to our Lord.

Prayers of Asking for God's Provision
("Give us today our daily bread.")

Here is an expanded version of some of the material presented in more condensed form in chapter 15.

It is important that our prayer lists not control or limit our praying. They are simply tools to help us be consistent and faithful. At the same time, I marvel at the wonderful way our Lord leads us in our praying if we are open to His guidance.

My prayer list includes the following categories of persons and ministries:

My family. I pray daily for each of my family members along with specific requests for them. Regardless of their present needs, I always pray about several things for them and for myself, including requests for God's provision and protection, His presence and His peace, His perspective and His power, His patience and perseverance. I pray the same for the members of our extended family, including the children and grandchildren of our eight brothers and sisters.

Our pastor and church family. I pray by name for our pastor and for other members of the pastoral team, our church leaders, our church family, and the ministry of our local church.

My ministry colleagues. For years I have prayed daily for my ministry colleagues by name. I believe it is one of the most important investments I can make in their lives and ministries. In addition, I have long employed a system for praying for the larger number of colleagues in the ministry. For example, when I was the president of a denomination, I prayed by name for every one of the hundreds of pastors at least once a year by simply praying for five of them each day.

Pastors and missionaries. I pray regularly for a significant list of friends who are serving the Lord as pastors or missionaries, including our national and international denominational leaders.

My support-group members. For years I have belonged to a small group of Christian brothers with whom I meet at least monthly and pray for regularly.

Ministry leaders. I pray for a long list of friends who are serving as national or international leaders in the ministry of our Lord Jesus Christ.

In addition, I pray regularly for a number of Christian leaders whom I have never had the privilege of meeting but whom I believe God has called to strategic ministry roles.

Other ministry colleagues and friends. Once again, it is a privilege to pray for many brothers and sisters in Christ on a regular basis. Jeannie and I have several scores of friends who are a part of our Ministry Prayer Team. As they faithfully pray for us, we enjoy praying for them.

Non-Christian neighbors and friends. One of the great privileges of praying for others is that of praying for neighbors and friends who, so far as can be determined, have never experienced the joy of following Christ. For years I have kept such a list. It has been a great joy to see many of those persons for whom I have prayed come to personal faith in the Savior.

Our nation and the world. I pray regularly for the leaders of our nation, state, and community, for various nations of the world, and for specific unreached people groups. I pray daily for at least three key "gateway cities" to the unreached people groups.

Personal requests. After praying for others, I usually pray for myself. Daily I ask for the Lord's provision of wisdom, love, generosity, purity, holiness, self-control, the fear of the Lord, a good name and reputation, freedom, faith, absence of anger, and a forgiving spirit. In addition, I ask that I may always bring to the Lord a humble spirit and a broken and contrite heart. And I pray that I may glorify the Lord both in life and in death.

Special and urgent requests. I close this segment of prayer by usually falling prostrate before the Lord in asking His provision for urgent requests others have shared with me. I keep these requests on a loose-leaf page with the dates they have been shared with me written to the left of the requests. Then in the right column I reserve space to record the date when the prayer was answered in an observable way.

I keep praying until I discern the Lord has answered according to His will. We should "always pray and not give up" (Luke 18:1); we should persist in prayer until the Lord answers in ways we can recognize, and we have the joy of seeing His will accomplished.

Appendix C

The National Prayer Accord

"Again, I tell you that if two of you on earth agree about anything you ask for, it will be done for you by my Father in heaven. For where two or three come together in my name, there am I with them" (Matt. 18:19–20).

I. We resolve to promote as prayer goals the outpouring of God's Spirit for:

> The revival of the church
> The advancement of Christ's kingdom

"'Not by might nor by power, but by my Spirit,' says the LORD Almighty" (Zech. 4:6).

II. We resolve to promote as a prayer rhythm . . .

> ONCE A WEEK
> Private or small-group prayer—one-half hour.

> ONCE A MONTH
> Individual-church prayer concert—one to two hours.

ONCE A QUARTER

Local, multiple-church prayer concert, wherein prayer for each church is offered for their neighborhoods, their towns and cities, the nation, and the world. It is recommended that these covenants be established among three to five like-minded churches, similar-size churches, and churches within a reasonable proximity to each other—two to three hours.

ONCE A YEAR

Join Christians from across the nation in simultaneous prayer by a nationally televised Prayer Concert, wherein heads of denominations, parachurch organizations, evangelistic and missions organizations, and evangelical institutions of higher learning gather to lead evangelicals in prayer for the church, the nation, and the world. Planned for the evening of the National Day of Prayer—two to three hours.

"If my people, who are called by my name, will humble themselves and pray and seek my face and turn from their wicked ways, then will I hear from heaven and will forgive their sin and will heal their land" (2 Chron. 7:14).

III. We resolve to promote time periods for prayer covenants.
      (among local congregations)

> First covenant: two years.
> Long enough period to examine its effect. Short enough period so that pastors/leaders do not feel trapped or unduly threatened.
>
> Second and renewable covenant: seven years.
> These covenants are to be "in such a latitude, as to keep at the greatest distance from entangling men's minds . . . as friendly, harmonious resolutions, with liberty to alter circumstances as shall be found expedient."

"They raised their voices together in prayer to God.... After they prayed, the place where they were meeting was shaken. And they were all filled with the Holy Spirit and spoke the Word of God boldly" (Acts 4:24, 31).

Some prayer subjects and strategies

- For localities and neighborhoods
  Pray for churches, local schools, teachers, town governments and officials, drug and alcohol issues, unwanted pregnancies, racial reconciliation, crime, local evangelistic strategies, and others. In a word, find the mind of God for one's own town or city.

- For our nation and the world
  Pray for governments and officials, heads of corporations, denominational leaders, heads of universities and colleges, mission leaders, national and international ministry leaders, and others. (See First Friday/Church Pray! 10/40 Window, Houses of Prayer, Pastors' Prayer Summits, March for Jesus, Day to Change the World, etc.)

- For ministry leaders
  Pastors, missionaries, lay evangelism, pastor-less churches, churches in crisis, evangelists, key laypersons, and others.

"For the earth will be filled with the knowledge of the glory of the LORD, as the waters cover the sea" (Hab. 2:14).

ENDNOTES

CHAPTER 1—RECOGNIZING THE UNLIMITED POTENTIAL OF PRAYER

1. Jim Cymbala and Dean Merrill, *Fresh Wind, Fresh Fire* (Grand Rapids: Zondervan, 1997), 16–17 (italics theirs).
2. Ibid., 27.
3. Tom Carter, comp., *Spurgeon at His Best* (Grand Rapids: Baker, 1988), 155 (selections from the 1873 edition of the *Metropolitan Tabernacle Pulpit,* 218).
4. John Munro, "Prayer to a Sovereign God," *Interest,* February 1990, 20.
5. Samuel Chadwick, quoted in *Prayer Powerpoints,* comp. Randall D. Roth (Wheaton, Ill.: Victor, 1995), 107.
6. E. M. Bounds, *Power through Prayer* (1912; reprint, Grand Rapids: Baker, 1972), 31.
7. *The Complete Works of E. M. Bounds on Prayer* (Grand Rapids: Baker, 1990), 162.
8. Ibid., 340–41.
9. Joseph Scriven, "What a Friend We Have in Jesus," in *Hymns for the Living Church* (Carol Stream, Ill.: Hope, 1974), 435.

CHAPTER 2—UNDERSTANDING THE PURPOSE OF PRAYER

1. *The Complete Works of E. M. Bounds on Prayer,* 319.
2. Phillips Brooks, quoted in *Prayer Powerpoints,* 30.

3. Augustine, quoted in ibid., 31–32.
4. Oswald Chambers, quoted in ibid., 32.
5. Martin Luther, quoted in ibid., 19.
6. Bill Hybels, *Too Busy Not to Pray: Slowing Down to Be with God,* ed. LaVonne Neff (Downers Grove, Ill.: InterVarsity, 1988), 8.
7. O. H. Hallesby, *Prayer* (1931; reprint, Minneapolis: Augsburg, 1956), 11 (italics his).
8. Rosalind Rinker, *Prayer: Conversing with God* (Grand Rapids: Zondervan, 1959), 9.
9. Roth, *Prayer Powerpoints,* 31.
10. Walter L. Liefeld, "When God Says 'No,'" *Interest,* February 1990, 27.
11. Rowland Hogben, quoted in David H. Adeney, "Personal Experience of Prayer II," in *Teach Us to Pray: Prayer in the Bible and the World,* ed. D. A. Carson (Grand Rapids: Baker, 1990), 309.
12. Ibid.
13. Hybels, *Too Busy Not to Pray,* 7 (italics his).

CHAPTER 3—SURVEYING THE AWESOME POWER OF PRAYER

1. John Wesley, quoted in *Prayer Powerpoints,* 18.
2. Martin Luther, quoted in ibid., 38.
3. Charles Finney, quoted in ibid.
4. Martin Luther, quoted in ibid.
5. S. D. Gordon, *Quiet Talks on Prayer* (New York: Revell, 1904), 9–10.
6. Thomas L. Constable, *Talking to God: What the Bible Teaches about Prayer* (Grand Rapids: Baker, 1995), 126–27.
7. Corrie ten Boom, *Clippings from My Notebook* (Minneapolis: World Wide, 1984), 22.
8. John Guest, *Only a Prayer Away: Finding Deeper Intimacy with God* (Ann Arbor, Mich.: Vine, 1985), 33–34.
9. Ibid., 34 (italics his).

CHAPTER 4—ENJOYING THE INTIMATE PRIVACY OF PRAYER

1. Charles R. Swindoll, *Growing Strong in the Seasons of Life* (Portland, Oreg.: Multnomah, 1983) 377.

2. David Brainerd, quoted in *Prayer Powerpoints*, 180.

3. Hallesby, *Prayer* , 11–12, 36.

4. Guest, *Only a Prayer Away*, 75.

5. Edmund Clowney, "A Biblical Theology of Prayer," in *Teach Us to Pray: Prayer in the Bible and the World*, 141.

6. Rinker, *Prayer: Conversing with God,* 22–23.

7. Constable, *Talking to God*, 32–33.

8. Margaret Magdalen, *Jesus, Man of Prayer* (Downers Grove, Ill.: InterVarsity, 1987), 62.

9. W. Bingham Hunter, *The God Who Hears* (Downers Grove, Ill.: InterVarsity, 1986), 71 (italics his).

10. John Baillie, "Excerpts from A Diary of Private Prayer," in *Devotional Classics: Selected Readings for Individuals and Groups*, ed. Richard J. Foster and James Bryan Smith (New York: HarperCollins, 1993), 127–28.

CHAPTER 5—DETERMINING THE PROPER POSTURE OF PRAYER

1. Warren W. Wiersbe, *Listen! Jesus Is Praying: An Expository Study of John 17* (Wheaton, Ill.: Tyndale, 1982), 24 (italics his).

2. Andrew Murray, quoted in *The Encyclopedia of Religious Quotations,* ed. and comp. Frank S. Mead (Westwood, N.J.: Revell, 1965), 239.

3. Dwight L. Moody, quoted in ibid.

4. *The Complete Works of E. M. Bounds on Prayer,* 87.

5. Hallesby, *Prayer*, 17.

6. Ibid., 20–21.

7. Napoleon Bonaparte, quoted in *The Encyclopedia of Religious Quotations,* 480.

8. Dean Merrill, "Whatever Happened to Kneeling?" *Christianity Today,* 10 February 1992, 24.

CHAPTER 6—CHERISHING THE PURITY OF PRAYER

1. Hybels, *Too Busy Not to Pray*, 89–90 (italics his).

2. Sammy Tippit, *The Prayer Factor* (Chicago: Moody, 1988), 105.

3. Gordon, *Quiet Talks on Prayer*, 69 (italics his).

4. Zane C. Hodges, "1 John," in *The Bible Knowledge Commentary, New Testament*, ed. John F. Walvoord and Roy B. Zuck (Wheaton, Ill.: Victor, 1983), 886.
5. Ibid.
6. Brother Lawrence, *The Practice of the Presence of God* (n.p., n.d.; reprint, with a foreword by Robert E. Coleman, Wheaton, Ill.: Institute of Evangelism, 1996), 34.
7. Hybels, *Too Busy Not to Pray*, 90.
8. Hallesby, *Prayer*, 11.
9. Ibid., 12.
10. Leith Anderson, *When God Says No* (Minneapolis: Bethany, 1996), 82–83 (italics his).

CHAPTER 7—DELIGHTING IN THE PRAISE AND WORSHIP OF PRAYER

1. Tippit, *The Prayer Factor*, 77.
2. Hallesby, *Prayer*, 12.
3. Alan Redpath, *Victorious Praying* (Westwood, N.J.: Revell, 1957), 11–12.
4. Marcus Dods, *The Prayer That Teaches to Pray* (New Canaan, Conn.: Keats, 1980), 21.
5. William Hendriksen, *Exposition of the Gospel According to Matthew*, New Testament Commentary (Grand Rapids: Baker, 1973), 328 (italics his).
6. Ibid (italics his).
7. Ibid., 327 (italics his).
8. Ibid., 327–28.
9. William Barclay, *The Gospel of Matthew* (Philadelphia: Westminster, 1956), 1:205 (italics his).
10. Charles H. Spurgeon, *Twelve Sermons on Prayer* (New York: Revell, 1890), 552.

CHAPTER 8—CLAIMING GOD'S PROMISES THROUGH PRAYER

1. R. Kelso Carter, "Standing on the Promises," in *Great Hymns of the Faith*, ed. and comp. John W. Peterson (Grand Rapids: Zondervan, 1968), 175.

2. Thomas Benton Brooks, quoted in *The Encyclopedia of Religious Quotations*, ed. and comp. Frank S. Mead (Westwood, N.J.: Revell, 1965), 338.

3. Richard Trench, quoted in ibid., 348.

CHAPTER 9—RECEIVING GOD'S PROVISION THROUGH PRAYER

1. Constable, *Talking to God*, 25.

2. Martin Luther, "A Mighty Fortress Is Our God," in *Great Hymns of the Faith*, ed. and comp. John W. Peterson (Grand Rapids: Zondervan, 1968), 36.

3. Rosalind Goforth, *How I Know God Answers Prayer* (Philadelphia: Sunday School Times, 1921), 27.

4. Dwight L. Moody, quoted in *The Encyclopedia of Religious Quotations*, ed. and comp. Frank S. Mead (Westwood, N.J.: Revell, 1965), 344.

5. John Piper, quoted in *Prayer Powerpoints*, 109.

CHAPTER 10—REALIZING GOD'S PROTECTION THROUGH PRAYER

1. Frances Havergal, "Like a River Glorious," in *Great Hymns of the Faith*, ed. and comp. John W. Peterson (Grand Rapids: Zondervan, 1968), 287.

2. Charles Wesley, "Love Divine," in ibid., 2.

3. Hybels, *Too Busy Not to Pray*, 117.

4. Ibid., 111.

5. R. Kent Hughes, *Ephesians: The Mystery of the Body of Christ* (Wheaton, Ill.: Crossway, 1990), 239–40 (italics his).

6. Ibid., 40.

7. Hallesby, *Prayer*, 27, 30.

CHAPTER 11—OVERCOMING THE PAROCHIAL THROUGH PRAYER

1. William Barclay, *The Gospel of John*, rev. ed.(Philadelphia: Westminster, 1975), 2: 255–56 (italics his).

2. *The Complete Works of E. M. Bounds on Prayer*, 273.

3. William Hendriksen, *Exposition of the Gospel according to John,* New Testament Commentary (Grand Rapids: Baker, 1954), 364 (italics his).
4. Joseph Aldrich, *Prayer Summits* (Portland, Oreg.: Multnomah, 1992), 74–75.
5. Brian H. Edwards, *Revival* (Durham: Evangelical, 1990), 190–93.
6. Kyu Nam Jung, "Prayer in the Psalms," in *Teach Us to Pray: Prayer in the Bible and the World,* ed. D. A. Carson (Grand Rapids: Baker, 1990), 42.
7. Tippit, *The Prayer Factor,* 83.
8. Roth, *Prayer Powerpoints,* 189.
9. Jack Hayford, quoted in ibid.
10. Charles Spurgeon, *The Power of Prayer in a Believer's Life,* ed. and comp. Robert Hall (Lynnwood, Wash.: Emerald, 1993), 120.
11. Wesley L. Duewel, *Touch the World through Prayer* (Grand Rapids: Zondervan, 1986), 11–14 (italics his).
12. Andrew Murray, *With Christ in the School of Prayer* (Westwood, N.J.: Revell, 1953), 110–11.
13. Spurgeon, *The Power of Prayer in a Believer's Life,* 94–96 (italics his).

CHAPTER 12—AVOIDING THE PHARISEES' APPROACH TO PRAYER

1. Murray, *With Christ in the School of Prayer,* 85.
2. Bounds, *Power through Prayer,* 7.
3. Quoted in *Prayer Powerpoints,* 33.
4. Catherine Marshall, quoted in ibid., 31.
5. John Dawson, quoted in ibid., 30.

CHAPTER 13—PERSISTING IN THE SCHOOL OF PRAYER

1. Charlie Riggs, *Learning to Walk with God* (Minneapolis: World Wide, 1986), 79.
2. Rinker, *Prayer: Conversing with God,* 23 (italics hers).
3. Evelyn Christenson, "Impact a Lost World with Prayer," *Pray,* September–October 1997, 17.
4. Wesley L. Duewel, *Mighty Prevailing Prayer* (Grand Rapids: Zondervan, 1990), 20–22.

5. Dutch Sheets, *Intercessory Prayer* (Ventura, Calif.: Regal, 1996), 204–205.

6. V. Raymond Edman, *He Leadeth Me* (Wheaton, Ill.: Scripture Press, 1959), 29.

7. Roy B. Zuck, "What Difference Does It Make?" *Kindred Spirit*, Fall 1986, 20.

8. Ibid.

9. William W. Klein, "When Does Praying Become Pestering?" *Moody Magazine*, November 1984, 60.

10. Thomas L. Constable, "What Prayer Will and Will Not Change," in *Essays in Honor of J. Dwight Pentecost*, ed. Stanley D. Toussaint and Charles H. Dyer (Chicago: Moody, 1986), 105.

11. Ibid., 107.

12. Charles R. Swindoll, *Laugh Again* (Dallas: Word, 1992), 203–204.

13. Leslie B. Flynn, *The Master's Plan of Prayer* (Grand Rapids: Kregel, 1995), 61.

CHAPTER 14—DEVELOPING YOUR PRAYER LIFE

1. Herbert Lockyer, *All the Prayers of the Bible* (Grand Rapids: Zondervan, 1959).

2. Walter A. Elwell, ed., *Topical Analysis of the Bible* (Grand Rapids: Baker, 1991), 607–632.

3. Kenneth Boa and Max Anders, *Drawing Near* (Nashville: Nelson, 1987), 18–110.

4. J.G.S.S. Thomson, "Prayer," in *The Illustrated Bible Dictionary* (Wheaton, Ill.: Tyndale, 1980), 1257–60.

5. Jung, "Prayer in the Psalms," 35–57. On the kinds of prayers in the Psalms also see Allen P. Ross, "Psalms," in *The Bible Knowledge Commentary, Old Testament*, ed. John F. Walvoord and Roy B. Zuck (Wheaton, Ill.: Victor, 1985), 785–88.

CHAPTER 15—PRACTICING YOUR DAILY PRAYER TIME

1. Boa and Anders, *Drawing Near*, 175–300.

CHAPTER 16—PREPARING TO BE MORE EFFECTUAL IN PRAYER

1. Franklin Graham, *Rebel with a Cause* (Nashville: Nelson, 1995), 139.
2. Henry T. Blackaby and Claude V. King, *Experiencing God* (Nashville: Broadman and Holman, 1990), 32.
3. Ibid.
4. Eric Liddell, quoted in *World Shapers*, comp. Vinita Hampton and Carol Plueddemann (Wheaton, Ill.: Shaw, 1991), 90.
5. Armin R. Gesswein, *With One Accord in One Place* (Harrisburg, Pa.: Christian, 1978), 32 (italics his).
6. Dick Eastman, *The Jericho Hour* (Orlando, Fla.: Creation, 1994), 139 (italics his).
7. Ibid. (italics his).
8. Steve Hawthorne and Graham Kendrick, *Prayer-Walking: Praying on Site with Insight* (Orlando, Fla.: Creation, 1993), 10.
9. C. Peter Wagner, *Churches That Pray* (Ventura, Calif.: Regal, 1993), 182–83.

CHAPTER 17—PROMOTING THE LORD'S AGENDA THROUGH PRAYER

1. Bill Bright, *The Coming Revival* (Orlando, Fla: New Life, 1995), 93–94.
2. Duewel, *Touch the World through Prayer*, 95–96.
3. Ibid., 96–97.
4. Curtis C. Mitchell, "The Practice of Fasting in the New Testament," *Bibliotheca Sacra* 147 (October –December 1990): 469.
5. Donald S. Whitney, *Spiritual Disciplines for the Christian Life* (Colorado Springs: NavPress, 1991), 156–70.
6. Lewis Sperry Chafer, *True Evangelism: Winning Souls by Prayer* (1919; reprint, Grand Rapids: Kregel, 1993).
7. Ed Silvoso, *That None Should Perish* (Ventura, Calif.: Regal, 1994), 31.
8. Tom Phillips, *Revival Signs* (Gresham, Oreg.: Vision, 1995), 173–74.
9. David Bryant, *The Hope at Hand* (Grand Rapids: Baker, 1995), 42–43.
10. Neil T. Anderson and Elmer L. Towns, *Rivers of Revival* (Ventura, Calif.: Regal, 1997), 185.

11. Phillips, *Revival Signs*, 178–79.
12. Jonathan Edwards (source unknown).
13. Robert Bakke, *The Concert of Prayer* (Minneapolis: Beacon, 1993), 147–48.

Bibliography

Anderson, Leith. *When God Says No.* Minneapolis: Bethany House Publishers, 1996.

Blackaby, Henry T., and Claude V. King. *Experiencing God.* Nashville: Broadman & Holman Publishers, 1994.

Boa, Kenneth, and Max Anders. *Drawing Near.* Nashville: Thomas Nelson Publishers, 1987.

Bounds, E. M. *The Complete Works of E. M. Bounds on Prayer.* Grand Rapids: Baker Book House, 1990.

Boyd, Malcom. *Are You Running with Me, Jesus?* New York: Rinehart and Winston, 1965.

Chafer, Lewis Sperry. *True Evangelism: Winning Souls by Prayer.* 1919. Reprint, Grand Rapids: Kregel Publications, 1993.

Christenson, Evelyn, with Viola Blake. *What Happens When Women Pray.* Wheaton, Ill.: Victor Books, 1975.

Christenson, Evelyn, with Sarah M. Peterson. *A Journey into Prayer.* Wheaton, Ill.: Victor Books, 1995.

Constable, Thomas L. *Talking to God: What the Bible Teaches about Prayer.* Grand Rapids: Baker Book House, 1995.

Cymbala, Jim, and Dean Merrill. *Fresh Wind, Fresh Fire.* Grand Rapids: Zondervan Publishing House, 1997.

Duewel, Wesley L. *Touch the World through Prayer.* Grand Rapids: Zondervan Publishing House, 1986.

_____ . *Mighty Prevailing Prayer.* Grand Rapids: Zondervan Publishing House, 1990.

Edwards, Jonathan. *The Works of Jonathan Edwards.* Vol. 5: *Religious Affections.* New Haven, Conn.: Yale University Press, 1959.

Flynn, Leslie B. *The Master's Plan of Prayer.* Grand Rapids: Kregel Publications, 1995.

Foster, Richard S. *Prayer: Finding the Heart's True Home.* San Francisco: HarperSan Francisco, 1992.

_____ , and James Bryan Smith, eds. *Devotional Classics: Selected Readings for Individuals and Groups.* New York: HarperCollins, 1993.

Gordon, S. D. *Quiet Talks on Prayer.* New York: Fleming H. Revell Co., 1904.

Guest, John. *Only a Prayer Away: Finding Deeper Intimacy with God.* Ann Arbor, Mich.: Vine Books, 1985.

Hallesby, O. H. *Prayer.* 1931. Reprint, Minneapolis: Augsburg Publishing House, 1956.

Hawthorne, Steve, and Graham Kendrick. *Prayer-Walking: Praying on Site with Insight.* Orlando, Fla.: Creation House Publishers, 1993.

Hughes, R. Kent. *Abba Father: The Lord's Pattern for Prayer.* Westchester, Ill.: Crossway Books, 1986.

Hunter, W. Bingham. *The God Who Hears.* Downers Grove, Ill.: InterVarsity Press, 1986.

Hybels, Bill. *Too Busy Not to Pray: Slowing Down to Be with God.* Edited by LaVonne Neff. Downers Grove, Ill.: InterVarsity Press, 1988.

Lockyer, Herbert. *All the Prayers of the Bible*. Grand Rapids: Zondervan Publishing House, 1959.

MacArthur, John, Jr. *Alone with God: The Power and Passion of Prayer*. Wheaton, Ill.: Victor Books, 1995.

Murray, Andrew. *With Christ in the School of Prayer*. Westwood, N.J.: Fleming H. Revell Co., 1953.

Pink, Arthur W. *Gleanings from Paul: Studies in the Prayers of the Apostle*. Chicago: Moody Press, 1967.

Piper, John. *A Hunger for God: Desiring God through Fasting and Prayer*. Wheaton, Ill.: Crossway Books, 1997.

Rinker, Rosalind. *Prayer: Conversing with God*. Grand Rapids: Zondervan Publishing House, 1959.

Stedman, Ray C. *Jesus Teaches on Prayer*. Waco, Tex.: Word Books, 1975.

Strauss, Lehman. *Sense and Nonsense about Prayer*. Chicago: Moody Press, 1974.

Swindoll, Charles R. *Intimacy with the Almighty*. Dallas: Word Publishing, 1996.

Towns, Elmer L. *Fasting for Spiritual Breakthrough*. Ventura, Calif.: Regal Books, 1996.

———. *Praying the Lord's Prayer for Spiritual Breakthrough*. Ventura, Calif.: Regal Books, 1997.

Tippitt, Sammy. *The Prayer Factor*. Chicago: Moody Press, 1988.

Tryon, Howard. *Praying for You*. Grand Rapids: Kregel Publications, 1996.

Whitney, Donald S. *Spiritual Disciplines for the Christian Life*. Colorado Springs: NavPress, 1991).

Wiersbe, Warren W. *Listen! Jesus Is Praying: An Expository Study of John 17*. Wheaton, Ill.: Tyndale House Publishers, 1982.

Scripture Index

Subject Index